RELEASE THE SUN

by William Sears

Bahá'í Publishing Trust
Wilmette, Illinois

This American edition first published in 1960 is a revised edition
of the book first published by the Bahá'í Publishing Trust of India
in 1957

Reprinted 1964, 1968, 1971, 1975, 1995, 1999

ISBN: 0-87743-027-6 (cloth)
ISBN: 0-87743-003-9 (paper)

Library of Congress Card Number: 60-8220

PRINTED IN THE UNITED STATES OF AMERICA

COVER DESIGN BY SUNI D. HANNAN
COVER ILLUSTRATION BY MAUREEN A. SCULLIN
All rights reserved 1995

FOREWORD

The following is the first in a series of three books which will tell the story of the central figures of the Bahá'í Faith.

This book, *Release the Sun*, gives the early history of the Bahá'í Faith up through the hour of the martyrdom of its Herald, the Báb.

Professor Edward Granville Browne of Pembroke College, Cambridge University wrote of this period in history, saying:

"I am very anxious to get as accurate an account of all the details connected with the [faith of the Báb] as possible, for in my eyes the whole [story] seems one of the most interesting and important events that has occurred since the rise of Christianity . . . and I feel it my duty, as well as pleasure, to try as far as in me lies to bring the matter to the notice of my countrymen . . . for suppose anyone could tell us more about the childhood and early life and appearance of Christ, for instance, how glad we should be to know it. Now it is impossible to find out much . . . but in the case of the Báb it is possible . . . So let us earn the thanks of posterity, and provide against that day now." *

This is an attempt to bring just such an account of the life of the Báb to the attention of the world. This same story has been set down in everlasting language for the scholar, in Nabíl's Narrative, *The Dawn-Breakers*, and in *God Passes By*, written by Shoghi Effendi Rabbani, the Guardian of the Bahá'í Faith.

Release the Sun does not present all of the drama of this epic, nor does it give word for word the exciting stories told during those memorable days. It merely offers a simplified version of a story too long neglected and overlooked by man in his search for peace of mind and satisfaction of soul.

WILLIAM SEARS
Wilgespruit, Transvaal, South Africa
September, 1957

* *The Chosen Highway*, Preface.

CONTENTS

PROLOGUE

.

A SMALL WHIRLWIND of dust moved quietly down the deserted street. It whipped a scrap of paper against a sleeping cat, frightening it out of the doorway into the house. Then all was motionless silence.

Suddenly a young child hurried around the corner and raced down the empty street. His bare feet kicked up little puffs from the hot earth.

"He's coming!" he cried out. "They're bringing him this way!"

People streamed from their houses with the panic of ants whose hill has been struck by a careless foot. The street was alive with thrilled and expectant faces. Their excitement increased as they heard the angry shouts of the approaching mob.

A river of men, women and children flowed noisily around the corner. The young man they were following was overwhelmed by their insults. The mob cried out with delight. They knew he would not escape them. He was a captive. His guards pulled him along in front of the crowd by a long rope tied to an iron collar which was fastened about his neck. He was being taken to the authorities so that his death warrant might be signed.

When he faltered in his steps, the guards helped him on his way by jerking savagely on the rope or by planting a well-aimed kick. Occasionally someone would dart out of the crowd, break

1

through the guards. and strike the young man with a fist or a stick. Cheers of pleasure and encouragement accompanied each attacker. When a stone or a piece of refuse hurled from the mob struck the young captive in the face, both the guards and the crowd would burst into laughter.[1]

"Rescue yourself, O great hero!" one of the pursuers called mockingly. "Break asunder your bonds! Produce for us a miracle!" Then he spat in derision at the silent figure.

The young man was returned to the barracks square, then a short time later was led to his place of execution. It was high noon in the public square of a sun-baked city.

The blistering summer sun flashed from the barrels of the raised muskets. The guns were pointed at the young man's breast. The soldiers awaited the command to fire and take his life.

Great crowds were still pouring into the public square. Thousands swarmed along the adjoining rooftops overlooking the scene of death. They were all hungry for one last look at this strange young man who had so troubled their country. He was either good or evil, and they were not sure which.

He seemed so young to die, barely thirty. Now that the end had come, this victim of all their hatred did not seem dangerous at all. He appeared helpless and gentle, yet confident and handsome. There was a look of contentment, even of eagerness, on his face as he gazed calmly into the hostile barrels of seven hundred and fifty cocked rifles.

THE PROMISE OF THE MESSIAH

THIS IS THE STORY of a modern search for the Holy Grail, the cup of everlasting life. It began in the land from which the three Kings came to Bethlehem guided by a bright star.

It was now the nineteenth century, and there was another sign in the heavens, a great fiery comet. Many were awed, many were frightened, many were cheered, for both the East and the West were caught up in a millennial zeal.[1] *

In Persia, home of the "three wise men," the excitement over the coming of a Messiah was greater than in any other land. In America and Europe, scholars wrote and spoke of the expected appearance of the promised Christ, but in Persia many people were actively searching for Him. They believed the Promised One to be already in their midst.

Among these devout searchers was Shaykh Ahmad, a kindly, gentle man. At the age of forty, he left his home and kindred in one of the islands to the south of the Persian Gulf, and set out to unravel the mystery of the coming Messenger. An inner voice kept urging him on. Eagerly, he devoured everything written on the subject. He questioned the great religious and scientific authorities until he felt that at last he knew the truth.

* See Appendix, Note One.

He was now filled with an eagerness to unburden his soul. He began to search for someone with whom he could share his great secret: his certainty of the time and place for the appearance of God's new Messenger, Who would fulfill all the promises given in the sacred Books.

Shaykh Ahmad made his way on foot to the city of Shíráz in southern Persia. Often and passionately in his public talks he extolled that city. Such was the praise he lavished upon Shíráz that his hearers, who were only too familiar with its mediocrity, were astonished at the tone of his language.

"Wonder not," Shaykh Ahmad told them. "Before long the secret of my words will be made clear to you. A number of you will live to behold the glory of a day which all the prophets of old have foretold and have yearned to witness.

There was no one to whom Shaykh Ahmad was able to pour out his knowledge in its entirety. He feared what the people might do to the One whose coming had set his heart on fire. He knew he must wait patiently until a kindred soul appeared with whom he could share his secret.

During those days, a young man named Siyyid Kázim was already on his way to visit Shaykh Ahmad. He had heard of this great man, and thought perhaps Shaykh Ahmad himself might be the Promised One. Siyyid Kázim lived near a famous tomb at Ardibil. One night in a dream he was told to arise and put himself under the spiritual guidance of Shaykh Ahmad whom he would find residing at Yazd.[2]

Siyyid Kázim began his journey to Yazd at once. When he reached his destination, Shaykh Ahmad greeted him affectionately. "I welcome you, O my friend! How long and how eagerly I have awaited your coming."

To him, Shaykh Ahmad confided all that he knew. He urged Siyyid Kázim to kindle in every receptive heart the fire that burned so brightly in his own.

"You have no time to lose," Shaykh Ahmad warned him. "Every fleeting hour should be fully and wisely used. Strive night and day to remove the veils of prejudice and orthodoxy that have blinded the eyes of men. For verily I say, the hour is drawing nigh."

By devoting his special attention to his followers, Shaykh Ahmad hoped to enable them to become the active supporters of the Cause of the Promised One when he appeared.

Shaykh Ahmad knew that the hour of his own death was approaching, so he called his followers together. "After me," he said, "seek for the truth through Siyyid Kázim. He alone understands my objective." [3]

Shaykh Ahmad died soon after, and Siyyid Kázim became the leader of his followers. Siyyid Kázim also found that there was no one sincere enough or worthy enough to hear all that Shaykh Ahmad had taught him. His followers were still tied to their homes, their families, their money, their businesses, their former beliefs.

"If the coming Promised One will exalt us and preserve all we hold dear," they told Siyyid Kázim, "then we are ready, nay eager, to accept. But, if His coming means forsaking all we cherish and perhaps even facing death, then our ears are deaf to the sweet music."

At long last Siyyid Kázim found one young man in whom he could place the greatest trust. The youth's name was Mullá Husayn. Such was the love and honor that Siyyid Kázim bestowed upon Mullá Husayn that some among his companions suspected that Mullá Husayn might be the Promised One to whom their master was unceasingly referring, the One whom he so often declared to be even now living in their midst unrecognized by them all.

"You behold Him with your own eyes," Siyyid Kázim told them, "and yet recognize him not!"

Mullá Husayn returned Siyyid Kázim's great love and respect. At times he himself secretly wondered whether or not Siyyid Kázim might be the One they awaited. Mullá Husayn, however, had a standard by which he planned to test whoever made such a stupendous claim. He would ask that a commentary be written upon the story of Joseph, a certain chapter in the sacred scripture, and written in a style and language entirely different from the prevailing standards.

One day Mullá Husayn, in private, asked Siyyid Kázim to write such a commentary. Siyyid Kázim refused.

"This verily is beyond me," he said. "However, He that great One who comes after me will, unasked, reveal it for you. That commentary will constitute one of the clearest evidences of His truth."

Mullá Husayn asked Siyyid Kázim why this chapter was called the "best of stories" in their holy Book. Siyyid Kázim replied, "It

is not the proper occasion for explaining the reason." His words
hinted that the future would unveil this truth.[4]

Another among his followers felt that Siyyid Kázim, in spite
of his denials, was the One foretold. He went so far as to declare
this publicly. Siyyid Kázim was most displeased. He would have
cast the speaker out of the company of his chosen followers had
he not begged for forgiveness.

"My knowledge is but a drop compared to the immensity of
His knowledge," Siyyid Kázim asserted. "My attainments are but
a speck of dust in the face of the wonders of His power."[5]

When Siyyid Kázim made this forthright denial, still another of
his followers was very distressed. For he, too, had believed Siyyid
Kázim to be the great announced Figure. He prayed earnestly
to God either to confirm the feeling in his heart or to deliver him
from such a fancy. The manner in which he was assisted is recorded
in his own words.

"One day at the hour of dawn, we went to the house of Siyyid
Kázim. He was fully dressed in his best attire and was about to
leave. He asked me to accompany him.

"He said, 'A highly esteemed and distinguished person has arrived. I feel it necessary that we both should visit him.'

"The sun had just appeared as we reached our destination. In
the doorway stood a youth. His face revealed an expression of
humility and kindliness which I can never describe. He quietly
approached us, extended his arms toward Siyyid Kázim and lovingly embraced him. His friendliness contrasted strongly with the
profound reverence which Siyyid Kázim showed him.

"He led us to an upper chamber. A silver cup had been placed
in the center of the room. After we were seated, our host filled the
cup and handed it to Siyyid Kázim. He spoke a verse from our
holy Book: 'A drink of a pure beverage shall their Lord give them.'

"How great was my amazement when I saw my teacher [Siyyid
Kázim] quaff without the least hesitation, that holy draught from a
silver cup, the use of which is forbidden to the faithful.

"Three days later, I saw that same young man arrive and take
his seat amidst assembled followers of Siyyid Kázim. He sat close
to the doorway, and with great modesty and dignity of bearing he
listened to the discourse of Siyyid Kázim.

"As soon as Siyyid Kázim saw him, he immediately discontinued speaking. One of his followers begged him to resume his talk about the coming of the Promised One.

"'What more shall I say?' replied Siyyid Kázim as he turned his face toward the young man. 'Lo, the truth is more manifest than the ray of light that has fallen on that lap.'

"I immediately observed that the ray of sunlight to which Siyyid Kázim referred had fallen upon the lap of that same youth we had so recently visited.

"One of Siyyid Kázim's followers asked, 'Why is it that you neither reveal His name nor identify His person? Why?'

"Siyyid Kázim replied that if he were to divulge His name, both the Beloved of God and he himself would be put to death instantly.

"I saw Siyyid Kázim actually point out with his finger the ray of light that had fallen on that lap, and yet none of those who were present seemed to apprehend its meaning. I was convinced that some mystery inscrutable to us all lay concealed in that strange and attractive youth.

"I often felt the urge to seek his presence, but every time I ventured an approach, a force I could neither explain nor resist detained me. My inquiries elicited the information that he was a resident of Shíráz and a merchant by profession. He had set my heart aflame, and the memory of him haunted me."

Siyyid Kázim became increasingly aware of the approach of the hour at which the Promised One was to be revealed. There is conclusive evidence that he referred time and again to this event. He was fond of saying: "I see him as the rising sun." He realized how thick the veils were that prevented even his own followers from understanding the truth. He kept warning them as John the Baptist had warned those who awaited Christ: "The kingdom of God is at hand." With care and wisdom he gradually began to remove all the barriers that might stand in the way of their full recognition of that hidden Treasure when it appeared.

"Beware, lest after my departure the world's fleeting vanities beguile you," he cautioned them. "Renounce all comfort, all earthly possessions and kindred, in your quest of Him. Detach yourselves from all earthly things and humbly beseech God to guide you. Never relax in your determination to seek and find Him. Be firm until the day He will choose you as His companions. Well is it with every one of you who will drink the cup of martyrdom in His path."

Siyyid Kázim promised some of his followers that they would

not only have the joy of seeing the coming Messenger of God face to face, but that they would see His Successor as well.

"For soon after the first trumpet blast, there shall be sounded yet another call, and all things shall be quickened and revived."

Repeatedly Siyyid Kázim told them that they would see not one, but two Messengers of God, the twin Revelations promised in all the holy Books for these "last days."

These two successive Messengers would be the fulfillment of the prophecy of the "second and third woe" mentioned in the Book of Revelation of St. John, which prophesies that the "third woe" would quickly follow the "second woe." [6] They would also be the fulfillment of the two trumpet blasts mentioned in the Qur'án which in the "last days" would quickly follow each other.[7]

Siyyid Kázim assured his followers that after the promised Dawn, the promised Sun would be made manifest. "For when the star of the Former has set," he said, "the Sun of the Latter will rise and illuminate the whole world."

His followers, Siyyid Kázim pointed out, were living in the very day of the prophecy which was fulfilled by these words. "In the year 1260 [1844] the earth shall be illumined by His light. . . . If thou livest until the year 1270 [1853] thou shalt witness how the nations, the rulers, the peoples, and the Faith of God shall all have been renewed." [8] *

In the last year of his life, Siyyid Kázim left the city of Karbilá to visit the holy Shrines nearby. He stopped at a prayer-house beside the highway to offer his noonday devotions. He was standing beneath the shade of a palm, when suddenly an Arab appeared. He approached Siyyid Kázim and spoke to him.

"Three days ago I was shepherding my flock in an adjoining pasture," he told Siyyid Kázim. "All of a sudden sleep overtook me. The Prophet appeared to me in my sleep. He said to me: 'Give ear to my words, O shepherd! Stay within the precincts of this prayer-house. In three days a man, Siyyid Kázim by name, will arrive accompanied by his friends. Tell him from Me: "Rejoice, for the hour of your departure is at hand. In Karbilá, three days after your return there, you will wing your flight to Me. Soon after shall He who is the Truth be made manifest. Then shall the world be illuminated by the light of His face."'"

---

* The year 1260 in the calendar of Islám is the year 1844 of the Christian calendar. 1270 is equivalent to 1853.

The companions of Siyyid Kázim were saddened by the thought of his approaching death. He comforted them with these words. "Is not your love for me really for the sake of that true One whose coming we all await? Would you not wish me to die, that the Promised One may be revealed?"

To his last breath, Siyyid Kázim urged his followers to persevere in their search. He returned to Karbilá, and on the day he arrived he became ill. Three days later he died, just as foretold in the shepherd's dream.

THE SEARCH BEGINS

MULLÁ HUSAYN was in Isfáhán at this time upon a special mission for Siyyid Kázim. He was sent to win the support of an eminent religious leader. Mullá Husayn was so successful that the priest changed his views. He became so fond of Mullá Husayn that he regretted his earlier discourtesy and sent an attendant to find out where he was residing. The attendant followed him, and saw Mullá Husayn enter a room devoid of furniture with but a single mat upon the floor. He watched Mullá Husayn offer his prayers and lie down on the mat with nothing to cover him from the cold but his cloak. Then he reported this to his master, whose admiration for Mullá Husayn increased so greatly that he sent his attendant back to him with a gift of one hundred tumans. Mullá Husayn returned the money, saying, "Tell your master that his real gift to me was the fairness and openmindedness with which he heard my message in spite of his exalted rank and my lowliness. Return this money, for I ask for neither regard nor thanks. We nourish souls for the sake of God. My prayer for your master is that earthly leadership may never hinder him from acknowledging and testifying to the truth." [1]

When Mullá Husayn returned to Karbilá, Siyyid Kázim was dead. Though his own heart was heavy, Mullá Husayn cheered and strengthened the disconsolate followers of his beloved leader. He called them all together to renew their ardor.

"What," he asked them, "were the dearest wishes and the last commands of our departed leader?"

From their reluctant lips Mullá Husayn extracted the following admissions: (1) That repeatedly and emphatically Siyyid Kázim had bidden them to quit their homes and scatter far and wide in search of Him to Whose coming he had so often alluded. (2) That the Object of their quest was now living amongst them and that His truth could be discovered only by the seeker who would persevere to the end. (3) That nothing short of prayerful endeavor, purity of motive, singleness of purpose, and ceaseless search would ever lead them to Him.

"We acknowledge our failure," they told him.

"Then why," Mullá Husayn demanded, "have you chosen to remain in Karbilá? Why is it that you have not dispersed and arisen to carry out Siyyid Kázim's earnest plea?"

To his entreaty they gave weak and evasive answers.

"Our enemies are many and powerful," one replied. "We must remain in this city and protect the honor of Siyyid Kázim."

"I must stay and care for the children and the family which Siyyid Kázim has left behind," another explained.

They all, however, agreed to the leadership of Mullá Husayn, saying, "Such is our confidence in you, that if you claim to be the Promised One, we shall all readily and unquestioningly submit."

Mullá Husayn was shocked. "God forbid!" he cried, "that I who am but dust be compared to Him!"

Mullá Husayn realized the futility of his efforts and spoke to them no more. He left them, and made his own plans to begin his quest for the Beloved of God.[2]

Mullá Husayn prepared for his search by withdrawing and spending forty days in retirement and prayer. His retreat was interrupted by the unexpected arrival of Mullá 'Alí and twelve other followers of Siyyid Kázim. They had been stirred by his words, and had decided to follow Mullá Husayn's example and begin their search as well.

On several occasions Mullá 'Alí approached Mullá Husayn to ask him where he was going and what his destination would be. Every time he neared Mullá Husayn, he found him so deeply wrapt in prayer that he felt it improper to venture a question. Mullá 'Alí decided to retire in a like manner from the society of men and prepare his own heart for the quest. His companions followed his example.

As soon as the forty days were up, Mullá Husayn left Karbilá. He was resolved never to cease his search until he was in the presence of the One he sought. The promises of Siyyid Kázim stirred in his memory. Many were the prophecies which he turned over and over in his mind.

"Verily in the year '60 [1260-1844] His Cause shall be revealed and His Name shall be noised abroad."

"In His name, the name of the Guardian ('Alí) precedeth that of the Prophet [Muhammad]."

"In 1260 the Tree of Divine guidance shall be planted."

"The ministers and upholders of His Faith shall be of the people of Persia."

It was now the year '60, so Mullá Husayn set out at once for Persia where he felt his search should begin. An inner prompting led him to Búshihr on the Persian Gulf. As he walked through the streets, his heart leaped with excitement for something told him that this city had once felt the footsteps of his Beloved. Mullá Husayn said that he could feel the sweet savors of His holiness in Búshihr. He did not remain in Búshihr because something suddenly turned him like a compass needle to the north. He set out at once on foot for the city of Shíráz.

When he arrived at the gate of the city, he directed his brother and his nephew, who had accompanied him, to go to the prayer-house and await his return.

"Something draws my heart into the city," he said, "but I shall meet you for evening prayers."

A few hours before sunset, Mullá Husayn's eyes fell upon a young man of radiant countenance. The youth advanced toward Mullá Husayn and greeted him with a smile of loving welcome. He embraced Mullá Husayn with tender affection as though he had been an intimate and lifelong friend.

At first Mullá Husayn thought him to be a follower of Siyyid Kázim, who on being informed of his approach to Shíráz, had come out to welcome him. Mullá Husayn recalls that memorable night as follows:

"He extended to me a warm invitation to visit His home, and there refresh myself after the fatigues of my journey. I asked to be excused, saying that my two companions were awaiting my return.

"'Commit them to the care of God,' was His reply. 'He surely will protect and watch over them.'

"Having spoken these words, He turned and bade me follow Him. I was deeply stirred by the gentle yet compelling manner in which that young man spoke to me. His gait, the charm of His voice, the dignity of His bearing, all seemed to enhance my first impression.

"Soon we were standing at the gate of a modest house. 'Enter therein in peace secure,' were His words as He crossed the threshold and motioned to me to follow Him. His invitation, uttered with power and majesty, penetrated my soul. I thought it a good sign to be addressed in such words, standing as I did on the threshold of the first house I was to enter in Shíráz. Might not my visit to this house, I thought to myself, enable me to draw nearer to the Object of my quest?

"A feeling of unutterable joy invaded my being. During the hour for prayer, I unburdened my heart: 'O my God! I have striven with all my soul, and until now have failed to find Thy promised Messenger. I testify that Thy word faileth not, and that Thy promise is sure!'

"It was about an hour after sunset when my youthful Host began to converse with me. 'Whom, after Siyyid Kázim, do you regard as your leader?'

"I answered Him: 'At the hour of his death, Siyyid Kázim exhorted each of us to forsake our homes, to scatter far and wide in quest of the promised Beloved. I have journeyed to Persia, and am still engaged in my quest.'

"'Has your teacher given you any detailed indications as to the distinguishing features of the Promised One?'

"I enumerated all the things that Siyyid Kázim had told us to look for in that Beloved One of God.

"My Host paused for some time, then with a vibrant voice He startled me with the words: 'Behold! All These signs are manifest in Me!'

"He then carefully considered each of the above signs separately, and conclusively demonstrated that each and all were indeed applicable to His person. I was greatly surprised and deeply moved. Politely I observed: 'He whose advent we await is a Man of unsurpassed holiness, and the Cause He is to reveal is a Cause of tremendous power.'

"No sooner had those words dropped from my lips than I found myself seized with fear and remorse, such as I could neither conceal nor explain. I bitterly reproved myself, and resolved to alter my attitude and to soften my tone. I vowed to God that should my Host again refer to the subject, I would, with the utmost humility, answer Him and say: 'If you be willing to substantiate your claim, you will most assuredly deliver me from the anxiety and suspense which so heavily oppress my soul. I shall truly be indebted to you for such deliverance.'"

The name of Mullá Husayn's host was 'Alí Muhammad. This young man had spent several years working as a merchant for his uncle in the city of Búshihr before coming to live at this time with his uncle in Shíráz. As Mullá Husayn looked upon the beautiful face of his host what thoughts must have coursed through his mind, for in his name the name of the Guardian ['Alí] preceded that of the Prophet [Muhammad]! He came from the land of Persia. He was announcing himself now in the year '60 [1844]. Was not all this foretold by Siyyid Kázim?

Mullá Husayn had two standards whereby he hoped to determine the truth of whoever claimed to be that great Messenger. The first was a treatise which he had composed himself. It dealt with the most difficult hidden teachings of Shaykh Ahmad and Siyyid Kázim. Whoever seemed capable of unravelling its mysteries would then be put to the test of revealing the commentary on the chapter of Joseph. Mullá Husayn recalls the suspense of that moment in these words:

"While I was thinking about these things, my distinguished Host again remarked: 'Observe attentively. Might not the Person intended by Siyyid Kázim be none other than I?'

"I thereupon felt impelled to offer Him my own treatise. 'Will you read this book of mine,' I asked Him, 'and look at its pages with indulgent eyes?'

"He opened the book, glanced briefly at certain passages, closed it, and began to speak to me. Within a few minutes He had, with vigor and charm, unravelled all its mysteries and resolved all the problems that had troubled me. He, further, informed me of certain truths which could not be found in any of the writings of Siyyid Kázim or Shaykh Ahmad. These teachings, which I had never heard before, seemed to be endowed with a refreshing vividness and power.

"'By the righteousness of God!' He exclaimed, 'It behooves in this day, the peoples and nations of both the East and the West to hasten to this threshold. It behooves them to arise, as earnestly and as spontaneously as you have arisen, and to seek with determination and constancy their promised Beloved.'

"Then He looked at me, smiled, and said: 'Now is the time to reveal the commentary on the Súrih [Chapter] of Joseph.'"

It all happened just as Siyyid Kázim had foretold it to Mullá Husayn. "The Beloved in that hour," he had promised, "will reveal the commentary on the story of Joseph, unasked!"

The Báb took up His pen and with incredible rapidity revealed the entire first chapter of His commentary on the chapter of Joseph. In this book, He prophesied His own martyrdom. The overpowering effect of the manner in which he wrote was heightened by the gentle intonation of His voice which accompanied His writing. Not for one moment did He interrupt the flow of the verses which streamed from His pen. Not once did he pause until it was finished.

The historian Comte de Gobineau writes, "that which one never tired of admiring was the elegance and beauty of the Arabic style used in those writings. They soon had enthusiastic admirers who did not fear to prefer them to the finest passages in the Qur'án." [3]

"I sat enraptured by the magic of His voice and the sweeping force of His revelation," Mullá Husayn said. "At last I reluctantly arose from my seat and begged leave to depart. He smilingly bade me to be seated, and said: 'If you leave in such a state, whoever sees you will assuredly say: "This poor youth has lost his mind."'"

At that moment the clock registered two hours and eleven minutes after sunset. It was on the eve of May 23, 1844.

"This night," the Báb told Mullá Husayn, "this very hour will, in days to come, be celebrated as one of the greatest and most significant of all festivals." [4]

Jesus first spoke of His Mission to simple fishermen. Now the Promised One of this age had given the first declaration of His Mission to this humble Persian student, Mullá Husayn. Never before in the history of a religion have the exact words of such an unforgettable meeting been preserved by an eye-witness. Mullá Husayn, however, has left in everlasting language a memory of that first announcement by 'Alí Muhammad, the Báb. He could never forget the inner peace and serenity which he had felt in the life-creating presence of the Báb. He spoke often to his companions of that wondrous night.

"I sat spellbound by His utterance," he said. "All the delights [of Paradise] I seemed to be experiencing that night. Methinks I was in a place of which it could be truly said: 'Therein no toil shall reach us, . . . but only the cry, Peace! Peace!'" Sleep had departed from Mullá Husayn as he listened to the music of his Beloved's voice.

"'O thou who are the first to believe in Me. Verily, I am the Báb, the Gate of God.'"

To Mullá Husayn, the first to believe in Him, the Báb gave the title: the Bábu'l-Báb, the gate of the Gate. In that hour, the Báb proclaimed that He was the One foretold in all the holy Books of the past. He said that He had come to usher in a new era, a fresh springtime in the hearts of men. His name, the Báb, meant the door or gate. His teaching, He said, was to open the door or the gate to a new age of unity in which men would recognize one God and worship in one religion—the same religion which all of God's prophets had taught from the beginning of time. It would be an age in which all men would live as brothers.

The Báb cautioned Mullá Husayn not to tell either his companions or any other soul what he had seen and heard. In the beginning, eighteen souls must spontaneously and of their own accord seek and accept Him and recognize the truth of His Revelation. When their number was complete, He would send them forth to teach the Word of God.

Mullá Husayn's long search was at an end. His own words can best describe the depth of that unique experience.

"I was blinded by the dazzling splendor of this new Revelation," he said, "and overwhelmed by its crushing force. Predominant among all my emotions was a sense of gladness and strength which seemed to have transfigured me. How feeble and impotent, how dejected and timid, I had felt previously! Then I could neither write nor walk, so tremulous were my hands and feet. Now, the knowledge of His Revelation had galvanized my being. I felt possessed of such courage and power that were the world, all its people and its rulers, to rise against me, I would alone and undaunted withstand their onslaught. The universe seemed but a handful of dust in my grasp. I seemed to be the Voice of Gabriel personified, calling unto all mankind: 'Awake, for lo! the morning Light has broken. Arise, for His Cause is made manifest. The portal of His grace is open wide; enter therein, O peoples of the world! For He Who is your Promised One is come!'

"In such a state I left His house and joined my brother and nephew. The words of the Báb were ringing their melody of joy in my heart: 'Render thanks unto God for having graciously assisted you to attain your heart's desire.'"

THE PROMISE IS FULFILLED

Mullá Husayn was faithful to the Báb's instructions. He told no one of his discovery, even though a large number of the followers of Siyyid Kázim soon gathered about him. They recognized a new spirit in Mullá Husayn's speech, and marvelled at it, unaware that the source of his knowledge and power flowed from the Báb Whose coming all of them were so eagerly awaiting.

"During those days," Mullá Husayn states, "I was summoned to visit the Báb on several occasions. Every time I visited Him, I spent the entire night in His presence. Wakeful until dawn, I sat at His feet fascinated by the charm of His utterance, and oblivious of the world and its cares. How rapidly those precious hours flew by! At each daybreak I would reluctantly withdraw from His presence. How eagerly in those days I looked forward to the approach of the evening hour. With what feelings of sadness and regret I beheld the dawning of day!

"In the course of one of these nightly visits, the Báb addressed me in these words: 'Tomorrow thirteen of your companions will arrive. To each of them extend the utmost loving kindness. Pray to God that He may graciously enable them to walk securely in that path which is finer than a hair and keener than a sword.'" [1]

Some of these companions, the Báb told Mullá Husayn, would become His chosen disciples. Others would be neither warm nor

18

cold, while still others would remain undeclared until that future day when He, for whom the Báb Himself was but the Herald, appeared.

The next morning, Mullá 'Alí, Mullá Husayn's close friend arrived in Shíráz, accompanied by twelve companions. He at once noted the great change which had taken place in Mullá Husayn. He was struck by the tranquil radiance of his face and suspected the truth.

"How is it," Mullá 'Alí asked, "that we see you teaching the people with the utmost tranquility and no longer searching? Agitation and expectancy have vanished from your face. I beg of you, bestow upon me a portion of what you have found, for only that can quench my thirst and ease the pain of longing in my heart."

Mullá Husayn refused. "Do not entreat me to grant this favor," he begged Mullá 'Alí. "Let your trust be in God, for He will surely guide your steps."

So great was the joy that shone from Mullá Husayn's face, that Mullá 'Alí could no longer bear to be deprived of that secret. By prayer and fasting he sought desperately to remove the veil that separated him from the Beloved. On the third night of his retirement, while wrapt in deep prayer, Mullá 'Alí had a vision. There appeared before his eyes a light, and lo! it moved off before him. Allured by its matchless beauty, he followed it until at last it led him to a certain door. He knew immediately that the Treasure was within. He awoke in a state of great rapture.

Although it was the middle of the night, he rushed to Mullá Husayn. His face was aglow with happiness. He threw himself into the arms of his friend. Mullá Husayn realized at once that Mullá 'Alí at last knew the truth. He knew where to find his Beloved.

He embraced Mullá 'Alí lovingly, and said: "Praise be to God Who hath guided us."

That very morning, at break of day, Mullá Husayn followed by Mullá 'Alí hastened to the residence of the Báb. At the entrance they were met by the Báb's much loved Ethiopian servant, who immediately recognized them. He greeted them with these words:

"Before break of day I was summoned to the presence of my Master who instructed me to open the door of the house and to stand expectant at its threshold.

" 'Two guests,' He told me, 'are to arrive early this morning.

Extend to them in My name a warm welcome. Say to them from Me: "Enter therein in the name of God." ' "

The first meeting of Mullá 'Alí with the Báb differed greatly from the first meeting of Mullá Husayn with the Báb. At the previous meeting the Báb had offered proofs of His Mission for Mullá Husayn to weigh and study. At this meeting, all such matters had been put aside and a spirit of intense love and ardent fellowship prevailed. The very chamber, said Mullá 'Alí, seemed to have been vitalized by His utterance. Everything in the room seemed to be vibrating with this testimony: "Verily, the dawn of a new day has broken. The Promised One is enthroned in the hearts of men. In His hand He holds the mystic cup of immortality, and blessed is he who drinks therefrom!" [2]

One by one, seventeen separate souls searched for the Báb, met Him, and accepted His teachings.

Among these disciples, there was one woman. She was called Táhirih, the Pure. She accepted the Báb without ever attaining to His presence. She saw Him in the world of vision, and became a staunch believer, a courageous teacher, and finally a martyr.

One night while conversing with Mullá Husayn, the Báb said to him, "Seventeen have thus far enlisted under the standard of the Faith of God . . . Tomorrow night the remaining Letter will arrive and will complete the number of My chosen disciples."

The next evening as the Báb, followed by Mullá Husayn, was returning to His home, a youth appeared. He was travel-stained and weary from his long journey. His name was Quddús. He approached Mullá Husayn, embraced him, and asked him if he had yet attained to his heart's desire.

Mullá Husayn tried to calm him. He advised him to rest for a while, saying that he would speak to him later. The youth, however, refused to rest. He looked past Mullá Husayn at the retreating figure of the Báb. Then turning to Mullá Husayn, he said: "Why do you seek to hide Him from me. I can recognize Him by His gait. I testify that none beside Him, whether in the East or the West, can claim to be the Truth. None other can manifest the power and the majesty that radiate from His Holy person."

Mullá Husayn marveled at these words. He pleaded with him to restrain his feelings, promising that the truth would be unveiled to him soon. Leaving him, Mullá Husayn hastened to join the Báb. He told Him of his conversation with the young man.

"Marvel not at this strange behavior," the Báb said, "We have in the world of the spirit been communing with that youth. We know him already. We indeed awaited his coming. Go to him and summon him forthwith to Our presence."

Mullá Husayn instantly recalled the prophecy given for the time of the end: "On the last Day, the men of the unseen shall, on the wings of the spirit, traverse the immensity of the earth, shall attain the presence of the Promised One and shall seek from Him the secret that will resolve their problems and remove their perplexities."[3]

Now when this eighteenth disciple, known as Quddús, had accepted Him, the Báb addressed them, saying: "Raise the cry: Awake! awake, for lo! the Gate of God is open, and the morning light is shedding its radiance upon all mankind! The Promised One has come, prepare the way for Him, O people of the world!"[4]

The Báb gave a special message of assurance to Mullá 'Alí. "Your faith must be immovable as the rock, must weather every storm and survive every calamity. Suffer not the denunciations of the foolish to turn you from your purpose. You are the first to leave the House of God, and to suffer for His sake. If you be slain in His path, remember that great will be your reward, and goodly the gift which will be bestowed upon you."

No sooner were these words uttered than Mullá 'Alí arose from his seat and set out to teach the Faith of the Báb.

True to the Báb's forewarnings, Mullá 'Alí was overtaken and beaten just beyond the gate of Shíráz. He was the first to suffer for the new Faith. He was also the first to bring news of the Báb to Táhirih. In Najaf he was arrested for fearlessly proclaiming the Faith. He was bound with chains and taken to Baghdád under sentence of death. He was cast into prison, tried again, and, still in chains, ordered to Constantinople. Some say he died enroute, some say he was later martyred. No one knows what eventually befell this hero of God.[5]

The Báb summoned all of the others to His presence and to each one He gave a special command and a special task. He spoke to all of them these parting words:

"O My beloved friends! You are the bearers of the name of God in this Day. . . . The very members of your body must bear witness to the loftiness of your purpose, the integrity of your life, the reality of your faith, and the exalted character of your devotion. . . .

"Ponder the words of Jesus addressed to His disciples as He sent them forth to propagate the Cause of God: 'Ye are even as the fire which in the darkness of the night has been kindled upon the mountain-top. Such must be the purity of your character and the degree of your renunciation, that the people of the earth may through you recognize and be drawn closer to the heavenly Father Who is the source of purity and grace.'"

In His parting message to His disciples the Báb once again called their attention to the One Who was soon to come after Him, and for Whom He was but the Herald. He sent each one of them back to his own province to teach.

"I am preparing you for the advent of a mighty Day," He told them. "Exert your utmost endeavor that, in the world to come, I Who am now instructing you, may, before the mercy-seat of God, rejoice in your deeds and glory in your achievements. Scatter throughout the length and breadth of this land, and with steadfast feet and sanctified hearts, prepare the way for His coming.

"Heed not your weaknesses and frailty: fix your gaze upon the invincible power of the Lord, your God, the Almighty. . . .

"Arise in His name, put your trust wholly in Him, and be assured of ultimate victory."

With such words as these, the Báb quickened the faith of His disciples and launched them upon their mission.[6]

THE PILGRIMAGE
AND THE PROCLAMATION

ONE MORNING shortly after this, at the hour of dawn, most of the disciples of the Báb left Shíráz to carry out the teaching tasks He had given them. The first disciple, Mullá Husayn, and the last, Quddús, remained with Him.

To these two the Báb disclosed His intention to go to Mecca. Just as Jesus had journeyed to Jerusalem, the stronghold of the Jews, to proclaim His Mission, so did the Báb make plans to go to Mecca, the heart of the Moslem world. As the hour of His departure arrived, He called Mullá Husayn to Him.

He Himself would visit Mecca and Medina, He told him, and there fulfill the Mission with which God had entrusted Him. He had chosen Quddús to go with Him and left Mullá Husayn behind to face the onslaught of a fierce and relentless enemy. He assured him, however, that until he had completely finished his work, no power on earth could harm him.

"He that loves you, loves God . . . Whoso befriends you, him will God befriend; and whoso rejects you, him will God reject. His Almighty arms will surround you and guide your steps." [1]

The Báb, accompanied by Quddús, departed for Búshihr on the Persian Gulf where they embarked upon a sailing vessel. After two

months of sailing on stormy seas, they landed on the coast of Arabia.
A fellow passenger during this voyage has recorded the following:

"From the day we embarked at Búshihr until we landed, whenever
I saw the Báb or Quddús, they were invariably together absorbed in
their work. The Báb was dictating and Quddús was taking down
whatever fell from His lips."

Neither the storms that raged about them, nor the sickness which
seized the other passengers, could disturb their serenity or interfere
with their work.[2]

The Báb entered the city of Mecca seated upon a camel, as Christ
had entered Jerusalem seated upon an ass. Quddús refused to ride
beside Him on the journey inland. He preferred, he said, to accompany Him on foot, holding the bridle of the camel. Each night from
sunset until dawn, Quddús would stand watch over His Beloved.

One day during His visit in Mecca, the Báb approached a man
named Muhít. The Báb recognized him as a distinguished follower
of Shaykh Ahmad. He knew that if Muhít were faithful to his master's instructions, he would now be energetically searching for the
Promised One. The Báb spoke to him.

"Oh Muhít!" He said, "Behold, we are both now standing within
this most sacred Shrine. . . . He Whose spirit dwells in this place can
cause Truth to be known from falsehood. . . . Verily, I declare, none
beside Me in this day, whether in the East or in the West, can claim
to be the Gate that leads men to the knowledge of God. . . . Ask Me
whatsoever you please; now, at this very moment, I pledge Myself
to reveal such verses as can demonstrate the Truth of My Mission."

This sudden, unexpected and direct challenge unnerved Muhít.
He was anxious to depart.

"I am expected at once in Medina," he said. He did not look at
the Báb as he spoke. Unable to remain in His presence, he fled in
terror from His face and hurried from the Shrine.[3]

The Báb found no one who would listen. They were indifferent,
antagonistic, or afraid. He made one last effort to awaken the people
in that holy city of the Muslims. He wrote a letter to the Sherif of
Mecca, hoping that through him He might reach the hearts of the
people.

In that letter, he set forth in clear and unmistakable terms the
distinguishing features of His Mission and called upon the Sherif to
arise and embrace His Cause.

The Sherif did not bother to read the letter or to share it with his friends who were all too much absorbed in their own affairs to respond to the call of the Báb.

Later, the Sherif admitted his indifference. "In the year 1844," he said, "I recall that a young man came to see me. He gave me a book, but I was too occupied to read it at that time. A few days later I met him again. He asked me if I had any reply to make to his message. Pressure of work had prevented me from reading the contents of that book, so I told him that I had no answer to give him." [4]

The Báb was treated as Christ had been treated, with ridicule and contempt. It was the same as it had been in those days when Jesus accused the leaders of His day, saying: "Woe unto you! . . . ye entered not in yourselves, and them that were entering in ye hindered." [5]

The people did not understand Him, whether He spoke plain truths or in symbols. The historian Nicolas writes that the Báb, throughout His Mission, had to act "as does a physician to children, who must disguise a bitter medicine in a sweet coating in order to win over his young patients. The people in the midst of whom he [the Báb] appeared were, and still are, alas, more fanatical than the Jews were at the time of Jesus. . . . Therefore, if Christ, in spite of the relative calm of the surroundings in which He preached, thought it necessary to employ the parable, the Báb was obliged to pour out one drop at a time, the filter of his divine truths. He brings up his child, humanity; he guides it, endeavoring always not to frighten it and directs its first steps on a path which leads it slowly but surely so that as soon as it can proceed alone, it reaches the goal preordained for it from all eternity." [6]

Before leaving the cities of Mecca and Medina, the Báb beseeched God to hasten the hour of His martyrdom so that by this sacrifice men might know the truth.

"The drops of this consecrated blood," He said, "will be the seed out of which will arise the mighty Tree of God, the Tree that will gather beneath its all-embracing shadow the peoples and kindreds of the earth. Grieve not, therefore, if I depart out of this land, for I am hastening to fulfill My destiny." [7]

THE PERSECUTION BEGINS

THE BÁB RETURNED with Quddús to Búshihr. A short time later He sent him on to Shíráz to bring greetings and instructions to His family and to the believers there. The Báb also sent some of His writings to be shared with them. He bade Quddús farewell with the greatest kindness.

"The days of your companionship with Me," He told him, "are drawing to a close. . . . In this world of dust, no more than a few fleeting months of association with Me have been allotted to you. . . .

"The hand of destiny ere long will plunge you into an ocean of tribulation. . . . In the streets of Shíráz, indignities will be heaped upon you, and the severest injuries will afflict your body. You will survive . . . and will attain the presence of Him who is the object of our adoration . . . [that great Figure Who is yet to come]."[1]

In a short time, Quddús arrived in Shíráz. He began to speak everywhere of the wonderous days he had spent with the Báb. He aroused the whole city with his inspired words. He became very friendly with an old man named Mullá Sádiq, and gave him a copy of one of the Báb's writings.

In this writing the Báb once again intimated that, just as Shaykh Ahmad and Siyyid Kázim had promised, there would be two Messengers of God following close upon each other in this day.

He was but the Herald and the servant of that great One yet to come.

The enthusiasm which greeted the teaching of Quddús and Mullá Sádiq alarmed the city. Thousands of protests poured into the office of the governor, Husayn Khán.

Quddús claims that the Báb is the author of a new Revelation, the governor was told. He has written a book which is divinely inspired. Now Mullá Sádiq has embraced this Faith, and is fearlessly summoning our people to accept as well.

The governor ordered the arrest of both Quddús and Mullá Sádiq. They were delivered in irons to him. The commentary which the Báb had written for Mullá Husayn on the night He had announced His Mission was turned over to the governor. It had been seized from Mullá Sádiq.

Husayn Khán ignored Quddús because of his extreme youth. He directed his questions to Mullá Sádiq who was older. Angrily he tapped the commentary of the Báb, which he held in his hand, showing his displeasure with it.

"Tell me," he asked Mullá Sádiq, "if you are aware of the opening words of this book. Do you know that the Báb addresses the rulers and kings of the earth in harsh terms? He says: 'Divest yourselves of sovereignty, for He who is the King in truth has been made manifest. The Kingdom is God's!' "

The governor's wrath increased. "Does this mean that my sovereign, the Shah, whom I represent as Chief Magistrate in this region, must lay down his crown because of the ravings of this unlettered youth? Does it also mean that I, the governor, must relinquish my position?"

Mullá Sádiq replied unhesitatingly, saying, that if the words spoken by the Báb were true and that He were indeed a Messenger of God, then everything else that was happening in the world was of little importance. Kingdoms and ages would pass into dust, but the Word of God would endure.

Husayn Khán was displeased with the answer. He cursed Mullá Sádiq and Quddús. He ordered his attendants to strip Mullá Sádiq of his garments and to scourge him with a thousand lashes. He then commanded that the beards of both men should be burned, their noses pierced, and that a cord should be passed through this incision.

"Let them be led through the streets of the city by this halter," he commanded. "It will be an object lesson to the people of Shíráz. It will teach everyone who is thinking of embracing this Faith just what the punishment for such action will be!"

Mullá Sádiq was so advanced in age that he knew that he could not possibly survive such torture. Yet he was calm and self-possessed. He raised his eyes to heaven and offered a last prayer.

"O Lord, our God! We have heard the voice of the One that called. He called us to His Faith, saying: 'Believe ye on the Lord your God!' We have believed, O God. Forgive us then for our sins, and cause us to die with righteousness."

An eye-witness to the torture of Mullá Sádiq has given the following testimony:

"I was present when Mullá Sádiq was being scourged. I watched them stroke the lash to his bleeding shoulders until he became exhausted. No one watching believed he could outlast fifty such savage strokes without dying. He was a very old man. We marveled at his courage.

"Yet when the number of strokes already exceeded nine hundred, his face still retained its original serenity and calm.

"When he was later being expelled from the city, I approached him with great admiration and asked him how he had been able to withstand such punishment.

"He replied: 'The first seven strokes were severely painful. To the rest I seemed to have grown indifferent. I was wondering whether the strokes that followed were actually being applied to my own body. A feeling of joy seized me. I was trying to repress my feelings and restrain my laughter.'"

Mullá Sádiq looked at this eye-witness, as though trying to convey to him an important truth which he felt all men should know: that suffering, pain and persecution are only unbearable to those who had no purpose in life, no hope for the future; if they were withstood for the love of God, then the pain became pleasure in this world, and the sufferings became a means of being closer to God in the next.

"I can now realize," he told him, "how the Almighty is able, in the twinkling of an eye, to turn pain into ease and sorrow into gladness. Immensely exalted is His power above the weak imagining of His mortal creatures."

Both Mullá Sádiq and Quddús withstood their torture with great fortitude. For Quddús, this was but the beginning of greater suffering to come. Exhausted and bleeding, they were driven out of Shíráz. They were warned at the city gates that if they ever returned, they would both be crucified.

Mullá Sádiq and Quddús were among the first followers of the Báb to suffer persecution on Persian soil.[2]

THE GENTLE ARREST

Husayn Khán's anger was not satisfied by the punishment he had inflicted upon Mullá Sádiq and Quddús. He now directed his attack upon the Báb Himself. He sent a mounted escort to Búshihr, and ordered them to arrest the Báb and to bring Him back in chains to Shíráz. This spectacle, he felt, would dampen the enthusiasm of the people for His Cause.

The guards set out at once to make the arrest. As they were marching across the wilderness enroute to Búshihr, they met a horseman. It was the Báb, Who had come to meet them. The leader of the escort has himself related the incident:

"As we approached him, he saluted us and asked our destination. I said that the governor, Husayn Khán, had commanded us to go to Búshihr to make an inquiry.

"He smilingly observed, 'The governor has sent you to arrest Me. Here I am. Do with me as you please.'

"I was startled by his remark and his straightforwardness. I could not understand his readiness to subject himself to Husayn Khán, thus risking his safety and life."

The commander of the escort was very taken with the Báb. He did not wish Him to fall into the hands of the governor. He pretended that he did not recognize the Báb, and ordered his men to move on.

"I tried to ignore him and prepared to leave," the commander reported, "but he approached me again. 'I know that you are seeking Me. I prefer to deliver myself into your hands rather than subject you and your companions to unnecessary annoyance for My sake.' "

The commander pleaded with the Báb, telling Him to flee from Husayn Khán. He told Him of the suffering and torture which the governor had caused Mullá Sádiq and Quddús.

"He is ruthless," the commander said. "I do not wish to be his instrument for persecuting you, an innocent person. Escape to Mashad."

"Deliver Me into the hands of your master," the Báb replied. "Be not afraid, for no one will blame you. Until My last hour is at hand, none dare assail Me, none can frustrate the plan of the Almighty. And when My hour is come, how great will be My joy to quaff the cup of martyrdom in His name." [1]

The commander bowed his head in consent and carried out the Báb's wishes. He ordered his escort to permit the Báb to ride on ahead of them as though they were a guard of honor rather than a party of arrest. They continued in this fashion until they reached Shíráz.

People turned around in the street to watch them and to marvel at this spectacle. The escort, which had been commanded to bring the Báb back in chains, had returned Him instead with every sign of the respect due to royalty.

Husayn Khán was furious. He rebuked the Báb publicly. In abusive language, he denounced His conduct.

"Do you realize what mischief you have caused?" he asked insolently. "Are you not the man who claims to be the author of a new revelation?"

The Báb's gentle manners and courtesy only added to the governor's anger. The historian Nicolas wrote: "We know that the Báb especially commended politeness and the most refined courtesy in all social relations. 'Never sadden anyone, no matter whom, for no matter what,' he enjoined."

". . . I have taught the believer in my religion," He says Himself, "never to rejoice over the misfortune of anyone." [2]

Lovingly, but firmly the Báb reminded Husayn Khán that as governor of the Province of Fárs his duty was to determine the truth about the affairs in his region and not to make unjust decisions without first investigating personally.

These words made the governor's temper flame. He repaid the Báb's courtesy by turning to his attendant and commanding him to strike the Báb in the face.

The blow was so violent that it dislodged the Báb's headdress. The governor ordered the Báb to remain confined within the home of His uncle, Hájí Mírzá Siyyid 'Alí, until he had decided what to do with Him. He instructed the uncle to be prepared to surrender the Báb to the governor's office for punishment at a moment's notice.

For a while, the Báb led a life of comparative peace. During this period His followers met Him in secret in the home of His uncle. One such visitor was the well-known scholar and priest 'Abdu'l-Karím.

'Abdu'l-Karím was from the village of Qazvín. He was a merchant, but, so great was his longing to know about God, that he gave up his business and devoted his life to study. Because of his great thirst for knowledge, he soon eclipsed his fellow students. He was elevated to the station of a teacher. He was told that he need no longer attend the classes, for he now knew as much as the wisest doctor of religion. Therefore, he, 'Abdu'l-Karím, could now teach others.

This troubled 'Abdu'l-Karím's heart very greatly, for he knew that in truth he knew nothing. If he were considered to be among the wisest of all, who was there on earth who really new anything about Almighty God at all? 'Abdu'l-Karím refused to teach others for he felt himself unworthy.

Night after night he would withdraw to his room and implore God for guidance. Of one of those nights, 'Abdu'l-Karím himself has related:

"I would remain absorbed in my thoughts each night until dawn. I neither ate nor slept. At times I would commune with God. 'Thou seest me, O my Lord, and beholdest my plight. I am deeply troubled when I see the divisions that have torn Thy religion. What is the truth? Wilt Thou not guide me and relieve my doubts? Whither am I to turn for consolation and guidance?'

"I wept so bitterly that I seemed to have lost consciousness. There suddenly came to me the vision of a great gathering of people. A noble figure was speaking to them: 'Whoso maketh efforts for us,' he said, 'in our ways will we guide them.' I was fascinated by his face. I arose and advanced toward him and was about to throw myself at his feet when the vision vanished. My heart was flooded with light. My joy was indescribable."

'Abdu'l-Karím set out at once for Karbilá. There he saw Siyyid Kázim. He was standing addressing a crowd just as 'Abdu'l-Karím had seen him in his dream. He was speaking those very same words. 'Abdu'l-Karím spent an entire winter in close companionship with Siyyid Kázim, who spoke constantly of the coming Messenger.

"The Promised One lives in the midst of this people," he declared. "The appointed time for His appearance is fast approaching. Purify yourselves that you may recognize His beauty. After my departure, arise and seek Him. Do not rest for a moment until you find Him."

On the day when 'Abdu'l-Karím parted from Siyyid Kázim, he told him: "Rest assured, O 'Abdu'l-Karím, that you are one of those who, in the day of His appearance, will arise for the triumph of His Cause. You will, I hope, remember me on that blessed day."

'Abdu'l-Karím returned to his home in Qazvín to await that wonderful day. A few years passed with no sign of the Promised One's coming, but 'Abdu'l-Karím's heart was assured.

He returned to his business as a merchant, but each night he would come home and withdraw to the quiet of his room. He would beseech God with all his heart, saying, "Thou hast, by the mouth of an inspired servant of Thine, promised that I shall attain unto the presence of Thy Messenger and hear Thy Word. How long wilt Thou withhold me from my promise?" Each night he would renew this prayer and would continue in his supplications until the break of day.

"One night I was once again so wrapt in prayer that I seemed to have fallen into a trance," he related. "There appeared before me a bird, white as snow, which hovered above my head and alighted upon the twig of a tree beside me. In accents of indescribable sweetness, that bird spoke these words: 'Are you seeking the Promised One, O 'Abdu'l-Karím? Lo, the year '60.' Immediately the bird flew away and vanished.

"The mystery of those words greatly agitated me. The memory of that voice lingered in my memory both sleeping and waking. When in the year '60 I heard of a wondrous personage in Shíráz, I hastened to that city.

"Eventually I attained the presence of the Báb. He turned to me and in the same sweet melodious voice of the white bird, He asked me: 'Are you seeking the Manifestation [Promised One]?"

'Abdu'l-Karím burst into tears and threw himself at the feet of the Báb in a state of profound ecstasy, much to the astonishment of his companions. The Báb took him lovingly in His arms, kissed his forehead, and invited him to be seated by His side. In a tone of tender affection, He succeeded in appeasing the tumult of his heart.[3]

In spite of Husayn Khán's close supervision, many such great figures came to visit the Báb. Stories of conversions similar to that of 'Abdu'l-Karím caused great excitement in Shíráz. Both the famous and the lowly were willing to take whatever risk was necessary to gain His presence. People met in groups on the street to discuss Him, some blaming, some approving.

Husayn Khán was infuriated at his helplessness and inability to stem the flow of the Báb's rising popularity.

THE ENCHANTMENT
OF THE KING'S MESSENGER

Mullá Husayn came to visit the Báb in Shíráz. Immediately strong voices were raised against him.

"Mullá Husayn has returned to Shíráz," they cried to the authorities. "Now, with his chief, the Báb, he is scheming some fierce onslaught against our time honored institutions!"

So grave and menacing was the situation, that the Báb instructed Mullá Husayn to return to his home province of Khurásán. He also dismissed all the rest of His companions except 'Abdu'l-Karím, whom He kept with Him to help transcribe His writings.

His disciples spread throughout the length and breadth of the land fearlessly proclaiming the regenerating power of the new-born Revelation.

Soon the fame of the Báb spread far beyond the circle of His disciples. It reached the authorities. They became alarmed at the enthusiasm with which the people everywhere accepted His message. An historical account states that the followers of the Báb were "ardent, brave, carried away, ready for anything. . . . every one of its members thought himself of no importance, and burned with a desire to sacrifice his life-blood and his belongings for the cause of Truth." [1] This was no longer a local matter, the authorities argued.

The same flood of persecution which surrounded Jesus, now gradually engulfed the Báb. The combined opposition of church and state unleashed what historians have called the most appalling wave of hatred imaginable. Soon the sands of Persia were stained by a freely given, red river of human martyrdom.

The officials arranged great public debates in Shíráz and invited the governor, the clergy, the military chiefs, as well as the people to attend. They hoped that in this manner they might discredit the young Prophet.

However, the Báb spoke such searching truths on these occasions, that day by day the crowds that followed Him greatly increased in number. His purity of conduct at an age when passions are intense impressed the people who met Him. He was possessed of extraordinary eloquence and daring. An historian of those times, Comte de Gobineau, writes: "From his first public appearances, they sent their most able mullás [religious leaders] to argue with him and confuse him. . . . instead of benefiting the clergy, they contributed quite a little to spread and exalt, at their own expense, the renown of this enthusiastic teacher." [2]

The Báb exposed, unsparingly, their vices and their corruption. Like Jesus, He proved their infidelity to their own belief. He shamed them in their lives. He defeated them with their own Holy Book in His hand.

Gobineau says further that the Báb was "of extreme simplicity of manner, of a fascinating gentleness; those gifts were further heightened by his great youth and his marvelous charm. He drew about himself a number of persons who were deeply edified. . . . He did not open his lips (we are assured by those who knew him) without stirring the hearts to their very depths." [3]

Sir Francis Younghusband in his book, *The Gleam*, writes of His "wonderful charm of appearance. Men were impressed by his knowledge and his penetrating eloquence of speech. . . . As soon as he ascended the pulpit there was silence." [4]

Another historical document states: "By the uprightness of his life the young Siyyid [the Báb] served as an example to those about him. He was willingly listened to . . . when he condemned the abuses in all classes of society. His words were repeated and elaborated upon and they spoke of him as the true Master and gave themselves to him unreservedly." [5]

These impressions of the Báb did not come from His followers and sympathizers alone. Comte de Gobineau states in his history of the times that "even the orthodox Muhammadans who were present [at these meetings when the Báb spoke] have retained an indelible memory of them and never recall them without a sort of terror. They agreed unanimously that [His] eloquence . . . was of an incomparable kind, such that, without having been an eyewitness, one could not possibly imagine." [6]

Soon all of Persia was stirring with stories about the Báb. The people eagerly hungered for more news. A wave of enthusiasm swept over the country. Leading figures of both State and Church either attended these meetings in person or delegated their most able representatives to inquire into the truth of the matter.

The *Journal Asiatique* states that the Faith of the Báb had many followers "in all classes of society, and many among them were of important standing; great lords, members of the clergy, military men and merchants had all accepted this doctrine." [7]

Those in authority began to ask searching questions. Finally the Crown itself became interested. Muhammad Sháh, the king, decided to investigate. He felt that he should know if the reports about this remarkable young man were true. So he summoned his Prime Minister.

"Who is there," he asked, "that can be trusted to make this investigation?"

After much consultation, the king and the Prime Minister chose someone in whom they both had the greatest faith. He was surnamed Vahíd. [8]

Vahíd was known to be the most learned, eloquent, and influential of all the king's people. If anyone could silence the Báb, it would be he. The great leaders of Persia all testified to his knowledge and wisdom. His father was one of the most celebrated religious doctors of that age, and now Vahíd had followed in his father's footsteps and even eclipsed him. His fame and popularity were known throughout the land. He was admitted to be outstanding among all the leading figures of Persia. Whenever he was present at a meeting, he was invariably the chief speaker. Furthermore, Vahíd, because of his wisdom, was frequently consulted by the government in times of trouble. [9]

He was living at that time in Tihrán as an honored guest of the king, therefore they thought at once of Vahíd when he sought an honest person to send on this important mission. The king was very disturbed. He wished to know what political significance the rise of this new Faith might have, so he gave Vahíd careful instructions.

"Go at once to Shíráz. Interview the Báb. Find out if these tales of wonder we hear are true. Then report to us personally and in detail what you discover."

The Prime Minister was not above planting a seed in Vahíd's mind before he left. "If you can discredit and unmask him, it will add greatly to your own stature," he told him.

Vahíd mounted the horse which had been given to him by the king and left immediately for Shíráz. On his way, he decided upon the questions which he would ask the Báb. These questions Vahíd felt would test the Báb's knowledge to the utmost, and upon the answers which He gave would rest, in Vahíd's opinion, the truth or falsehood of His claim to be a Messenger of God.

When Vahíd arrived in Shíráz, he met an intimate friend whose name was 'Azím. "You have met the Báb," Vahíd said to his friend. "What do you think of him? Are you satisfied with him? Is he a charlatan?"

"Meet him yourself," 'Azím replied. "Make your own decision. But, as a friend, I would advise you to be careful. You will regret any discourtesy which you show to him."

Vahíd arranged to meet the Báb, Who welcomed him with affection. For nearly two hours Vahíd courteously directed question after question at the Báb. He pointed out the most obscure passages of Holy Scripture. He dwelt upon the mysterious prophecies and traditions which must be fulfilled at the time of the coming of the Promised One. He spoke at great length of certain difficult and vague metaphysical themes.

The Báb listened patiently to Vahíd's learned and detailed references, quietly noting his questions. Vahíd suddenly felt ashamed of this long and showy display of his own learning. Later he reported:

"Quietly the Báb began to speak. He gave brief but persuasive answers to each of my questions. The conciseness and clarity of his replies excited my admiration and wonder. My feeling of personal superiority vanished. I was embarrassed by my own presumptuousness and pride. I felt so abased that I hurriedly asked permission to retire. I told him: 'If it please God, I shall in my next interview submit the rest of my questions and conclude my inquiry.'"

Vahíd withdrew. As soon as he left the Báb he hastened to the home of his friend 'Azím and told him what had happened during the first interview to cause his own deep humiliation.

Vahíd was confident that his inquiry into the Faith of the Báb would end with the second interview. He had his questions clearly in mind. They were direct and to the point this time. He would be polite, as 'Azím suggested, but firm.

However, when he entered the Báb's presence and began to speak with Him, Vahíd found himself discussing things which had nothing whatsoever to do with his inquiry.

All the questions which he had intended to submit to the Báb had disappeared from his memory. Then later, to his greater surprise, he found that the Báb was answering those forgotten questions. He spoke with that same brevity and lucidity which had so excited his admiration before.

"I seemed to have been in a daze during the first part of that interview," he later observed. "Then, when I realized what the Báb was saying, that he was answering my unasked questions, I awoke with a start. I was thrilled. Yet, in spite of my attraction to him, a voice kept whispering to me: 'Might not this all be a mere accidental coincidence?' I became so agitated that I could not collect my thoughts. I refused to remain. A second time I begged leave to retire."

Vahíd returned to 'Azím again and told him what had happened. 'Azím spoke frankly to this most learned of the Persians.

"Would that schools had been utterly abolished," he said, "and that neither of us had ever entered one, if through our little-mindedness and conceit this acquired knowledge is withholding us from the redeeming Grace of God, and is causing pain to Him Who is the bearer of His Message."

Vahíd admitted that pride in his own knowledge had been like a curtain which separated him from the Báb. 'Azím entreated him, "This time go with humility and detachment from all that you have learned in the past. Perhaps he will relieve your doubt and perplexity."

This third and final interview has been reported in detail by

Vahíd not only for the king and Prime Minister, but also for posterity. Vahíd states:

"I resolved that in my third interview, I would not ask aloud for proof of his mission. Instead, in my innermost heart, I would request the Báb to write a commentary upon a special chapter of Holy Scripture which had always interested me.

"'If he does this,' I told myself, 'and if it's style and truth distinguish it from the standards current amongst men, then I shall acknowledge his truth. I shall even embrace his cause. However, if he fails, I shall denounce him.'

"As soon as I was ushered into the Báb's presence, a sense of fear, for which I could not account, seized me. My limbs quivered as I beheld his face. On repeated occasions I had been in the presence of the king without feeling the slightest trace of timidity, but I was now so awed and shaken that I could not remain standing on my feet.

"The Báb beheld my plight. He arose from his seat and came to me. He took my hand and seated me beside him.

"'Seek from Me' he said. 'Whatever is your heart's desire.' 'I will readily reveal it to you.'

"I was helpless. I felt powerless to speak. He looked at me, smiled, and said, 'Were I to reveal unto you the commentary on the Súrih of Kawther, would you acknowledge that My words are born of the Spirit of God? Would you recognize that My utterance can in no wise be associated with sorcery or magic?'

"Tears came to my eyes as I heard him speak these words. All I was able to say were the words: 'O our Lord, with ourselves we have dealt unjustly: if Thou forgive us not and have not pity upon us, we shall surely be of those who perish.'"

Then the Báb called for his pen-case and some paper. He began to reveal the commentary which Vahíd's inmost heart had requested.

No less than two thousand verses were revealed by the Báb on that occasion. The bewildering rapidity with which they were written was even less remarkable than their matchless beauty and profound meaning.[10] Even more startling to Vahíd was the fact that this explanation which the Báb gave was the one which he himself had discovered after long meditation. He believed himself to be the only one who had reached this hidden meaning, and he had never made it known to anyone.[11]

Vahíd's report on this interview communicates his sense of wonder: "How am I to describe this scene of inexpressible majesty? Verses streamed from His pen with a rapidity that was truly astounding. The incredible swiftness of His writing, the soft and gentle murmur of His voice, the stupendous force of His style, all amazed and bewildered me. He continued in this manner until the approach of sunset, not pausing until the entire commentary was completed. Then he laid down His pen and asked for tea to be brought. Soon after, He began to read it aloud in my presence. My heart leaped madly as I heard Him pour out, in accents of unutterable sweetness, those treasures hidden in that holy chapter.

"I was so entranced by its beauty that three times I was on the verge of fainting. The Báb revived my failing strength by sprinkling rose-water upon my face. When He had completed His recital, the Báb arose to depart."

With 'Abdu'l-Karím, Vahíd devoted three days and three nights to transcribing the newly revealed commentary. They verified all the prophecies and traditions in the text and found them to be entirely accurate.

Vahíd summed up his report on his investigation of the Báb by saying: "Such was the state of certitude to which I had attained that nothing could shake my confidence in the greatness of His Cause."

Vahíd discharged his responsibility to the king, writing a detailed and personal account of his investigation of the Báb.

Vahíd himself did not return to the capital. He began to summon the people to accept the new Messenger of God. Such was his enthusiasm and fervor, that other learned doctors decided Vahíd must have suddenly lost his mind. A history of the times states that Vahíd "wrote without fear or care a detailed account of his observations to the . . . chamberlain in order that the latter might submit it to the notice of the late king, while he [Vahíd] himself journeyed to all parts of Persia, and in every town and station summoned the people from the pulpit-tops in such wise that other learned doctors [leaders] decided that he must be mad, accounting it a sure case of bewitchment." [12]

When the report was given to the king that Vahíd had investigated the Báb, found His Cause to be the truth, and had accepted it himself, the king was greatly troubled. He spoke confidentially to his Prime Minister.

"We have been told," he said, "that Vahíd has become a follower of the Báb. If this is true, it would be wise for us to cease belittling the cause of this young man from Shíráz."

Immediately the Prime Minister began to attack Vahíd for having fallen under the spell of a sorcerer, but the king would still not hear any evil spoken of this great figure. He rebuked the Prime Minister.

"Vahíd is a man of noble lineage. He is also a man of great learning and great virtue."

Husayn Khán, at whose home Vahíd stayed during his interviews with the Báb, also attacked him openly. To him also the king sent an imperial command which read: "It is strictly forbidden to any one of our subjects to utter any such words as would detract from the exalted rank of Vahíd. He will never incline his ear to any Cause unless he believes it will be for the advancement of the best interests of our realm."

Thus ended the story of the king's investigation of the Cause of the Báb. Vahíd, acknowledged as the most outstanding of the leaders of Persia, selected as his personal messenger by the king himself, embraced the Faith of the Báb and began to teach it. To Husayn Khán, the governor, who challenged him, saying, "Have you fallen under the enchantment of the Báb's magic spell?" Vahíd replied: "No one but God can captivate the heart of Vahíd. He alone can change the hearts of men. Whosoever can ensnare my heart is of God and His word is unquestionably the voice of Truth." [13]

Vahíd was but one of many illustrious figures who were being attracted to the Faith of the Báb. The Prime Minister and the people of the royal court tried to belittle each of these new believers in the eyes of the king.

One day as the Shah was riding on horseback, an old man crossed the street in front of him. Undisturbed by the presence of the king, the old man approached him and greeted him cheerfully. The king was very much taken with the old man's courtesy, dignity and manner. He replied to the greeting and invited the old man to come and visit him at the palace.

Before they had returned to the royal residence, those close to the king began whispering to him.

"Does your Majesty not realize that this old man is none other than one of the famous and newly converted followers of the Báb?

He has proclaimed himself so. He has publicly announced his undying loyalty to the cause of that youth."

The king knew they were jealous and envious of the attention he had bestowed upon the old man. He was displeased with them, and at the same time confused by their constant backbiting.

"How strange!" he exclaimed. "Whoever is distinguished by learning, by uprightness of conduct, and by courtesy of manners, my own court immediately denounces as a follower of the Báb? Why? Why is this?" [14]

Because of the orders of the king, Husayn Khán was no longer able to express his hatred of Vahíd openly; therefore, he began quietly to undermine Vahíd's friendship with the king. In the days to come this treachery would lead to Vahíd's martyrdom in his native town of Nayríz.

THE AVENGING HAND OF GOD

THE FEW MONTHS which the Báb spent as a prisoner in the house of His uncle, Hájí Mírzá Siyyid 'Alí, were to be His last days of friendship and tranquility. They were now drawing rapidly to a close.

What memories must have stirred in His mind as He shared those last free hours with His family and friends. This uncle had shown great love for the Báb throughout His entire life. In His early childhood, the Báb lost His father, and was brought up by this same uncle. Anxious to give Him every advantage, Hájí Mírzá Siyyid 'Alí had placed the Báb under the care of a tutor while He was still a child.

Those days have been preserved for history through the words of that tutor: "The sweetness of His speech utterance still lingers in my memory. I felt impelled to take Him back to His uncle . . . to tell him how unworthy I felt to teach so remarkable a child.

"I have brought Him back to you," the tutor told Hájí Mírzá Siyyid 'Alí. "And commit Him into your protection. He is not to be treated as a mere child. I can already discern evidences in Him of a mysterious power."

The Báb's uncle scolded Him and said, "Have you forgotten my instructions? Return to school and follow the example of your fellow pupils. Do not speak out, but observe silence and listen to every word spoken by your teacher."

The little boy promised to obey faithfully, but it was impossible to restrain His spirit. The tutor said frankly, "Day after day He continued to display such remarkable signs of wisdom that I felt helpless to teach Him." [1]

A well-known priest went to the home of the Báb's uncle at this time. He has given the following account of that visit:

"Early one morning I heard from the prayer-room, which was next to mine, a tiny sweet voice. It was a little child's voice raised in prayer. Such prayers, such a voice, such devotion that I was absolutely enraptured. I waited patiently until dawn and then I saw a boy of about seven years of age. As soon as I gazed upon the child, I saw such a beautiful expression that I felt sure that I could never find another like Him in the whole human race."

The priest followed the boy to the tiny school that He attended. He could not forget that face. He went to the tutor and inquired about the child.

"What do you think of this boy?" he asked.

The tutor spoke with great feeling. "What can I say about this child! He comes to my school as a pupil, but in reality, He is the teacher and I am the pupil. If you could but hear the wonderful things He says in the classroom. Such deep and important questions He speaks about. What can I say about this child? To me He seems to be ready to give out a message to the world."

The admiration of the tutor for this little boy increased the priest's interest and wonder. He returned to the home of the Báb's uncle and told him what the tutor had said. The uncle then confided to the priest the dream which he had had about his nephew when the Báb was five years old.

"I dreamed that a pair of scales hung from heaven," he said. "On one side of the scales was one of the Prophets. On the other side, this child was placed by an invisible hand. Then, the side with the child slowly weighed down the other." [2]

The Báb's uncle was finally persuaded to take the boy out of school. With the greatest of love and care the uncle raised the child. When He was seventeen the Báb left Shíráz for Búshihr where He engaged in business for His uncle as a merchant. During this time He won the esteem of all the merchants because of His honesty and kindness.

An eye-witness who met the Báb in those days has said: "I often heard those who were closely associated with Him testify to the purity of His character, to the charm of His manners and to His high integrity. A trust was confided to His care to dispose of, at a fixed price. When the Báb sent the payment, it far exceeded the amount fixed. The owner wrote the Báb asking the reason. The Báb replied, "What I have sent you is entirely your due. There is not a single farthing in excess of what is your right. There was a time when the trust you delivered to me attained this value. Failing to sell it at that price, I now feel it my duty to offer you the whole of that sum." [3]

When the Báb was twenty-two, He married and had one child, a son, whom He named Ahmad. The child died the year before the Báb proclaimed His Mission. He wrote movingly of the passing of His son whom He had loved dearly.

"O God, my God!" He said. "Would that a thousand Ishmaels were given to Me, this Abraham of Thine, that I might have offered them, each and all, as a loving sacrifice unto Thee. Grant that the sacrifice of My son, My only son, may be acceptable unto Thee. Grant that it be a prelude to the sacrifice of My own, My entire self, in the path of Thy good pleasure. Endow with Thy grace My life-blood which I yearn to shed in Thy path. Cause it to water and nourish the seed of Thy Faith. Endow it with celestial potency, that this infant seed of God may germinate in the hearts of men, that it may thrive and prosper, that it may grow to become a mighty tree, beneath the shadow of which all the peoples of the earth may gather." [4]

The wife of the Báb understood His mission from the very beginning. The Báb confided to her the secret of His future sufferings. He unfolded to her eyes the significance of the events that were soon to take place, and told her not to disclose this secret to anyone. He counselled her to be patient and resigned to the Will of God.

In order to lighten the burden of her woes in the days to come, He entrusted her with a special prayer. The reading of this prayer, He promised, would remove her difficulties.

"In the hour of your perplexity," He directed her, "recite this prayer ere you go to sleep. I Myself will appear to you and will banish your anxiety." [5]

These peaceful days within the circle of His family were now at an end. He would soon be caught up in a whirlwind of adversity which would never cease until it had carried Him swiftly to the field of martyrdom.

The governor of Shíráz, Husayn Khán, exerted every effort to involve the Báb in fresh embarrassments. He was outraged because Vahíd's acceptance to the Báb had for a time tied his hands. He feared to offend the king. Yet he could not bear to see the Báb moving about once again free and unmolested. The sight of the constant stream of followers and friends who were once more entering His house enraged him.

The Báb was very courageous in proclaiming His Faith. He sent a message to one of the leading figures of the city of Zanján, saying: "He Whose virtues the late Siyyid Kázim unceasingly extolled, and to the approach of Whose Revelation he continually alluded, is now revealed. I am that Promised One." [6]

Husayn Khán decided to employ spies to watch the Báb secretly for evidence of the slightest mistake on His part. The governor sent repeated letters to the Prime Minister, Hájí Mírzá Áqásí, expressing his grave concern at the huge numbers who were embracing His Cause. The Prime Minister responded promptly to the governor's entreaties. He told Husayn Khán that he was sick and tired of the turmoil in Shíráz.

"Have done with the reformer," he ordered. "Have him killed immediately and secretly." [7]

One of Husayn Khán's agents came to him with the news that the people gathered about the Báb were now so many as to constitute a public menace. The spy reported: "The eager crowd that presses in each night to see him surpasses in number those that gather every day before the seat of your government. Among them are men who are celebrated for their exalted rank as well as for their profound learning. So great has become their love for the Báb, that none of your subordinates other than myself is willing to acquaint you with the truth about conditions."

Husayn Khán's anger was now directed not only at the Báb and His companions, but also at his own untrustworthy assistants. The spy suggested a plan.

"If you will permit me," he said, "I will surprise the Báb at midnight and will deliver him in handcuffs along with certain of his companions who can be made to confirm the truth of my statements."

The governor refused. "I know better than you what has to be done," he said. "Watch me, I will show you how to deal with him."

Husayn Khán summoned the chief constable.

"Go to the house of the Báb's uncle," he commanded. "Quietly and unobserved, scale the wall, climb to the roof and from there suddenly enter his home. Arrest the Báb and bring him here to me. Bring all who are in his company, and seize all the books you can find."

Husayn Khán slowly closed his fingers into a fist as though he were crushing some hated thing. "I swear that this night I shall have the Báb executed before my eyes," he said. "I shall slay him with all his companions. That should quench the fire they have kindled in my region. It will be a final warning to all who seek to disturb the peace of this land. By this act tonight, I will stamp out this grave menace once and for all." [8]

Later that night the chief constable, as instructed, broke into the house, arrested the Báb, and seized all documents. He ordered the Báb and His companions to accompany him to the house of the governor.

The Báb was calm and unruffled. He knew the hour of separation had struck. He quoted words from the chief constable's Holy Book. "That with which they are threatened is for the morning." He paused significantly. "Is not the morning near?"

The chief constable did not understand that by those words the Báb foretold the beginning of suffering on both sides. He conducted the Báb and His friends into the street where he put them under guard.

As they were approaching the market-place, they heard cries of excitement. People were rushing frantically from the city as though fleeing from an appalling calamity.

The constable was filled with dread as an awesome sight passed before them. A long train of coffins was being hurried through the streets. Each coffin was followed by a procession of men and women loudly uttering cries of anguish. The chief constable stopped one of the mourners.

"What has happened?" he cried. "In the name of God, answer me! What dreadful thing has struck our city?"

"Flee for your life," he was warned. "Cholera! A violent plague has suddenly broken out. The city has been devastated. Already since the hour of midnight, it has taken the lives of over a hundred people. All of us have abandoned our homes and are calling upon God to aid us!"

The chief constable rushed his prisoners through the streets to the home of the governor. The house was deserted. The governor had fled.

"Where has he gone," the chief constable asked.

"Out of the city," he was told. "Already three of his servants have died of the plague. Several members of his family are now dangerously ill. He has forsaken them and sought refuge in a garden outside the city."

The chief constable decided to take the Báb to his own home. He would keep Him and His friends there until he received further instructions from the governor.

As he approached his home, he heard the sound of weeping. He became terrified. As he rushed forward, he remembered those words of the Báb's spoken such a short time before: "That with which they are threatened is for the morning, is not the morning near?" The constable was told that his own son had been stricken with the cholera and was almost dead. He was crushed by the news.

Perhaps, he told himself, the manner in which he and the governor had treated their prisoner was responsible for this suffering. He turned and approached the Báb. He threw himself at His feet and implored Him to save the life of his son.

"Do not punish him for the guilt which his father has committed," he pleaded. "I repent of what I have done. I swear that at this very moment I have resigned my post under Husayn Khán."

The Báb comforted the constable. He directed him to take some of the water which He had poured out. He told him to give it to his son to drink.

"It will save his life," He promised.

The chief constable followed directions, and shortly after his son recovered. As soon as the constable saw the signs of recovery in his son, he sat down and wrote a long letter to Husayn Khán. He told the governor the entire story of that night of panic, and begged him to cease his attacks on the Báb.

"Have pity on yourself," he wrote, "as well as on those who are entrusted to your care."

The governor replied: "Release him."

Husayn Khán insisted however that the Báb leave the city of

Shíráz at once.[9] If he could not triumph over Him personally, he could at least drive Him out from the circle of His friends.

By this harsh action, Husayn Khán brought the days of his own peace and prestige to an end. History records that a short time later he was dismissed from office. From the day of his dismissal, he fell victim to several misfortunes. No one was willing to come to his assistance. In the end his plight was so tragic that he was unable to earn his daily living. Sunk in misery and shame, he languished until his death.

The Báb Himself foretold the governor's downfall. In a letter written to the Shah, He said of Husayn Khán: "his cruelty has drawn the punishment of heaven."[10]

The Báb was obedient to the decree of Husayn Khán. He made plans to leave Shíráz at once. Thus, in the summer of 1846, He bade farewell to His native town, to His family, and to His friends.

He left His family in the care of His uncle, Hájí Mírzá Siyyid 'Alí. He embraced His uncle lovingly in parting.

"I will again meet you," He promised him, "amidst the mountains of Adhirbáyján, from whence I will send you forth to obtain the crown of martyrdom. I Myself will follow you, . . . and will join you in the realm of eternity."[11]

THE KINDLY GOVERNOR

THE BÁB DEPARTED for Isfáhán, a city noted for the learning of its clergy. Here He found that the first one to have embraced His Faith was a humble sifter of wheat. As soon as he had been given the Message of the Báb he accepted and devoted his life to teaching others. A few years later, when he heard that some of his fellow believers were being martyred, he left his work, arose and carrying his sieve in his hand hurried through the bazaars of Isfáhán.

"Why leave in such a hurry?" his friends asked.

"I am going to join the glorious company of those who are willing to give their life for their faith. With this sieve which I carry with me, I intend to sift people in every village through which I pass. Whoever I find ready to embrace this Cause I will ask to join me and hasten to the fold of martyrdom."

Such was the devotion of this youth, that the Báb referred to him with great love, saying that Isfáhán was a city distinguished by the religious fervor of its inhabitants, the learning of its priests, and high and low alike shared the eager expectancy of the coming of the Promised One. Yet, when the Messenger of God appeared, the learned, the wise and the religious rejected Him. Of all the inhabitants of that seat of learning, only one person, a sifter of wheat, was found to recognize the Truth.

This, the Báb said, was the fulfillment of the prophecy of the

Promised One which said, "the lowliest of the creatures shall become the most exalted, and the most exalted shall become the most
debased." [1]

As the Báb approached the city of Isfáhán, He wrote a letter to
the governor of that province, Manúchihr Khán. The letter was so
courteous and friendly, and of such exquisite penmanship, that it
immediately attracted the attention of the governor. Unlike Husayn
Khán, he was not opposed to knowing more about this Young Man.
He decided to take the Báb under his protection until he could
investigate the truth of His claim.

Manúchihr Khán instructed the chief priest of the Province to
meet the Báb and to take Him into his own home. He told him
to treat the Báb with great kindness and consideration.

The chief priest was very displeased at being given this task.
However, he was afraid to offend the powerful Manúchihr Khán,
so he complied grudgingly to the request. Yet even he admitted
that in spite of his anger, from the very first night, he fell under
the spell of the Báb.

The Báb's presence in Isfáhán caused even more excitement than
it had caused in Shíráz. An unceasing stream of visitors and friends
flowed from every quarter of the province to the house of the
chief priest. Some came out of curiosity, some came to gain a deeper
understanding of His message. Some came, as they had to Jesus,
to seek a remedy for their ills or suffering.[2] All were welcomed and
were helped according to their needs.

The governor himself, Manúchihr Khán, came one night to visit
the Báb. He asked Him to write a commentary upon the specific
mission which Muhammad had come to earth to discharge.

The Báb instantly took up His pen and began to write. In less
than two hours, He filled about fifty pages. The governor was
deeply impressed with the originality, vigor, and accuracy of that
commentary.

With masterly insight, the Báb once again expressed the central
theme of His teaching: that the people had looked for the arrival
of the Day of the Promised One, and now that Day had come.
He argued with such force and courage that those who heard Him
were amazed.[3]

The governor was enthusiastic. "Hear me!" he called to the people
present at that meeting. "I take you as my witnesses. I solemnly
testify to my belief in the superhuman power with which this youth

is blessed. It is a power that no amount of learning can ever impart."

With these words, the governor brought the meeting to a close.

The brother of the chief priest writhed in envy at this statement. He was jealous of the attentions which the governor and his brother showered upon the Báb. His bitter enmity and savage cruelty to both the followers of the Báb and to the followers of the One Whom the Báb said would come after Him, were to earn him in the future the title: "Raqsha—the female serpent."

He plotted with the other priests of the region to undermine the Báb's growing power. It was easy to win their support, for they firmly believed that unless they arose to stem the tide of this popular enthusiasm for the Báb, the foundations of their own livelihood and future might be swept away.

At first they refrained from outright hostility. Instead, they began circulating wild rumors and base accusations concerning the teachings of the Báb. They made certain that these false rumors reached the capital at Tihrán and were especially made known to the Prime Minister, Hájí Míráz Áqásí.

The Prime Minister was already fearful that the king might be inclined to befriend the Báb because of Vahíd's acceptance of Him. He knew that such a friendship between the Sháh and the Báb might easily lead to his own downfall. He was even more afraid that the governor of Isfáhán, Manúchihr Khán, might try to arrange an interview between them, as the governor enjoyed the complete confidence of the king. Hájí Míráz Áqásí knew therefore that he must prevent such a meeting. He wrote a strongly worded message to the chief priest at Isfáhán, and lashed out at him for playing host to the Báb.

"We expected you to resist this teaching with all your might," he said. "Instead you befriend an arch-enemy. You have sheltered and glorified the author of a contemptible and dangerous movement."

The Prime Minister wrote to all the other priests of Isfáhán as well. Although he had previously ignored them, now he showered his attention and favors upon them. He made lavish promises to them. They knew what he wanted, and by his gifts to them, he welded them together against the Báb.

The chief priest still was afraid to come out openly against the Báb because of the governor, Manúchihr Khán. He did, however, take steps to lessen the ever-increasing number of visitors who thronged each day at the door of the Báb. The chief priest's brother secretly encouraged the other priests to attack the Báb directly. He induced them to begin preaching against Him from the pulpit.

When Manúchihr Khán heard of this, he immediately had the Báb brought into the safety of his own home. This protective gesture by the governor further inflamed the priests of Isfáhán. They called for a great gathering of all their numbers. Once assembled, they issued a written document to be signed and sealed by all the religious leaders of the city. It condemned the Báb to death. About seventy of the leading members of the clergy set their seal to this document.

Two of the priests refused to sign it. It was an abusive document, they said. The chief priest did not sign it because he feared the governor's wrath. Instead of signing it, he wrote on the document in his own handwriting saying that he could find no fault with the Báb's character or person. Then he added: "However, the extravagance of his claims and his disdainful contempt for the things of this world incline me to believe that he is devoid of reason and judgement."

The governor was secretly informed of the plan of the priests to execute the Báb, so he conceived a plan of his own. He issued a statement that he was sending the Báb to Tihrán. Then he gave instructions for the Báb to leave Isfáhán at sundown and openly proceed toward Tihrán under a protective escort of five hundred of his own mounted bodyguard. He gave further orders that at each three mile post, one hundred of the soldiers should return to Isfáhán. To the captain of the last hundred, a man in whom the governor placed complete confidence, he gave instructions to send back twenty of the one hundred soldiers at every further mile post. Of the remaining twenty, ten should be dispatched to Ardistán to collect taxes. The final ten, all of whom were his most trusted hand-picked men, should return in disguise with the Báb to the governor's home in Isfáhán.

The instructions were carefully carried out. In order to assure the safety and comfort of the Báb upon His return the governor, Manúchihr Khán, had Him occupy his own private apartment. He served the meals himself, and waited upon the Báb at all times for a period of four months.

Three orders to slay the Báb had already been issued. One by the Prime Minister, one by Husayn Khán, and one by the priests of

Isfáhán. Each had failed. It had been exactly as the Báb had told the military escort of Husayn Khán when they had come to arrest Him on the way from Búshihr:

"No one knows the mystery of My Cause. No one can fathom its secrets. Until My last hour has come, none can frustrate the plan of the Almighty."

One day, while the Báb was seated in the private garden of the governor, Manúchihr Khán approached Him. He said, "The Almighty has endowed me with great riches. Now that I have recognized the truth of your Message, I desire to offer all of my possessions to further the interests of this Faith."

Manúchihr Khán had a plan already devised. "It is my intention," he told the Báb, "to go at once to Tihrán and do my best to win over the king. His confidence in me is firm and unshaken in spite of the Prime Minister. I am certain that he will embrace this Faith and arise to promote it.

"I will also try to induce the king to dismiss the profligate Hájí Míráz Áqásí. His folly has brought our land to the brink of ruin.

"I hope," he concluded, "to be enabled to attract the hearts of the kings and rulers of the world to this wonderful Cause."

The Báb was deeply moved. "May God reward your noble intentions," He said. "So lofty a purpose is to me even more precious than the act itself. Your days and mine are numbered, however; they are too short for Me to witness, and allow you to achieve, the realization of your hopes."

The Báb told Manúchihr Khán that the Faith of God would not be spread by noble and wealthy figures. Rather, He said, it would triumph through the efforts of the poor, the persecuted, and the lowly. Through the blood they shed in the path of their Lord, and through the sacrifice and suffering of those humble people, the Faith of God would be spread throughout the world. The Báb made Manúchihr Khán a promise as a reward for his love and service.

"God," He said, "will in the world to come shower upon you inestimable blessings, but of your earthly life there remain only three months and nine days."

As the days of his life drew to a close, the governor spent more and more time with the Báb.

"I feel a great happiness flooding my life," he told the Báb one day, "but I am apprehensive for You. I fear to leave You to the mercy of my successor, Gurgín Khán. He will discover Your presence in this house and will grievously ill-treat You."

"Fear not," the Báb assured him. He quoted words akin to those spoken by Christ and Muhammad under similar circumstances, saying:

"Of My own will have I chosen to be afflicted by My enemies that God might accomplish the thing destined to be done."

Manúchihr Khán was satisfied with these words. His heart was refreshed. He knew now that he had not spent his own days on earth in vain. He had met and believed in the Promised One. His ears had not been stopped by his own learning, nor had his eyes been blinded by his own wealth. Serene and confident, he died three months and nine days later after a slight fever.

Mir Muhammad Husayn, the brother of the chief priest who so bitterly persecuted the Báb and His followers in Isfáhán, did not escape the avenging finger that so remorselessly sought out these persecutors. He was expelled from Isfáhán, and, despised, wandered from one village to another. He finally contracted a loathesome disease from which he sickened and died, a disease so foul smelling that his own wife and daughter could not bear to attend him.

Almost immediately Gurgín Khán, Manúchihr Khán's successor, was informed of the Báb's presence in the governor's residence. He verified it, then sent an urgent letter to the king.

"Four months ago it was believed that your Majesty had summoned the Báb to Tihrán. He left here under escort. Now it is discovered that he had been hidden in the residence of Manúchihr Khán, my predecessor, all this time. It is known that the governor himself extended this secret hospitality to the Báb and believed in Him. Whatever your Majesty now wishes done, I shall be pleased to perform."

The king was still convinced of the loyalty of his dear friend Manúchihr Khán. He felt certain that the governor had been waiting for a favorable occasion when he could arrange a meeting between himself and the Báb. Now, his sudden death had interfered with this plan.

The king, therefore, decided to carry out what he believed to have been the wish of his friend, the governor. He would meet the Báb at last.

THE KING'S SUMMONS

Muhammad Sháh, king of Persia, was torn between two conflicting desires. He wanted to meet the Báb. He was anxious to see in person this young Man Who could win over to His Faith someone as learned and gifted as Vahíd, and a man of such nobility, stature and wealth as Manúchihr Khán. He was eager to know more of this young Prophet Who could so powerfully affect such illustrious people. Yet he was alarmed at the same time. He was frightened of what might happen if the Báb gained too much popularity. His Prime Minister, Hájí Mírzá Áqásí, constantly warned him to beware of the Báb. The priests at Court spoke of the Báb in the same manner the religious authorities had spoken of Jesus, saying: "He is a political revolutionary. He will undermine your state and destroy your influence over your subjects."

The king wavered. He blew hot and cold. Prompted by the Prime Minister, he at one time issued instructions to do away with the Báb, then later withdrew them. Now, thinking it would have pleased his friend, the late Manúchihr Khán, the king again expressed his eagerness to meet the Báb in person. Therefore, he summoned the Báb to the capital city of Tihrán.

The historian Nicolas wrote: "The Sháh, whimsical and fickle, forgetting that he had, a short time before, ordered the murder of the Reformer [the Báb], felt the desire of seeing at last the man who had aroused such universal interest."[1]

The king's order read: "Send the Báb in disguise, in the company of a mounted escort. Exercise the utmost consideration towards Him in the course of his journey, and strictly maintain the secrecy of His departure. Visit no towns or villages enroute."

The king said he wished to protect the Báb from His enemies in this manner. In reality, the Prime Minister had arranged the plan for an entirely different reason. He preferred the Báb to remain in disguise and hidden for fear of the influence that he might exercise upon the inhabitants of the cities through which he passed.

The captain of the escort was told, "Beware lest anyone discover his identity or suspect the nature of your mission. No one but you, not even the members of his escort, should be allowed to recognize him. Should anyone question you concerning him, say that he is a merchant whom you have been instructed to conduct to the capital, and of whose identity you are completely ignorant."

Late one night, in accordance with the instructions of the king, the Báb set out for Tihrán.

Enroute to the capital, the Báb's guards discovered His identity in spite of the precautions, and became His supporters. His alluring charm, combined with a compelling dignity and loving kindness, won them over and transformed them. In their eagerness to serve and please Him, they told Him: "We are strictly forbidden by the government to allow you to enter any village or house. We are told to proceed by an unfrequented route directly to Tihrán so that you shall come in contact with no one. However, if it be your wish, we are ready to ignore these instructions and escort you through the streets of every town."

The Báb replied that He preferred to go by way of the country, for the cities were unholy. The people paid tribute to the shrines with their lips while with their acts they heaped dishonor upon them. Outwardly they reverenced, but inwardly they disgraced.

The Prime Minister sent a message which intercepted the party one day's journey from Tihrán and commanded the guard not to take the Báb to Tihrán, but to the village of Kulayn instead, and to hold Him there until further instructions. The Prime Minister was determined that the Báb should never reach the capital.

The Prime Minister continually reminded the king of the religious revolts that had taken place in the past in Mirman and Khurásán, and warned him that the Báb was just such a dangerous threat to the peace of the realm. The Prime Minister's influence over the king was unlimited.

Comte de Gobineau, the French historian, wrote: "His [the king's] disposition, naturally weak, had become very melancholy and, as he craved love and could not find it in his family either with his wives or children, he had centered all his affection upon the aged Mullá [Hájí Mírzá Áqásí], his tutor. He made of him his only friend, his confidant, then his first and all-powerful minister, even his god!" [2] The *Journal Asiatique* states that the Prime Minister gained such power over the king that one could truly say that the Prime Minister was the real sovereign.[3] P. M. Sykes in his *A History of Persia* states, "Hájí Mírzá Áqásí, who had been its virtual ruler for thirteen years was utterly ignorant of statesmanship . . . yet too vain to receive instruction . . . brutal in his language; insolent in his demeanor; indolent in his habits; he brought the exchequer to the verge of bankruptcy and the country to the brink of revolution."

Hájí Mírzá Áqásí finally persuaded Muhammad Sháh, to send the Báb to a remote fortress called Máh-Kú.

According to one historian, the king had been suffering from illness for some time. The Báb had promised to heal him if He were permitted to come to Tihrán. Hájí Mírzá Áqásí feared that if the Báb should bring about such a cure, the king would no longer be under his thumb.[4]

He induced the king to write to the Báb as follows: "Much as we desire to meet you, we find ourselves unable, in view of our immediate departure from our capital, to receive you befittingly in Tihrán. We have signified our desire that you be conducted to Máh-Kú." [5]

The Báb had written earlier to the king asking for an audience with him. He had requested permission to come to the capital so that before the king and all the religious leaders of the land, He might present the proofs of His Mission. He agreed to leave the decision of its truth or falsehood entirely in the hands of the king. He said that He would accept the judgement of the king as final; and in case of failure, was ready to sacrifice His head.[6]

Both the Prime Minister and the king had originally welcomed this letter. They were convinced that once the Báb was faced by the noted religious leaders of the land, they could humiliate Him and divest Him of all prestige. However, when they received the news of His overwhelming victories in debate at Shíráz, and especially when word came of the conversion of both Vahíd and Manúchihr Khán to His Faith, they were no longer eager, or even willing, to have Him at the capital.

When the king's message reached the Báb, telling Him of His transfer to the prison of Máh-Kú, He knew whose hand was behind the cruel order.

"You summoned Me from Isfáhán to meet the doctors [religious leaders] and for the attainment of a decisive settlement," He wrote the Prime Minister. "What has happened now that this excellent intention has been changed for Máh-Kú and Tabríz?" [7]

In these words, the Báb foreshadowed the suffering He was to face in the northern city of Tabríz where He would be summoned from prison, once to be beaten and a second time to be slain.

Thus the king broke his promise to meet the Báb, and the Royal party including the young son of the king, Prince Farhad Mírzá, left with the Sháh and the Prime Minister for a lovely park in the neighborhood of Tihrán. While there the prince approached the Prime Minister and asked him, "Hájí, why have you sent the Báb to Máh-Kú?"

The Prime Minister replied, "You are still too young to understand certain things, but know this: had he come to Tihrán, you and I would not at this moment be walking free from care in this cool shade."

The historical document *Journal Asiatique* records: "As the order of the Prime Minister, Hájí Mírzá Áqásí, became generally known . . . from Isfáhán to Tihrán everyone spoke of the iniquity of the clergy and of the government towards the Báb; everywhere the people muttered and exclaimed against such an injustice."

The Báb was ordered to proceed first to Tabríz. He refused to accept the funds provided by the government for the expense of the journey. All of the allowances that were given by the Prime Minister, the Báb bestowed upon the poor. For His own needs, He used the money which He had earned as a merchant.

Rigid orders were given to avoid entering any of the towns on the journey to Tabríz. When the party at last approached the gate of the city, the leader of the escort, Muhammad Big, approached the Báb.

"The journey from Isfáhán," he said, "has been long and arduous. I feel I have failed to do my duty toward you, and have failed to serve you as I should have. I can only ask for your pardon and forgiveness."

"Be assured I account you a member of My fold," the Báb told him. "They who embrace My Cause will bless and glorify you, and will extol your conduct and exalt your name."

The rest of the guards followed the example of their chief, and with tears in their eyes, bade the Báb a last affectionate farewell. Reluctantly, they delivered Him to the soldiers of the governor of Tabríz.

THE TUMULT IN TABRÍZ

THE NEWS of the Báb's arrival at Tabríz caused great excitement. Huge crowds set out to meet Him at the gate. They were eager to extend their welcome to Him. The officials, into whose custody the Báb had been delivered, refused to allow the people to draw near and receive His blessing.

One youth, however, was unable to restrain himself. He ran through the gate of the city, past the officials, and rushed out over a mile towards the Báb. He approached the horsemen who were marching in advance and joyously welcomed them.

"You are the companions of my Beloved One," he cried, "I cherish you as the apple of my eye."

They granted him permission to meet the Báb. As soon as the young man's eyes fell upon Him, a cry of exultation broke from his lips. He fell upon his face and wept profusely. The Báb dismounted, put His arms about the young man and embraced him.

Of all the believers of Tabríz, that youth alone on that day succeeded in reaching the Báb and being blessed by His hand. All of the others had to content themselves with seeing Him from afar. A mere glimpse had to satisfy their longing.

An immense crowd of people thronged the gate of the city to witness the entry of the Báb. Some were merely curious, while others were earnestly trying to find out if the Báb were in truth such a wondrous figure as they had been told. Still others were moved by their faith and devotion, and sought to attain His presence so they could assure Him of their loyalty.

As He walked along the streets, the cries of welcome rang out on every side. The great majority of those who saw Him shouted aloud: "God is most great!" They cheered Him on His way.

So great was the clamor which His arrival had raised that a crier was sent out among the people to warn them of the danger of continuing this behavior.

"Whoever shall make any attempt to approach the Báb," the people were warned, "or seek to meet him, at any time, all that person's possessions shall be seized and he shall be imprisoned." [1]

The Báb was placed in a room of the Citadel, a fortress-like structure. A detachment of soldiers stood guard at the entrance. In spite of the rigid orders of their superiors, these soldiers soon became His friends. They were entirely obedient to the instructions of the Báb, and permitted whomever He wished to visit Him. They were in reality a protection against the onrush of the multitude who thronged about the house, the Báb said, but they were powerless to prevent those Whom He desired to meet from attaining His presence.

This same detachment of soldiers who now guarded and protected Him, would in a future day, and in a mysterious manner, be chosen to discharge the volley that would cause His death; but only after another squadron of soldiers would find themselves powerless to kill Him, a thing described by the historian Nicolas as "unique in the annals of the history of humanity." [2]

One day, shortly after the Báb's arrival in Tabríz, one of His devoted followers, named 'Alí-Askar, went to see Him. 'Alí-Askar was warned by his friends not to go.

"Don't you know that such a foolish attempt on your part will not only involve the loss of your possessions, but will also endanger your very life?"

"I am going," he said.

He refused to heed their counsel, and made his way to the house where the Báb was imprisoned. Nothing could keep 'Alí-Askar from the presence of the Báb, even if it meant giving up his life.

In the days past, he had journeyed many miles with Mullá Husayn, the first follower of the Báb. They had taught together in many towns. Time after time, 'Alí-Askar would complain bitterly to Mullá Husayn of his own earlier failure to recognize the Báb and meet Him in Shíráz. This was a source of great sorrow to 'Alí-Askar.

"Grieve not," Mullá Husayn told him. "The Almighty will no doubt compensate you in Tabríz for the loss you sustained in Shíráz." Mullá Husayn spoke very confidently. "Not once," he said, "but seven times can He enable you to partake of the joy of His presence, in return for one visit which you have missed."

Now that the Báb was in Tabríz, 'Alí-Askar would allow nothing to keep them apart. As he approached the door of the house in which the Báb was confined, he was immediately arrested along with the friend who accompanied him.

A command was sent from the Báb to the guards: "Suffer these visitors to enter, inasmuch as I Myself have invited them to meet Me."

This message silenced the guards at once. 'Alí-Askar and his friend were ushered into the Báb's presence. He greeted them affectionately and made them welcome. He gave them many instructions to carry out. He assured them that whenever they wished to visit Him, no one would bar their way.

'Alí-Askar said, "Several times I ventured to visit the Báb, so that I might ask questions about the work with which He had entrusted me. Not once did I encounter any opposition on the part of those who were guarding the entrance to His house.

"I had forgotten the words which Mullá Husayn had spoken to me until the time of my last visit to the Báb. How great was my surprise when, on my seventh visit, I heard Him speak these words: 'Praise be to God, Who has enabled you to complete the number of your visits, and Who has extended to you His loving protection.' "

An eye-witness has related the following: "During the first ten days of the Báb's imprisonment in Tabríz, no one knew what would befall Him next. The wildest rumors were circulating about the city.

"One day I asked Him whether He would be kept in Tabríz or whether He would be transferred to still another place.

"He answered me, saying: 'For a period of no less than nine months, we shall remain confined in [Máh-Kú]. From thence we shall be transferred to [Chiríq].'

"Five days after the Báb had uttered this prediction, orders were issued to transfer Him and me to the castle of Máh-Kú and to deliver us into the custody of the Warden, 'Alí Khán."

With saddened hearts the people of Tabríz watched the Báb depart from the city. Many were confused by His apparent helplessness and docility. They turned away, as the people had turned away from Christ, and they believed no more. They whispered among themselves as they had whispered in Jerusalem when Christ was delivered in turn to Caiaphus and Pilate.

"If this is the Promised One, why is He subjected to the whims of the men of earth?"

THE HIGH STONE PRISON

THE BÁB was delivered into the custody of the warden, 'Alí Khán, at Máh-Kú, where He was shut up inside a four-towered, stone castle-fortress, high on the summit of a mountain. Below the fortress, on the west, flowed the river Araxes, the boundary between Persia and Russia.

The Prime Minister, Hájí Míráz Áqásí, had chosen Máh-Kú for the Báb's imprisonment for only one reason. It was a wild and inhospitable region, inhabited by people who had always been the bitter enemies of the Persians. The Prime Minister had bestowed many favors upon this rebellious region and it was now under his complete control.[1] Hájí Mírzá Áqásí felt certain that by this imprisonment he could cut the Báb off permanently from His followers, and separate Him from their activities. In this way, His Cause would be stifled at its birth and soon extinguished. Few, if any, would ever try to penetrate that unfriendly country.

His plan was a failure. The hostility of the native people of Máh-Kú was gradually softened by the gentle manner of the Báb. Their opposition to His teaching was melted by the wisdom of His words. Each morning they would come from the village of Máh-Kú and gather on the road below His prison and call out to Him, asking His blessing on their daily work.

The Báb Himself wrote of those early days in Máh-Kú: "My

companions are two men and four dogs." But His teachings reached the multitudes who gathered outside. He would dictate to Siyyid Husayn of Yazd, who had been brought with Him in captivity from Tabríz. On a quiet day, the sound of His voice could be clearly heard by the people below the fortress. One of the eye-witnesses of those days has written: ". . . Mountain and valley echoed with the majesty of His voice. Our hearts vibrated in their depths to the appeal of His utterance." [2]

The warden, 'Alí Khán, did his best to discourage this practice, but he was unable to dampen their enthusiasm. He refused to permit any of the villagers to enter the Báb's presence. He would not allow any of the Báb's followers who came to the mountain to remain, even for one night, in the village of Máh-Kú. Hájí Mírzá Áqásí had warned 'Alí Khán of the danger of falling under the spell of the Báb's charm. "He is an agitator," the Prime Minister had said.

'Alí Khán found himself increasingly helpless to resist his attraction to the Báb. During the nine months of the Báb's imprisonment from the summer of 1847 until April in 1848, his hostility underwent a series of transformations from enmity to devotion. From that moment on, 'Alí Khán tried by every means in his power to make up for his past hatred.

One day he went to the Báb: "A poor man waiting outside the gate of Máh-Kú yearns to attain Your presence," he said. "May I have your permission to bring him to this place so that he may meet You? By this act, I hope that You will forgive me, and that the memory of my cruel behavior toward You and Your friends in the past may be forever washed away."

His request was granted. 'Alí Khán did all he could to soften the rigor of the Báb's imprisonment. At night he would still close the gate of the village, but in the daytime those whom the Báb wished to see were allowed to visit Him, converse with Him, and receive His instructions.

A. L. M. Nicolas writes: "All historians [unfriendly as well as friendly] . . . tell us that in spite of the strict orders to keep the Báb from communicating with the outer world, the Báb received great numbers of disciples and strangers in his prison." [3] Another has reported: "So great multitudes continued to come from all quarters to visit the Báb, and the writings which emanated from his inspired pen during this period were so numerous that they amounted in all to more than a hundred thousand verses." [4]

During this nine-month period in Máh-Kú, the Báb composed His most comprehensive book, the Persian Bayán. In it the Báb defined His Mission as two-fold: to call men back to God, and to announce the coming of the Promised One of all ages and religions. This great Prophet, He said, would appear soon after Himself. The station of this Figure-to-come was so exalted, the Báb told His followers, that "if one should hear a single verse from Him and recite it, it is better than that he should recite the Bayán a thousand times." [5]

He urged His followers to remember these words and to seek and find this great Figure upon His own passing. He implied that His Faith and that of the One to come after Him were indentical; they were one Faith: He was the Herald, the One to come was the Author. This Truth was now in the stage of seed. In the day of Him Who was yet to come, its perfection would become apparent.[6]

Repeatedly He told His followers that He was but the preparation for that great Day of God promised in all the scriptures. Christ had warned His disciples of the last days in these words: "Watch therefore: for ye know not what hour your Lord doth come." [7] The Báb echoed this warning, saying: Be awake on the day of the appearance of Him Whom God will manifest." [8]

The Báb's constant prayer during those months of captivity in Máh-Kú was that He might be able to prepare the soil of men's hearts for the coming of this great world Shepherd. "O my God!" He said, "Through Him destroy all tyrants . . . annihilate, through His justice, all forms of oppression." [9]

The Báb said that He spoke of His own suffering only so that it might be "an example to [My followers] so that they may not act toward Him [Who is to come] as the believers in the Qur'án have acted toward Me." [10]

"Of all the tributes I have paid to Him Who is to come after Me," the Báb wrote in Máh-Kú, "the greatest is this, My written confession, that no words of Mine can adequately describe Him, nor can any reference to Him in My Book, the Bayán, do justice to His Cause." [11]

He left no question whatsoever in the minds of His followers as to His own station: He was the Dawn, the One to come was the

Sun. "Were He to appear at this very moment," proclaimed the Báb, "I would be the first to adore Him, and the first to bow down before Him." [12]

The historian Nicolas states that when the Báb was asked for proofs of His mission, His answer was admirable for its precision and clearness, His explanations new and original, and His literary work of profound interest. [13]

For nine months the Báb wrote almost continuously. His followers came from all parts of Persia to visit Him. After a stay of three days they were encouraged by the Báb to return to their homes and continue the work of teaching and consolidating the Faith. Not only was the Báb able to meet His followers, in spite of the isolation imposed upon Him by the Prime Minister, but more important, He was given the time and opportunity to set down in permanent form the fundamental truths of His Mission.

In His solitary chamber He was not permitted to have even a lighted lamp. The winter was so severe that the water with which He washed Himself would freeze in drops upon His face.

It was during this time that Mullá Husayn decided to visit Him at Máh-Kú. [14] He had been teaching the Cause industriously in the city of Mashhad, greatest center of pilgrimage in all Persia. Half of the city derived its living from the flow of visitors. All these people were now joined together against this teacher who might possibly deprive them of their livelihood. To denounce abuses of religion might be all right in any other city, they said, but it was certainly improper to denounce them in Mashhad where everyone of every class was thriving upon them. It was all very well for the Promised One to come, and perhaps He had the right, but He certainly was a public nuisance. Mullá Husayn was told plainly, by actions as well as words, that it might be very thrilling to undertake the conquest of the world with the Báb, but there was a big risk involved, not to mention fatigue and danger, especially now, while everyone was enjoying perfect peace in a fine city where business was good and one could earn a living with ease and security.

Mullá Husayn abandoned Mashhad in disgust. He was hungry for the pure, holy presence of the Báb. He told his friends: "I have resolved to go on foot the entire distance that separates me from my Beloved. I shall not rest until I have reached my destination."

Warden 'Alí Khán saw Mullá Husayn approaching Máh-Kú one

morning at sun-up. He went out to greet him, bringing a horse so
that he might finish the final stage of his journey in ease.

Mullá Husayn refused the mount. "No," he said, "I have vowed
to accomplish the entire journey on foot. I will walk to the summit
of this mountain and will there visit your Prisoner."

When Mullá Husayn reached the gate of the prison he saw the
Báb standing at the threshold. The Báb stretched forth His arms
and affectionately embraced him.

One day as they stood together on the roof of the prison looking
out over the mountains of Ádhirbáyján, the Báb quoted the following prophecy to Mullá Husayn: "The things which will happen in
Ádhirbáyján are necessary for us, nothing can prevent their occurrence. Remain therefore in your homes, but if you hear that an
agitator has appeared then hasten towards him."

He turned toward Mullá Husayn and quoted another prophecy,
saying: "The following verse is also divinely inspired: 'Shíráz will
be thrown into a tumult; a Youth of sugar-tongue will appear. I
fear lest the breath of His mouth should agitate and upset Baghdád.'"

Part of this prophecy had already taken place, He told Mullá
Husayn. The mystery of the rest would be known in the year 1853.

The Báb gazed toward the west where the river Araxes wound
its way below the castle. He quoted yet another prophecy: "Treasures lie hidden beneath the throne of God; the key to those treasures is the tongue of poets." He looked at Mullá Husayn and said:
"That is the river, and this is the bank thereof, of which the poet
Háfiz has thus written: 'O Zephyr, shouldst thou pass the banks of
the Araxes, implant a kiss on the earth of that valley, and make
fragrant thy breath. Hail, a thousand times hail, to thee, O abode
of Salmá!'

"But for the shortness of your stay," the Báb told Mullá Husayn,
"We would have shown you the 'abode of Salmá,' even as We have
unveiled to your eyes the 'banks of the Araxes.'"

By the 'abode of Salmá' the Báb meant the prison of Chiríq to
which He was soon to be transferred, and which stands by the town
of Salmás.

He then related to Mullá Husayn many things which would take
place in the future. He told him not to disclose them to anyone.

As the Báb bade His last farewell to Mullá Husayn, He said
to him: "You have walked on foot all the way from your native

province to this place. On foot you likewise must return. . . . your days of horsemanship are yet to come. You are destined to exhibit such courage, such skill and heroism as shall eclipse the heroes of old."

The Báb instructed Mullá Husayn to visit the believers in each of the villages on his way back. "Inflame their hearts anew, . . ." He told him, "and fortify their faith in this Revelation.

"A few days after your departure, they will transfer Us to another mountain. Ere you arrive at your destination, the news of Our departure from Máh-Kú will have reached you."

The prediction of the Báb soon came to pass. Those who had been sent by the Prime Minister to watch secretly and report what was taking place at Máh-Kú, sent back alarming news.

"The once unfriendly people of Máh-Kú are now showing the greatest respect and love for the Báb," they confessed. "People come from everywhere to visit him. Even 'Alí Khán, the warden, has been enchanted by him. He treats the Báb as his host rather than his prisoner."

Both fear and rage impelled the Prime Minister to issue an order for the instant transfer of the Báb to the more rigid prison of Chiríq, called "the grievous mountain."

Mullá Husayn was in Tabríz when the news of the Báb's transfer to Chiríq reached him.

The Báb said farewell to the people of Máh-Kú. Their hearts were heavy at the sad sight of His departure. The One they had come to love so much was now going out of their lives forever. During His nine months of captivity among them, they had recognized to a remarkable degree the power of His personality and the greatness of His character.

THE SCOURGING AT TABRÍZ

THE BÁB was subjected to a closer and more rigorous confinement at Chiríq. The Prime Minister gave strict and explicit orders to the warden, Yahyá Khán, who was a brother-in-law of the king. He told Yahyá Khán that no one was ever to enter the presence of the Báb. There were to be no exceptions to this rule. The warden was warned to profit by the failure of 'Alí Khán at Máh-Kú, and never to disregard the orders he had received, even for a minute, if he valued his life.

Yet, in spite of this open threat to his own safety, Yahyá Khán found himself powerless to obey. He too soon felt the fascination of his Prisoner. He forgot completely the duty he was expected to perform. Love for the Báb claimed his entire being, until he would have preferred to be slain rather than to cause Him the slightest discomfort.

The villagers who lived in Chiríq were more fanatic in their hatred of the Báb than those who had lived at Máh-Kú, but they also gradually fell under the transforming influence of His presence. The spirit which He radiated was a life-creating thing. It changed hate into love, enemies into friends.

This is confirmed by the following historical account: "His qualities were so rare in their nobility and beauty, His personality so gentle and yet so forceful, and His natural charm was combined

72

with so much tact and judgment, that after His Declaration He quickly became in Persia a widely popular figure. He would win over almost all with whom He was brought into personal contact, often converting His gaolers to His Faith and turning the ill-disposed into admiring friends." [1]

The size of the crowds who had visited Him at Máh-Kú was dwarfed by the number of those who flocked to Him at Chiríq. Yahyá Khán would not refuse admittance to anyone who wished to see Him. So many sought His presence that there was no room to accommodate them all. They had to be housed at Old Chiríq, an hour's distance away.

M. Mochenin who was on duty for a foreign organization in that region says in his memoirs: "The multitude of hearers was so great that the court was not large enough to hold them all; most of them stayed in the streets and listened with religious rapture." [2]

Whatever provisions were required for the Báb were purchased in Old Chiríq. One day honey was purchased for Him. The price seemed exorbitant. He refused it and said: "Honey of a superior quality could no doubt be purchased at a lower price. It behooves you in all your transactions to follow in My way. You must neither defraud your neighbor nor allow him to defraud you." He insisted that the honey be returned and one better in quality and cheaper in price be brought in its place. [3]

During those days a dervish walked all the way from India to seek the Báb. As soon as he met Him, he embraced His Faith. He told the following story:

"I was an official in India occupying a fine position. In a dream a young man gazed at me and won my heart completely. I arose and started to follow Him. He looked at me intently and said: 'Divest yourself of your gorgeous attire, depart from your native land and hasten on foot to meet Me in Ádhirbáyján. In Chiríq you will attain your heart's desire.' I followed his directions and have now reached my goal."

This fulfilled the words of the prophecy given for the last days that: men should come from the far places, guided by the spirit, until they met their Promised One. [4]

This was but one of many remarkable events which followed upon each other with swift succession. They caused the turmoil in Chiríq to eclipse that of Máh-Kú. A continuous stream of seekers and followers flowed back and forth through this old prison city.

Men of distinguished merit, eminent members of the clergy, and even government officials were openly and rapidly embracing the Faith of the Báb.

One of the most outstanding literary figures of the land, who was also a high government official, accepted the Báb's teaching and devoted both his person and his pen to the spreading of His Faith. He was called Dayyán by the Báb. Previously, Dayyán had denounced the Báb and His Message. Then one night he had a dream, after which he wrote to the Báb, saying, "I have definite things in my mind. I request you to reveal to me their nature." A few days later he received a reply penned by the Báb in which He described the dream and revealed the exact words that were in Dayyán's mind. The accuracy of that reply brought about his complete conversion. He went on foot to the mountain to meet the Báb. This meeting excited in him a fiery ardor which lasted to the end of his life.

The Báb knew that the hour of his deeper affliction was approaching. He told all of His followers who had gathered in Chíríq to disperse and to return home to their most important work, teaching. He instructed the believer from India to return to his native land and work unceasingly for the spread of the Faith. He obeyed the Báb at once, and alone, clad in simplest attire, staff in hand, he went down the mountainside and walked all the way back to his own country, teaching in every village along the way.

Calmly the Báb waited for the inevitable edict of Hájí Mírzá Áqásí. It was not long in coming. When the news of all these startling events reached the capital, the Prime Minister was violent in his anger. He had failed again. He knew he must not fail a third time. He demanded that the Báb be transferred at once from the prison to the city of Tabríz. Strict orders were given to avoid any contact with those towns to which the Báb's influence had already spread. He was to be brought to Tabríz by an unsuspected route by way of the village of Urúmíyyih.

Such a secret, however, could not be kept. On His arrival in Urúmíyyih, the prince Malik Qásim Mírzá respectfully received Him, and gave the Báb a guard of footmen to hold back the gathering crowd. The people were crushing against each other in their eagerness to catch a glimpse of so marvelous a Prisoner.

Arrangements were made for the Báb to go to the public bath. The prince was anxious to test the power and courage of his Guest, having heard such wondrous tales about Him. He ordered his groom to offer the Báb one of his wildest horses to ride.

The groom feared that the Báb, Whom he loved, might suffer harm from this untamed animal. He secretly approached the Báb and told Him the story, and tried to induce Him to refuse to mount this steed.

"It has already overthrown the bravest and most skillful of horsemen," he said.

"Fear not," the Báb replied. "Do as you have been bidden and commit Us to the care of the Almighty."

The villagers learned of the plan of the prince. They filled the public square the next morning, eager to witness the test and learn what would befall the Báb.

The wild horse was brought from his stable. The bridle was cautiously given to the Báb by the frightened groom. The Báb quietly stepped toward the animal. Gently, He caressed the steed, and then slowly placed His foot in the stirrup. The horse stood motionless as the Báb mounted. He rode the animal to the public bath. All along the way people tried to rush in from every side to marvel at such a miracle, and to offer their belief in His Faith. On His return from the bath He again mounted the same horse, and was once again acclaimed by the townspeople.

As soon as the Báb left the public bath, the people of Urúmíyyih rushed to take away all the water from that place and carry it in containers to their homes in all parts of the village. There were some who remembered the closing words of a prophecy given for the time of the Promised One's coming which said that the lake of Urúmíyyih will boil up, will overrun its banks, and inundate the town.⁵

When the Báb was told that many people had spontaneously arisen to accept His Faith because of these remarkable events, which they considered to be miracles, He sadly quoted the words: "Think men that when they say, 'We believe,' they shall be let alone and not put to the proof?"

This comment was fully justified by the attitude of these same people of Urúmíyyih when later they heard the news of the dreadful treatment which the Báb had suffered at Tabríz. Hardly a handful of those who had so eagerly proclaimed their belief in His Cause on that day remained faithful. Miracles, the followers of His Faith were to learn, are but a secondary proof and of value only to those who witness them; of themselves miracles have no lasting value. It was now as it had been in the time of Christ, for when Jesus miraculously healed the ten lepers only one remained to thank Him. He said: "Were there not ten cleansed? but where are the nine?" [6]

Tales of what had happened in Urúmíyyih raced ahead of the Báb and His escort, causing a great wave of enthusiasm. Tabríz, in particular, was in the throes of the wildest excitement. Word of the Báb's coming ignited the imagination of the people and roused the fierce animosity of the religious leaders.

Such was the fervor of the public feeling that the authorities decided to confine the Báb in a place outside the gates. Precautions were taken, warnings were published, restrictions were enforced, yet all these only served to aggravate a situation which had already become critical. The Báb had captured the fancy of the people and nothing the officials or clergy could do was able to diminish their ardor.

Hájí Mírzá Áqásí issued an order from the capital. He demanded that all the leading religious dignitaries, as well as the government officials, hold an immediate gathering. His words made clear the grave nature of this crisis. The religious leaders, he said, must decide at once upon the most effective measures for extinguishing this fire which the Báb had kindled. They must bring to an abrupt end the Báb's power over the public. There must be no mistakes. The Báb must be summoned before this important gathering, and there He must be humiliated in such a manner as would permanently undermine His influence.

The Báb was well aware of the Prime Minister's purpose. On the second night after His arrival in Tabríz, the Báb told His friends that on the morrow, in the presence of the king's eldest son, the assembled religious leaders, and the notables of the city, He would publicly proclaim His mission. [7]

The meeting was arranged according to the plan of the Prime Minister. It took place in the residence of the governor. An officer of the army was sent to bring the Báb into the presence of the gathering. Already a multitude besieged the outside entrance. Crowds had been waiting since early dawn to catch a glimpse of the Báb's face. They pressed forward in such large numbers that a passage had to be forced through the crowd for the Báb to enter.

When He came into the hall, He saw that every seat was occupied except one, which had been reserved as the seat of honor for the heir to the throne, the king's son. The Báb courteously greeted the assembly. He knew they planned to humiliate Him by making Him stand. Without hesitation He walked to that seat of honor and sat down.

A silence, long and intense, fell over the gathering. Their plans had been frustrated, and their anger was apparent in their faces. At last the stillness was broken by the presiding officer of the gathering.

"Who do you claim to be?" he asked the Báb. "What is the message which you have brought?"

It was the story of Christ retold. When Jesus was taken into the judgment chamber before the priests with their pre-planned investigation, He was asked: Art thou the Christ? He replied: I am.[8] There could no longer remain any doubt of His mission.

In like manner, with similar words, the Báb replied to this assembly which also wished to hear Him condemn Himself by making this staggering claim. Three times He repeated it in their presence. "I am," exclaimed the Báb, "I am, I am the Promised One! I am the One Whose name you have for a thousand years invoked, at Whose mention you have risen, Whose advent you have longed to witness, and the hour of Whose Revelation you have prayed God to hasten. Verily I say, it is incumbent upon the people of both the East and the West to obey My word and to pledge allegiance to My person."

A witness to that stirring event has said: "Immediately after He declared Himself to be the Promised One, a feeling of awe seized those who were present. The pallor of their faces betrayed the agitation of their hearts."

It was recorded of that meeting in yet another place: "The majesty of His gait, the expression of overpowering confidence which sat upon His brow—above all, the spirit of power which shone from His whole being, appeared to have for a moment crushed the soul out of the body of those whom He had greeted."

A hush fell over the hall. At last, unable to bear the tension any longer, one of the assembly arose and shouted angrily at the Báb.

"You wretched and immature lad of Shíráz! Do you wish to arouse a turmoil here?"

The Báb turned to the presiding officer. "Your honor," He said,

"I have not come hither of My own accord. I have been summoned to this place."

The authorities asked no truly sincere questions about His Mission or His teachings. Instead, they indulged in a series of insulting and flippant inquiries which had nothing to do with His Faith, but were designed solely to humiliate their Prisoner.

After patiently bearing their abuse and insults throughout the session, the Báb quoted their own Holy Book to them, saying: "Praise be to God, the Lord of all the worlds!" Immediately after, He arose and abruptly left the hall.

At once, the religious authorities began to spread the most unfavorable and false reports of the Báb's part in that trial. They said His answers were both childish and unsatisfying, that they were not even the replies of a sane man, let alone those of a promised Redeemer.

Fortunately for history, two European scholars, following much investigation, have preserved an unbiased account of those proceedings. The first was Dr. T. K. Cheyne, a Christian clergyman and student of that period. He has written:

"As for the Muslim accounts [of that trial], those which we have before us do not bear the stamp of truth; they seem to be forgeries. Knowing what we do of the Báb, it is probable that he had the best of the argument, and that the leaders and functionaries who attended the meeting were unwilling to put on record their own fiasco." [9]

The second was Professor Edward G. Browne, of Cambridge University. He called the questions which these religious leaders had asked the Báb "frivolous and even indecent." He writes of that trial: "That the whole examination was a farce throughout, that the sentence was a foregone conclusion, that no serious attempt to apprehend the nature and evidence of the Báb's claim and doctrine was made, and that from the first to last a systematic course of browbeating, irony, and mockery was pursued, appear to me to be facts proved no less by the Muhammadan than by the Bábí accounts of these inquisitorial proceedings." [10]

Even the presiding officer at that gathering, Hájí Mullá Mahmud, was displeased at the way the priests had conducted the meeting. He did not wish his name associated with it.

"How shameful is the discourtesy of this people," he said. "What possible connection could there be between such idle questions and the honest consideration of such an important issue as the Báb's claim?"

A. L. M. Nicolas referring to an earlier inquisition of the Báb by such hostile religious leaders, says they conditioned their belief in His Truth by His ability to explain three miracles to them: (1) How could the Imám Javád travel in the twinkling of an eye from Arabia to Persia in the body; (2) How could the Imám 'Alí be in sixty different places at one instant; (3) How did the heavens revolve rapidly during the reign of a tyrant and slowly during that of an Imám? "It was the solution of these insanities," says Nicolas, "that they proposed to the Báb. I shall not dwell on them any longer . . . one will easily understand the emptiness and arrogance of all those minds." [11]

The Báb was brought to the home of Mírzá 'Alí-Asghar, the head of the religious court. He was given over to the governor's bodyguard for humiliating punishment. The guard refused.

"This is not a government affair," he insisted. "It is the concern of the clergy."

Impatient at the delay, Mírzá 'Alí-Asghar himself decided to inflict the punishment upon the Báb with his own hands. It would then be done, and at least the Báb's triumph would appear less spectacular in the eyes of the people.

Just as Jesus had fallen under the scourge of Pilate following His examination in the judgement hall where He proclaimed Himself as the Redeemer of men, the Báb also was subjected to the same indignity, following the same trial, and the same great proclamation. Eleven times the rod of the bastinado was applied to His feet. He was struck across the face with one of the blows. It caused a great wound.

Dr. Cormick, an English physician who was residing in Tabríz, was called to treat the Báb. He has set down his impression of the Báb, gained during those meetings.

"He was a very mild and delicate looking man . . . with a melodious soft voice which struck me much . . . . on my saying that I was willing to know something about his religion as I might perhaps be inclined to adopt it. He regarded me very intently on my saying this, and replied that he had no doubt of all Europeans coming over to his religion. In fact," the doctor added, "his whole look and deportment went far to dispose one in his favor." [12]

The Báb was not released after His scourging. He was marched back under heavy guard to the prison of Chiríq. However, He left behind Him in Tabríz the memory of a great victory. Many who had been opposers became followers. Many, pointing a finger at the cruel behavior of the religious leaders, recalled the well-known prophecy about the Promised One: "In that day most of His enemies shall be the [religious authorities]."

To those who felt great anguish because of the cruelties inflicted upon the gentle Báb, these words of His brought comfort, "Be patient . . . for verily God hath vowed to establish Thy glory in every land, amongst all who dwell on earth."

The trial in Tabríz had enabled the Báb to set forth clearly the fundamental features of His Faith. It had also enabled Him to destroy, in brief and convincing language, the arguments of His enemies.

As Jesus had said: My teaching is not Mine, but His that sent Me; the Báb, too, made it plain that His message was an outpouring from One greater than Himself. His purpose was to proclaim the Word of God as a Messenger of God. The people were free to believe or not, as they chose.

When the Báb returned to the prison-fortress of Chiríq, He wrote a moving letter denouncing the treacherous Prime Minister, Hájí Mírzá Áqásí. It foretold his downfall soon to come. This was written as a warning to all such leaders who, refusing the truth themselves, had shut the door in the face of those whose destiny they held in their power.

The Báb gave the letter to one of His disciples and told him to deliver it personally into the hands of Hájí Mírzá Áqásí. The letter was called: "The Sermon of Wrath." It began with the words: "O thou who hast disbelieved!" [13]

From that hour, the dreadful consequences, which had already befallen so many who had persecuted the Báb and His followers began to descend upon the ring-leaders of His Tabríz torture.[14]

The head of the religious court, Mírzá 'Alí-Asghar, who with his own hands had scourged the Báb in the prayer-house, was despised and feared by a people who had sickened of his leadership and which prayed to be delivered from his evil ways. Mírzá 'Alí-Asghar was suddenly struck with paralysis. After enduring long and excruciating pain, he died a miserable death. Following his death, his office was permanently abolished in Tabríz. The very name of the institution which had been associated with his name became abhorred by the people and was used as an insult.[15]

The king himself, Muhammad Sháh, did not escape this retribution. He had been weak enough to listen to the promptings of the Prime Minister and had refused to meet the Báb, in spite of His personal letter, requesting such an audience. The king instead had banished the Báb to a remote mountain prison. No sooner had he agreed to issue that order than he was afflicted with an abrupt reversal of fortune. Several parts of his kingdom broke out in revolt. His health declined rapidly. Finally, at the early age of forty, he fell a victim to a complication of maladies which the Báb had foretold would in the end devour him.

The Prime Minister, Hájí Mírzá Áqásí, who had been the chief conspirator in the outrages committed against the Báb, was made the major target of this avenging wrath. Scarcely a year and six months from the moment he first came between the Báb and the king and prevented their meeting, he was hurled from power. While the Báb was still in the prison to which Hájí Mírzá Áqásí had condemned Him, and from which He had sent the "Sermon of Wrath," the Prime Minister was dismissed in disgrace from his post. He was stripped of all his dishonestly acquired property and riches.

C. R. Markham's *History of Persia* says, "Hájí Mírzá Áqásí, the half-crazy old Prime Minister . . . was sedulously collecting wealth for himself at Tihrán, at the expense of the wretched country. The governorships of provinces were sold to the highest bidders, who oppressed the people in a fearful manner." [16]

When knowledge of the enormity of his graft and thefts became known, he had to flee for shelter from the anger of his countrymen. Hájí Mírzá Áqásí had expelled the Báb from His home and banished Him to a far place, now he, in turn was expelled from his native country and banished to Iraq where he fell a victim to disease and sorrow. "Gnawing grief shortened his life," says the *Journal Asiatique.*[17]

History has recorded these words of the last days of Hájí Mírzá Áqásí: "He met his death in circumstances of abject poverty and unspeakable distress." [18]

THE MASSACRE AT THE FORT

OF SHAYKH TABARSÍ

MUHAMMAD SHÁH WAS DEAD. The new ruler was the seventeen-year-old Nasiri'd-Dín Sháh. Hájí Mírzá Áqásí was toppled from power. The new Prime Minister was Mírzá Taqí Khán.

The young king was even less friendly than his father. The new Prime Minister was more iron-hearted in his rule, and his hatred for the Báb was more implacable than that of Hájí Mírzá Áqásí. He unchained a combined assault by the civil and religious powers against the Báb and His leading disciples. He was determined not to make the mistake of the former Prime Minister and wait too long.

The news of the Báb's triumph over His examiners at Tabríz spread rapidly throughout all of Persia. It awakened new zeal in the hearts of His supporters. They redoubled their efforts to spread His teachings. It enkindled a corresponding reaction among His enemies. Encouraged by the new Prime Minister, persecutions unprecedented in their violence swept over the nation, engulfing the staunchest of the Báb's followers. This brief but triumphant period may well be called the bloodiest and most dramatic in the rise of His Faith.

No story of the life of the Báb would be complete unless it told about His disciples who sacrificed everything in life, proving their love and devotion for His Cause. Some preceded the Báb in death, some followed shortly after. Almost every one of His chief followers was struck down during this raging period of persecution.

Quddús was imprisoned in the town of Sárí, and Mullá Husayn set out to rescue him. A messenger had come from the Báb to Mullá Husayn bearing the Báb's turban.

"Adorn your head with My green turban, . . ." the message said, "and with the Black Standard unfurled before you, hasten to lend your assistance to My beloved Quddús."

Mullá Husayn immediately left the province of Khurásán and headed for Sárí. His small party marched under a black banner which Mullá Husayn raised up so that all who wished to join him would know that these were followers of the Báb.

That emblem waved continuously over his small band for eleven months. It summoned all who gazed upon it to renounce the world and embrace the Cause of God. This was the same standard prophesied for the last days: "Should your eyes behold the Black Standards proceeding from Khurásán, hasten ye toward them, even though ye should have to crawl over the snow, inasmuch as they proclaim the advent of the Promised [One], the Vicegerent of God." [1]

Mullá Husayn and his party arrived at a junction on the highroad to Mázindarán. They encamped under the shadow of a big tree by a running stream.

"We stand at the parting of the ways," he told his companions. "We shall wait here for some sign telling us which road to take."

One day a fierce gale arose and struck down a large branch from the big tree. Mullá Husayn, watching, observed: "The tree of the sovereignty of Muhammad Sháh has been uprooted and hurled to the ground."

On the third day after he had uttered that prediction, a messenger arrived from Tihrán reporting the death of the king. The following day Mullá Husayn gathered his companions and pointed in the direction of Mázindarán and Sárí.

"This is the way that leads to our martyrdom," he said. "Whoever is unprepared, let him return home now. I, together with seventy-two of my companions, shall suffer death for the sake of the Báb. Whosoever is unable to renounce the world, let him at this very moment depart, for later on he will be unable to escape."

Twenty chose to return, feeling themselves powerless to withstand the trials to which Mullá Husayn continually alluded. The others approached the town of Bárfurúsh.

The news of their coming alarmed the Sa'ídu'l-'Ulamá, the chief religious leader of that city. Nicolas says in his history that all the clerics of Bárfarúsh were filled with hate for the followers of the Báb because of the many conversions which Quddús had been able to make in their city, as many as three hundred in one week.² The Sa'ídu'l-'Ulamá told the town crier to summon all the people to the mosque at once. When an immense throng had gathered, he ascended to the pulpit. He flung his turban to the ground, tore open the neck of his shirt, and angrily began to incite the people to arise against Mullá Husayn and his party.

"Awake!" he thundered. "Our enemies are at our very doors. Let both young and old arm themselves against these wreckers of our Faith. Tomorrow, at the hour of dawn, let all arise and march out to exterminate their forces."

The entire congregation arose in response to his appeal and made every preparation for the dawn, arming themselves with any weapon they could find or devise.

The next morning immediately after offering his morning prayers, Mullá Husayn called his companions together and told them to discard all their possessions.

"Leave behind all your belongings," he urged them. "Content yourself with only your steeds and your swords, so that all may witness your abandonment of all earthly things. Then may they realize that this little band of God's chosen companions has no desire to safeguard its own property, much less covet the property of others."

Instantly all obeyed. They unburdened their steeds without a word. A prominent merchant, who had joined the band at Níshápur, had brought with him a satchel full of very precious turquoise. Yet, at a word from Mullá Husayn, he was the first to cast aside his treasure as an example to the others. He hurled it into a ditch without a backward glance.

A short distance from Bárfurúsh, Mullá Husayn and his companions encountered a multitude of people who blocked their way along the road to Sárí. In the face of the uproar from this angry populace, some of the companions began to unsheath their swords.

"No," Mullá Husayn told them. "Not yet. Not until the aggressor forces us to protect ourselves must our swords leave their scabbards."

The mob armed with knives, clubs, axes, guns, swords and every conceivable weapon moved forward toward that small group. They had set out from Bárfurúsh at the break of day determined to meet and slay Mullá Husayn's party, and to plunder their possessions. The Sa'ídu'l-'Ulamá had remained behind in the safety of his home after urging the others to attack.

This was but one of a series of such onslaughts which were taking place througout the country, all encouraged by the Prime Minister, Mírzá Taqí Khán. The following historical report indicates the gravity of the situation: "The minister with the utmost arbitrariness, without receiving any instructions or asking permission, sent forth commands in all directions to punish and chastise the Bábís [followers of the Báb]. Governors and magistrates sought a pretext for amassing wealth, and officials a means of acquiring profits; celebrated doctors [of religion] from the summits of their pulpits incited men to make a general onslaught; the powers of the religious and civil law linked hands and strove to eradicate and destroy this people." [3]

This was to be the first of three occasions on which the followers of the Báb withdrew to a chosen retreat, erected defenses, and defied further pursuit. They would fight for their lives with determined skill and strength; but they would not attack. Even in the midst of a fierce conflict they would not drive home an advantage nor strike an unnecessary blow. [4]

Browne, in his *Year Among the Persians*, says that on one of these occasions even the women took part, and when their shelter was attacked, like the Carthagenian women of old, they cut off their long hair and bound it around their make-shift weapons to afford them the necessary support. "The desperate resistance offered by the [followers of the Báb] must therefore," he says, "be attributed less to the strength of the position which they occupied than to the valor with which they defended themselves." [5]

Separated as they were from their imprisoned leader, the Báb, His followers did not yet understand His clear teaching on the matter of physical violence and warfare. Therefore, they followed after the pattern of their previous religious teaching: do not attack, but defend. In the book *A Traveler's Narrative*, edited by Professor E. G. Browne of Cambridge University, it states: "In towns where these [followers of the Báb] were but a limited number, all of them with bound hands became food for the sword, while in cities where they were numerous they arose in self-defense in accordance with their former beliefs, since it was impossible for them to make enquiry as to their duty." [6]

His followers had not yet read the Báb's words: "The slaying of a soul is outside the religion of God; . . . and if anyone commands it, he is not and has not been of the Bayán [the Báb's Book and symbol of His followers], and no sin can be greater for him than this." [7]

As the huge crowd moved menacingly toward them at Bárfurúsh, Mullá Husayn's companions pleaded with him.

"Allow us to defend ourselves."

"Not yet," Mullá Husayn replied.

The mob poured down upon that small group and as they neared, opened fire. Six of the defenseless party were struck down by that first blast. Mullá Husayn's companions were impatient.

"We have risen and followed you," they said, "with no other thought than to sacrifice our lives in the path of God. But we pray you, allow us to defend ourselves so that we do not fall disgracefully before this savage mob."

Mullá Husayn was still patient, hoping there might be found some way to avoid this bloodshed. A bullet struck his nearest companion, Siyyid Ridá, in the chest and killed him instantly.

Ridá was a man of humble and loving disposition. His devotion to the Báb was deep and sincere. He had walked on foot beside Mullá Husayn all the way from Khurásán. At the sight of this much-loved companion fallen dead at his feet, Mullá Husayn could no longer remain silent.

"O God," he cried out. "Behold the plight of my companions! Witness the welcome which these people have given us. Thou knowest that we cherish no other desire than to guide them to the way of Truth."

Unsheathing his sword, Mullá Husayn spurred on his horse as the attack of the mob was unleashed in full force. He commanded his followers to defend themselves.

On this plain of Bárfurúsh the words which the Báb had spoken to Mullá Husayn at Máh-Kú began to come true: "Your days of horsemanship are yet to come. You are destined to exhibit such

courage, skill and heroism as will eclipse the mightiest deeds of the
heroes of old."

Mullá Husayn struck terror into the hearts of that unruly mob.
One of the killers took refuge behind a small tree. He held his
musket in front of his body to shield himself as Mullá Husayn
swept down upon him. Mullá Husayn recognized him as the slayer
of Ridá, his friend. Mullá Husayn rushed on and, with a single
sweeping slash of his sword, he cut through the trunk of the tree,
through the musket, and severed the body of his enemy in two.

The historian Nicolas states that "anger redoubled the strength
of Mullá Husayn who with one single blow of his weapon cut in
two the gun, the man and the tree." He adds: "The Muslims themselves do not question the authenticity of this anecdote." [8]

One of the enemies of Mullá Husayn on that day has recorded
his impression of that dreadful attack: "Then I saw Mullá Husayn
unsheathe his sword and raise his face toward heaven . . . 'Now
have they made it our duty to protect ourselves,' he said. Then he began to attack us on the right and on the left. I swear by God that on
that day he wielded the sword in such wise as transcends the power
of man. Only the horsemen of Mázindarán held their ground and
refused to flee. And when Mullá Husayn was well warmed to the
fray, he overtook a fugitive soldier. The soldier sheltered himself
behind a tree, and further strove to shield himself with his musket.
Mullá Husayn dealt him such a blow with his sword that he clave
him and the tree and the musket into six pieces." [9]

The astounding force of that blow ended the opposition. The mob
fled in panic, crying "Peace! Peace!"

Mullá Husayn forced his way through the ranks of that retreating
mob, unmindful of the bullets that rained about him as he passed.
He galloped his horse toward Bárfurúsh. He rode straight to the
residence of the Sa'ídu'l-'Ulamá. Three times Mullá Husayn circled
the house calling for him to come out.

"Let that contemptible coward emerge from his inglorious retreat," he cried out. "Has he forgotten that the one who preaches
a holy war must himself march at the head of his followers and by
his own deeds sustain their enthusiasm?"

Peace was at last restored. Mullá Husayn addressed the people
of Bárfurúsh. "What have we done that you should arise against
us? Why should you think it meritorious in the sight of God to shed
our blood? Have we ever spoken one word against the truth of your

Faith? Is this the hospitality which your own Prophet, Muhammad, has commanded you to show to believer and unbeliever alike?"

Mullá Husayn shamed them with his words, then he assembled his companions and they continued on their way toward Sárí and the rescue of Quddús.

The Sa'ídu'l-'Ulamá came out of hiding as soon as Mullá Husayn departed with his friends. He immediately planned an attack upon them at the place where they had encamped for the night, at the Sabzih-Maydán caravanserai.

That evening at sunset, Mullá Husayn gathered his companions together.

"Is there one among you," he asked, "who is willing to arise and risk his life for the sake of God and ascend to the roof of the caravanserai and sound the call to prayer?"

In this way, Mullá Husayn told them, they would demonstrate to the people that they were not enemies, but friends; that they were lovers of Islám.

A youth gladly responded. No sooner had the melodious words of "God is great!" echoed over the countryside than a bullet struck him, killing him instantly.

"Let another arise," Mullá Husayn urged them, "and, with the selfsame renunciation, proceed with the prayer which that youth was unable to finish."

Another young man mounted to the roof and began to chant the words: "I bear witness that Muhammad is the Apostle of God!" His testimony was cut short by another bullet which struck him down.

Although Muhammad, Himself, had commanded that everyone should "Honor thy guest though he be an infidel," still these companions who were lodged for the night in the village caravanserai were being slain for observing out of respect and love His sacred call to prayer. Mullá Husayn entreated them to show their loyalty and thus expose the unfaithfulness of those who were attacking them.

A third youth, at the bidding of Mullá Husayn, attempted to complete the prayer which his two martyred companions had left unfinished. He, too, suffered the same fate. As he approached the end of his prayer, and with power and vigor called out the words, "There is no God but God," he in his turn, fell dead.

Such ruthless behavior impelled Mullá Husayn to throw open the gates of the caravanserai. He leaped onto his horse, gave the signal to charge, and at the head of his companions he swept out upon the assailants who had been massing before the gates. They fled before the fury of his onslaught. It was the story of Bárfurúsh repeated: again the enemy fled in panic, again they pleaded for peace, again they implored for mercy.

This was to be the first in a series of such encounters which were to last for nearly a year. The believers met every attack with a counter-attack and time after time humiliated their opponents. They would rally to the encouraging cry of Mullá Husayn, which all took up in turn:

"Mount your steeds, O heroes of God!"

Mullá Husayn and his companions finally arrived at the small shrine Shaykh Tabarsí about fourteen miles from Bárfurúsh. They hoped that by withdrawing, the onslaught against them might cease, and that after a reasonable time they might be permitted to go on their way to Sárí in peace.

The Sa'ídu'l-'Ulamá rejoiced. He felt that he had his hated enemies trapped at last. He vowed they would never escape. He called upon the government to help him annihilate them.

The night preceding the arrival of Mullá Husayn and his companions at the fort of Shaykh Tabarsí, the keeper of the shrine had a strange dream. He saw a holy man with seventy warriors and many companions arrive at Tabarsí. He dreamed that they remained in that place and engaged in the most heroic of battles, triumphing over the forces against them, and that finally, the Prophet of God Himself arrived one night to speak with them.

When Mullá Husayn appeared the next day, the keeper recognized him and told him of his dream. Mullá Husayn replied: "All that you witnessed will come to pass. Those glorious scenes of your dream will soon be enacted before your eyes."

The keeper threw in his lot with Mullá Husayn and the heroic defenders of what came to be known as the fort Shaykh Tabarsí.

Realizing that they would never be set free, but that orders had been issued to exterminate them, Mullá Husayn and his companions erected defenses about Tabarsí to help protect themselves.

Mullá Husayn was feeling very sad because of his failure to reach Sárí and rescue Quddús, when word came that Quddús was approaching the fort. The messengers Mullá Husayn had sent to

Sárí were successful in securing his release from the official in whose home he had been held captive.

Inside this fort the followers of the Báb were to hold out against assault, starvation, and treachery; they would outwit and outfight the entire army of the king; this God-intoxicated handful would be pitted against a trained army, well equipped, supported by the masses of the people, blessed by the clergy, headed by a prince of royal blood, backed by the resources of the state, and acting with the enthusiastic approval of the king himself.

When Quddús entered the fort, he asked Mullá Husayn to determine the exact number of the assembled companions. One by one Mullá Husayn counted them off as they passed in through the gate: three hundred and twelve in all. He was on his way to make his report to Quddús when a young man who had come on foot from Bárfurúsh rushed through the gate and begged to be allowed to join them. Thus, the number reported to Quddús was exactly three hundred and thirteen.

Quddús said to them: "Whatever the tongue of the Prophet of God has spoken concerning the Promised One must needs be fulfilled."

Then the companions were reminded of the prophecy given for this day, that "the assembling of three hundred and thirteen chosen supporters" would be yet another proof which would herald the coming of the Promised One on earth.[10]

The fury of the Sa'ídu'l-'Ulamá of Bárfurúsh was increased when the news of Quddús' presence in the fort reached him. Impelled by an implacable hatred, he sent a burning appeal to the king.

"A revolt has taken place," he told the Sháh. "This wretched band of agitators strikes at the very foundation of your kingdom. They have built a fort, and in that massive stronghold they have entrenched themselves, preparing to direct a campaign which will sweep you from your throne. What greater triumph could begin your new rule than to wipe out this hateful group which has dared to conspire against you. Should you fail to rise against them, I feel it my duty to warn you that the day is fast approaching when not only this province, but the whole of Persia will have cast aside your authority and surrendered to their cause."[11]

The king was alarmed and responded by sending an army of twelve thousand men to drive this small band from the fort of Tabarsí and to destroy them all. Food and water were cut off from them and soon the companions were reduced to grave conditions. The army was installed upon a hill overlooking the fort.

As Quddús stood with Mullá Husayn watching the army of the king, he said, "The scarcity of water has distressed our companions. God willing, this very night a downpour of rain will overtake our opponents, followed by a heavy snowfall, which will assist us to repulse their planned attack."

That night as the great mass of soldiers prepared to launch an assault upon the fort, a torrential rain overtook them. It ruined their ammunition. They broke ranks and took shelter, abandoning all plans of attack. Rainwater was quickly gathered inside the fort to quench the thirst of the friends.

The following historical record of that period has been preserved: "A snowfall such as the people of the neighborhood even in the depths of winter had never experienced added considerably to the annoyance which the rain caused." These storms brought hardship and ruin to the camp of the king's soldiers, but refreshment to the fort.

One of the most memorable encounters took place one morning just before dawn. The companions were sorely distressed and constantly harried by the outright attacks as well as by the snipers. One morning the gates of the fort were thrown open to meet an attack.

"Mount your steeds, O heroes of God!" came the command from Mullá Husayn.

This stirring call rallied all hearts. Preceded by Quddús, they rushed full charge toward the stronghold of the prince, the leader of the army of the king. Mullá Husayn thrust his way right into the royal quarters. The prince had already thrown himself from a back window into the moat, and had escaped barefooted, leaving the army bewildered and routed by a handful of Mullá Husayn's companions.

Comte de Gobineau in his account states that "in a few moments his [the prince's] army already in such confusion, was scattered by the three hundred men of Mullá Husayn! Was not this the sword of the Lord and of Gideon?"

In the prince's quarters, the companions found coffers filled with gold and silver. They looked at them, then left them behind, taking only the abandoned sword of the prince which they gave to Mullá Husayn whose own sword had been struck by a bullet.

A detachment of soldiers, meanwhile, surrounded Quddús and fired a volley at him, wounding him in the mouth and throat. Mullá Husayn rushed to his aid. He seized the sword of Quddús, and brandishing this blade in one hand and the captured sword of the prince in the other, he attacked the enemy and aided by one hundred and ten of his fellow disciples, put the soldiers to flight. Quddús recovered from his wound, minimizing its importance.

Each time the enemy was routed, Quddús would remind the companions of their real purpose. "We have repulsed them," he said, "no need to carry the punishment further. Our purpose is to protect ourselves in the hope that God may enable us to continue our work of teaching and regenerating the hearts of men. We have no intention whatever of causing unnecessary harm to any one."

Repeatedly the companions of Mullá Husayn and Quddús tried to persuade their enemies to permit them to go on their way without the shedding of further blood. Even one of the leaders of the king's army has testified to this. When questioned at a later date by prince Ahmad Mírzá about Tabarsí and Mullá Husayn, 'Abbás-Qulí Khán gave this account:

"One day Mullá Husayn stood forth in the open field, and leaning upon a lance which he held in his hand, said, 'O people, why without enquiry, and under the influence of passion and prejudiced misrepresentation, do ye act so cruelly toward us, and strive without cause to shed innocent blood? Be ashamed before the Creator of the universe, and at least give us passage, that we may depart out of this land.' Seeing that the soldiers were moved, I opened fire, and ordered the troops to shout so as to drown out his voice. Again I saw him lean on his lance and cry: 'Is there anyone who will help me?' Three times, so that all heard his cry. At this moment all the soldiers were silent, and some began to weep, and many of the horsemen were visibly affected. Fearing that the army might be seduced from their allegiance, I again ordered them to fire and shout. Then I saw Mullá Husayn unsheathe his sword, raise his face toward heaven and heard him exclaim: 'O God, I have completed the proof to this host, but it availeth not.' Then he began to attack us on the right and on the left." [12]

Mullá Husayn was slain during the course of the struggle to defend the fort of Tabarsí. True to his forecast, he fell a victim to the enemy fire, along with seventy-two of his friends.

The scarcity of water compelled the companions to dig a well inside the fort. Mullá Husayn, who was watching the completion, said with a smile, "Today we shall have all the water we require for our bath. Cleansed of all earthly defilements, we shall seek the court of the Almighty. Whoso is willing to join me, let him prepare himself to partake of the cup of martyrdom ere dawn."

That afternoon he had washed himself thoroughly, clothed himself with freshly washed garments, and placed the Báb's green turban upon his head. A great happiness appeared to surround him. He spent a long time in conversation with Quddús. He visited with each one of his companions that evening, cheering them and encouraging their hearts.

Soon after midnight, the morning star appeared in the skies. Mullá Husayn, gazing at it, recognized it as a star that "heralded the dawn of reunion with his Beloved."

He mounted his charger and ordered that the gate of the fort be thrown open. He rode out at the head of his companions, to cry: "O Lord of the Age!" So intense and powerful was this shout in praise of the Báb that forest, fort, and camp vibrated to its resounding echo.

Mullá Husayn charged the barricades from behind which the army planned to launch their most concentrated offensive. One after the other he crushed his way through them until all seven of the barricades had fallen. His gallantry and courage were never greater, but his days of horsemanship and heroism were now at an end.

With victory complete, Mullá Husayn's steed became entangled in the rope of a tent. Before he could free himself, he was struck in the breast by a bullet which had been fired from the ambush of a neighboring tree. One of the leaders of the enemy, 'Abbás-Qulí Khán, had fled and hidden in the sheltering branches rather than face the attack of Mullá Husayn. Seeing him in distress, he fired the fatal shot.

Mullá Husayn dismounted, staggered a few steps, then fell exhausted to the ground, unconscious. Two of his companions bore him back to the fort.

Quddús said, "Leave me alone with him."

The friends retired. One of them standing near the door heard Quddús speak gently to Mullá Husayn with the greatest love.

"You have hastened the hour of your departure, and have

abandoned me to the mercy of my foes. Please God I will ere long join you and taste the sweetness of heaven."

What a short time had passed since that night in Shíráz when the Báb had spoken to Mullá Husayn, saying: "O thou who art the first to believe in Me, verily, I say I am the Báb, the Gate of God." On that never-to-be-forgotten night, the Báb had called upon all men to awake! teach the Word of God! quicken the souls of men!

Now Mullá Husayn lay dying in the fort of Tabarsí. His last words, addressed to Quddús were directed beyond him to the Beloved of his heart, the Báb. Softly, he said, "Are you pleased with me?"

Quddús opened the door and came out to the companions of Mullá Husayn. "I have bade my last farewell to him," he said. They knew then that Mullá Husayn was dead. They entered to say farewell, moved to tears by the faint smile of happiness that still lingered upon his face. Such was the peacefulness of his countenance, that he seemed to have fallen asleep.[13]

Quddús attended to the burial. He clothed Mullá Husayn in his own shirt and gave instructions to bury him in a spot adjoining the Shrine at the fort of Tabarsí. A Traveller's Narrative says that "his mortal remains still repose in the little inner room of the Shrine of Shaykh Tabarsí where, at the direction of [Quddús], they were reverently laid by the hands of his sorrowing comrades in the beginning of the year A.D. 1849." [14] As Quddús placed Mullá Husayn's body in its last resting place, he said: "I pray God to grant that no division ever be caused between you and me."

In every encounter, Mullá Husayn had distinguished himself by acts of valor and chivalry. His great learning, his high sense of justice, his tenacity of faith, and his unswerving devotion to God marked him as an outstanding figure among those who have borne witness to the power of the Faith of the Báb.

The historian Gobineau said of him, "At last, he passed away. The new religion which found in him its first martyr, lost, in the same stroke, a man whose moral strength and ability would have been of great value to it, had he lived longer. The [opposing forces] naturally feel a hatred for the memory of this leader, which is as deep as the love and veneration shown for him by the [followers of the Báb].[15]

The Christian clergyman, Dr. T. K. Cheyne, wrote, "Frail of form, but a gallant soldier and an impassioned lover of God, he [Mullá

Husayn] combined the qualities and characteristics . . . seldom found united in the same person." [16]

The death of Mullá Husayn caused inexpressible sorrow to the Báb, a sorrow that gave rise to eulogies and prayers equivalent to thrice the volume of the Qur'án. In one of His prayers, the Báb declared that the very dust of the ground where the remains of Mullá Husayn lie buried is endowed with such a potency as to bring joy to the disconsolate and healing to the sick. [17]

That great Figure (Bahá'u'lláh) Whose coming the Báb unceasingly proclaimed, wrote at a later date, that but for Mullá Husayn the Cause of God would not have been established.

Mullá Husayn was thirty-six when he was slain. After his burial Quddús gave instructions to inter the bodies of the thirty-six who had fallen with him that night in one and the same grave near the shrine.

"Let the loved ones of God," Quddús said, as they were lowered into the earth, "take heed of the example of these martyrs of our Faith. Let them be as united in life as these are now in death."

Quddús was now in sole command of those in the fort. When their supply of provisions was nearly exhausted, Quddús distributed the last of the rice among them, and warned them of the hardships that lay ahead.

"Whoever feels himself strong enough to withstand the calamities that are soon to befall us, let him remain with us in this fort. And whoever perceives in himself the least hesitation and fear, let him betake himself away from this place. The way will soon be barred before our faces, and we shall fall a victim to devastating afflictions."

The very night Quddús gave this warning, one fearful soul betrayed his companions. He wrote a letter to 'Abbás-Qulí Khán, the king's general, informing him that Mullá Husayn was dead. "He was the pillar upon which the strength and security of the fort depended. They are worn with famine and are being grievously treated." The letter was carried by a messenger, who, with his share of the rice given him by Quddús, stole out of the fort during the night.

The welcome news of the death of Mullá Husayn nerved 'Abbás-Qulí Khán to a fresh attack. Fearing that the messenger might spread the report of Mullá Husayn's death and thus rob him of some of the glory of victory, he killed him instantly. He massed his soldiers for an advance and, at the head of two detachments, he had the fort surrounded.

Quddús understood at once what had happened. "A betrayer has announced the death of Mullá Husayn," he said. "Sally out and administer a befitting chastisement."

Nineteen of the companions plunged headlong into the ranks of the enemy. They were pitted against no less than two regiments of infantry and cavalry. They counter-attacked with such fury that 'Abbás-Qulí Khán, the slayer of Mullá Husayn, became terrified and fell from his horse. In his panic and haste, he left one of his boots hanging from the stirrup. He ran away half-shod and thoroughly frightened. He fled to the prince and confessed the ignominious reverse he had suffered at the hands of those nineteen companions of Mullá Husayn.

This same 'Abbás-Qulí Khán later wrote of these defenders of Tabarsí: "In truth, I know not what had been shown unto these people, or what they had seen, that they came forth to battle with such alacrity and joy. The imagination of man cannot conceive the vehemence of their courage and valor."

Gobineau records that the army "built large towers as high as the various levels of the fortress or higher and, through a continuous plunging fire, they rendered the circulation of the [followers of the Báb] within their fort extremely dangerous . . . but in a few days, [they], taking advantage of the long nights, raised their fortifications so that their height exceeded that of the attacking towers of the enemy." [18]

"Exasperated by these evidences of unquenchable fervor, the commanding officer erected a great tower upon which he placed his biggest cannon, and directed his fire into the heart of the fort.

"The faithful seeing this," an historical document tells us, "began to dig subterranean passages and retreat thither. But the ground of Mázindarán lies near the water and is saturated with moisture, added to which rain fell continually, increasing the damage so those poor sufferers dwelt amidst mud and water till their garments rotted away with damp." [19]

Outraged at their failure to conquer this pitiful band of untrained students, the leading officers of the army, under the command of the prince, gathered a huge force and constructed trenches and barricades. They brought up more cannon and cannon-balls.

They hurled flaming projectiles into the fort and gave orders to begin a heavy bombardment.

Gobineau states in his book, "In a very short time, the outer defenses of the fortress were dismantled; nothing was left of them but falling girders, smoked and burning timbers, and scattered stones." [20]

While the bombardment was in process, Quddús emerged from his shelter and walked to the center of the fort. His manner was one of the greatest tranquillity. A cannon-ball fell suddenly into the fort. It embedded itself in the earth before him, then rolled free. It came to a stop in front of him. Calmly Quddús placed his foot on it and rolled it back and forth.

"How utterly unaware," he said, "are these boastful aggressors of the power of God's avenging wrath. Do they seek to intimidate the heroes of God, in whose sight the power of kings is but an empty shadow?"

Quddús turned to his friends. "Beware," he cautioned them, "lest fear and selfishness steal away your glorious station. Each one of you has his appointed hour, and when that hour is come neither the assault of the enemy nor the pleading of your friends will be able to retard or advance it. If you allow your hearts to be frightened by the booming of these guns which with increasing violence will shower their projectiles on this fort, you will have cast yourself out of the stronghold of God's protection."

This appeal breathed much-needed confidence into every heart, for their troubles were mounting. Their food was at last reduced to the flesh of the horses they had brought away from the camp of the enemy. Later they had to content themselves with grass snatched from the ground. Finally, they consumed the bark of trees and the leather of their saddles, their belts, their scabbards, and their shoes. They even subsisted on the ground bones of the horses fallen in battle. For eighteen days their only sustenance was a mouthful of water each morning.

"God knows," one of the survivors has testified, "that we had ceased to hunger for food." Quddús quickened their enthusiasm and brightened their hopes each day at sunrise and at sunset, by telling of the beauty and greatness of the Báb.

Many lost their lives, but the dwindling band still remained unconquered. Their actions fulfilled several prophecies which foretold of the coming of God's Prophet in the last days. One of the most significant spoke of the "halting of those who had believed in the Lord about Tabarsí, and their martyrdom." [21]

The young king at last grew impatient. "An army which we thought could fight a lion or a whale cannot fight a handful of weak and defenseless men," he said. "It has achieved nothing!"

He and his Prime Minister, Mírzá Taqí Khán, burst forth against their army leaders. In the most bitter terms they accused them of rank incompetency. They threatened to punish them with the same treatment which had been planned for the followers of the Báb. The king, in his anxiety and anger, threatened the lives of every person in the province around the fort of Shaykh Tabarsí. "I shall exterminate them to the last man!" he said.

The prince and 'Abbás-Qulí Khán knew that it was useless to try and explain to an angry king that although the defenders of the fort were not professional soldiers, it had proved impossible to force their surrender. 'Abbás-Qulí Khán himself expressed this dilemma by admitting in his own words that the companions of Quddús were: "Scholars and men of learning . . . strangers to the roar of the cannon, the rattle of musketry, and the field of battle . . . Notwithstanding this, it seemed as if in time of battle a new spirit were breathed into their frames . . . the imagination of man cannot conceive the vehemence of their courage and valor. They used to expose their bodies to the bullets and cannon-balls not only fearlessly and courageously, but eagerly and joyously, seeming to regard the battle-field as a banquet." [22]

The prince was informed of the threats which the king had made. He was afraid that any further delay in subduing Quddús and his companions might result in the loss of his prestige, perhaps his own life. Therefore, he resorted to treachery. He despaired of conquering, so he conceived a plan of betrayal.

The prince sent a Qur'án to Quddús and swore by that Holy Book that he would set free all the defenders of the fort and permit them to go their way. They would not even be molested, the prince promised. He himself, at his own expense, he vowed, would arrange for their safe departure with honor to their homes. Quddús received the Book, kissed it reverently, and quoted from the sacred words: "O our Lord, decide between us and between our people with truth; for the best to decide art Thou." Then he read the pledge, and assembled his companions. "Prepare to leave the fort," he said. "By our response to their oath, we shall test the sincerity of their intentions."

At the gate of the fort, they mounted the horses which were to take them to the camp of the prince. A dinner was placed before Quddús and his starving friends. He refused to touch it, knowing that the hour of death was upon him. The prince repeated his promise: "My oath is irrevocable and sacred," he said.

One of the companions whispered to Quddús, "I am of the opinion that what his tongue professes, his heart does not believe at all."

Quddús, who shared this view, told his companions to disperse that very night before it was too late. They implored him not to send them away from his side.

"Weep not," was his final word, "the reunion which will follow this separation will endure eternally. We now commit our Cause to the care of God."

This was the final scene of that somber tragedy at Tabarsí. The prince violated his sacred pledge. Quddús and his companions were seized, stripped of their meager possessions, and some were sold as slaves. Others were slain outright, killed by the spears and swords of the officers who were hungry for revenge.

One account states, "the whole world marvelled at the manner of their sacrifice . . . their deeds . . . their fortitude and bodily endurance." [23]

No less than nine of the Báb's first eighteen disciples, known as the Letters of the Living, fell in this disaster.

The historian Nicolas speaks of the futile attempt of the civil and religious authorities to erase all trace of that gallant spot. "All the fortifications constructed by the followers of the Báb," he says, "were razed to the ground, and even the ground was leveled to remove any evidence of the heroic defense of those who had died for their Faith. They imagined that this would silence history."

Quddús was bound with chains and taken by the prince on foot to Bárfurúsh, the city of the cowardly high-priest, the Sa'ídu'l-'Ulamá. Bárfurúsh was also the city in which Quddús had been born.

The Sa'ídu'l-'Ulamá was not afraid now to come out of his home. With all the religious leaders of Bárfurúsh, he went to welcome the prince, and to extend his congratulations on their triumphal return. The entire town was hung with flags to celebrate the victory. Bonfires blazed at night. Three days of festivities took place.

The prince gave no indication to the high-priest as to what was to be done with Quddús. The prince himself was extremely reluctant to ill-treat his captive further. He had captured Quddús by treachery, but now that his prestige was secure, he did not wish any further shame to be attached to his share in this hateful episode.

The prince made up his mind to conduct Quddús to Tihrán and deliver him into the hands of the king. This, he felt, would relieve him of the responsibility of deciding Quddús' fate. What was more important, it would also bring additional honors to him along the route of march. However, the unquenchable hostility of the high-priest interfered with this plan. When the high-priest saw that Quddús might slip from his grasp, he appealed to the mob once more, as he had appealed to them on that first day when Mullá Husayn and his companions had appeared on the plain of Bárfurúsh. He encouraged their basest sentiments. He whipped them into a frenzy. The whole of Bárfurúsh was aroused by the persistency and viciousness of his call to action.

"I have vowed to deny myself both food and sleep," he cried from the pulpit, "until such a time as I am able to end the life of Quddús with my own hands."

The crowd rallied around him and became so ugly that the prince feared that his own safety might be in danger. He summoned all the priests of Bárfurúsh in to consult upon measures to quiet and restrain the populace.

Quddús was also summoned into their presence. At that moment, the prince realized that the hatred of the entire city was solidly against him. He sighed, and spoke words reminiscent of those of Pontius Pilate: "I wash my hands of all responsibility for any harm that may befall this man. You are free to do what you wish with him. You will yourselves be answerable to God on the day of Judgment."

As soon as he had spoken these words, the prince surrendered Quddús into the hands of the chief priest. He mounted his horse and as his final act of cowardice, fled from the city, turning his back upon Quddús.

There was now no restraint upon the people. They pounced upon Quddús with uncontrolled violence. He was stripped of his clothes. He was paraded through the streets barefooted, bareheaded, and loaded down with chains. He was followed each step of the way by a howling mob. They jeered at him, spat upon him, and flung refuse at him.

Amidst his last tortures, Quddús asked the pardon of God for nis persecutors. "Forgive the trespasses of these people, O God," he cried. "Deal with them in Thy mercy, for they do not know the secret we have already discovered. Show them the way of Truth, O God, and turn their ignorance into faith."

In his hour of agony, one of the traitors who had deserted the fort passed Quddús. He saw how helpless Quddús now was. Emboldened, he came forward and struck him in the face.

"If what you speak is of God," he scoffed, "free yourself."

Quddús looked quietly into his eyes. "May God forgive you your deed," he said, "inasmuch as you have added to the measure of my suffering."

When the family of Quddús heard of his agonies, they recalled the prophetic words he had spoken to them many years before in that same city.

His step-mother, who had been kind and loving to him, had urged him to marry. "I long to witness your nuptials," she told him, "but I fear this longing will always remain unfulfilled."

Quddús replied: "The day of my wedding is not yet come. That day will be unspeakably glorious. Not within the confines of this house, but out in the open air, under the vault of heaven, in the public square before the gaze of the great multitude, I shall celebrate my nuptials and witness the fulfillment of all my hopes."

Now that promise had come true. As he approached the public square, Quddús remembered those long-ago tender years, and the words he had spoken. He raised his voice. "Would that my mother were with me now, and could see the splendor of my nuptials!"

In the middle of the night, a devoted friend gathered what still remained of Quddús' burned and mutilated body. He buried them in a place not far from the scene of his martyrdom.

Nabíl in his history declares that the story of Mullá Husayn, Quddús, and the defense of the fort of Tabarsí "must ever remain as one of the most moving episodes of modern times." [24]

The words spoken by Quddús in the fort of Tabarsí now made themselves felt, fulfilling his prediction: "How utterly unaware are these boastful aggressors of the power of God's avenging wrath."

After the passing of but a short time, the Sa'ídu'l-'Ulamá was struck down by the same fate that had crushed Husayn Khán, Mírzá 'Alí-Asghar, Muhammad Sháh, and Hájí Mírzá Áqásí. Thus still another leader in the plot against the Báb and his followers was seized in the grip of destruction.

He became afflicted with a strange disease for which there was no cure. In spite of the furs which he wore, in spite of the fire which burned constantly in his room, he could never become warm. Even as he trembled with the cold, his fever was so high that nothing could quench his burning thirst.

He died of his illness, and his beautiful house was abandoned until it crumbled into ruins. Little by little the practice grew of dumping refuse upon the site where it had once so proudly stood.

Nicolas points out in his history, "This so impressed the people [of that district] that when they quarrel among themselves, the final insult frequently is, 'May thy house meet the same fate as the house of the Sa'ídu'l-'Ulamá!'" [25]

The news of the tragic fate which had overtaken the heroes of Tabarsí reached the Báb in His prison at Chiríq. It brought great sadness to His heart. He penned a eulogy in honor of Quddús and Mullá Husayn. In it He wrote that He, too, would soon join these twin immortals; each of whom by his life and his death had shed imperishable luster upon the Faith of God.

He instructed one of His followers to visit Tarbarsí and Bár-furúsh.

"Arise," He said, "and . . . in the guise of a traveler, . . . visit on My behalf, the spot which enshrines [their] bodies. . . . Bring back to Me, as a remembrance of your visit, a handful of that holy earth which covers the remains of My beloved ones, Quddús and Mullá Husayn. Strive to be back ere the day of Naw-Rúz [New Year] that you may celebrate with Me that festival, the only one I probably shall ever see again." [26]

A WONDER AMONG WOMEN

ONE OF THE MOST courageous of all the followers of the Báb was a woman. She was among His chosen disciples. She was known as Táhirih, which means "The Pure One." The members of her family ranked high among the religious leaders of Persia. Her father was one of the most famous of all. From her earliest childhood, she was regarded by her fellow-townsmen as a prodigy. Her knowledge and gifts were so outstanding that her father often was heard to lament, "Would that she had been a boy, for he would have shed illumination upon my household, and would have succeeded me." [1]

She was renowned for both her intelligence and her beauty. Her brother, 'Abdúl-Vahháb said, "None of us, her brothers or her cousins dared to speak in her presence, her learning so intimidated us; and if we ventured to express some hypothesis upon a disputed point of doctrine, she demonstrated in such a clear, precise and conclusive manner that we were going astray, that we instantly withdrew confused." [2]

A. L. M. Nicolas' historical account tells us that "her reputation became universal throughout Persia, and the most haughty 'ulamás [scholars] consented to adopt some of her hypotheses and opinions."

One day while visiting in the home of her cousin, she discovered some books in his library which interested her very much. They were written by Shaykh Ahmad and his successor, Siyyid Kázim.

Her cousin warned her that her father would be very displeased if he found her reading them.

"He is opposed to these modern thinkers," he told her.

However, she persuaded him, and took the books home to study. Her father raised violent objections, had heated discussions with her, and criticized and denounced the writings of Shaykh Ahmad. She eagerly read all of their books that she could find. Shaykh Ahmad was dead, but Siyyid Kázim was still living in Karbilá, so Táhirih began corresponding with him. His letters excited in her an ever keener interest in the coming of a promised Messenger. She had a great longing to go to Karbilá to study under Siyyid Kázim.

She knew that her father would never grant his permission. However, with the help of her uncle, she secured permission to visit the Shrines at Karbilá and Najaf. Her family willingly granted permission for this, believing that a pilgrimage might bring her back to her senses and to more orthodox ways. They did not suspect that her true purpose in going was to meet Siyyid Kázim.

She made the journey in 1843. She looked forward to studying under Siyyid Kázim. During those days she thought only of his promise: the approaching appearance of a new spiritual Teacher in the world. Táhirih told her uncle that she wished to be the first woman to serve Him when He appeared.

"Oh, when will the day come," she said, "when new laws will be revealed on earth! I shall be the first to follow those new Teachings and to give my life for my sisters!" [3]

Táhirih's grief was very deep when she reached Karbilá and found that Siyyid Kázim had died just ten days before her arrival. Her sorrow softened when she was permitted to stay in his home, and was given access to all his writings, some of which had never been published. She studied them eagerly. In each one of them she discovered that same thrilling promise of a great Figure soon to appear on earth.

While she was in Karbilá, Táhirih met Mullá Husayn who was just starting out on his search for the Promised One. Her hopes were set ablaze. She, like Mullá Husayn, spent her time in prayer and meditation.

One night in a dream, a young man appeared before her. He raised his hands toward heaven and in a beautiful voice recited many wonderful verses, one of which she wrote down. She awakened with a feeling of joy which flooded her being.

One day, some time later, a friend placed in her hands certain writings of the Báb. As her eyes looked down upon a page, she discovered the exact same words she had written down from her dream. To her intense delight she realized that the Message of the Author was true.

Táhirih wrote immediately to the Báb, telling Him that she believed Him to be that promised Messenger foretold in all the holy Books, and so long and eagerly awaited. To the one who delivered the letter for her, she added: "Say to Him, from me, 'The effulgence of Thy face hath flashed forth, and the rays of Thy visage arose on high. Then speak the word, "Am I not your Lord?" and "Thou art, Thou art!" we will all reply.'" [4]

Her acceptance of the Báb brought immediate and violent protests from her father, her uncle, her husband, and her brothers. Because of the illustrious name of her family, they all tried to quiet her and to curb her teaching.

Táhirih was aflame with the message of the Báb. She won many to His Faith in Karbilá. The following description has been recorded of her early days of teaching in that city: "All who met her were ensnared by her bewitching eloquence and felt the fascination of her words. None could resist her charm; few could escape the contagion of her belief. All testified to the extraordinary traits of her character, marveled at her amazing personality, and were convinced of the sincerity of her convictions." [5]

Táhirih was not content with a passive sympathy for the Faith of the Báb. She openly confessed her belief in Him. She tried to awaken those around her to the coming of a great new day in the affairs of all mankind. Many people began to share her enthusiasm and flocked to listen to her.

When the learned religious leaders of Karbilá learned that she was an ardent follower of the Báb and was teaching His Faith in the very center of their religious life, they complained bitterly to the government.

They were especially angered when Táhirih wanted to celebrate the birthday of the Báb which fell within the month of the commemoration of the martyrdom of the Imám Husayn. She discarded her mourning garb and attired herself in clothes which showed her happiness. [6]

Officials were dispatched at once to arrest her, but they seized a friend of hers by mistake. Táhirih wrote immediately to the governor and told him that she was the one for whom they were looking and to release her friend.

The governor put Táhirih's residence under guard so that no one could go in or out for three months.[7]

Her family heard of these happenings and tried to persuade her to return to Qazvín. Failing in this, they urged her to be more calm and reserved and not let her conduct reflect on the good name of the family.

Word came to her that the disciples of the Báb were gathering for a great conference in Khurasán, Persia, so Táhirih started on her way immediately.

Before her departure from Karbilá she unburdened her heart by writing a letter to each of the priests of that city, condemning their bigotry. These leaders gave to women a rank little higher than that of animals and even denied them the possession of a soul. Táhirih ably defended her Faith in this letter and exposed their unjust and backward views.[8]

She stopped at Baghdád enroute eastward. She was accompanied from Karbilá by the mother and sister of Mullá Husayn in whom she had kindled a great love for the Faith.

The very day that Táhirih arrived in Baghdád she began teaching the Cause. She spoke with such power and eloquence that those who had seen and heard her before she became a follower of the Báb were amazed. They said: "This is not the same woman we knew before."

Her lectures began to attract very large audiences from among the peoples of all religions. One of the most outstanding of her characteristics was her ability to arouse a keen desire in her listeners to investigate the truth of the Báb's mission for themselves. Within a short time her extraordinary attraction had won many supporters. A large number had followed her from Karbilá to Baghdád in order to attend her classes.

The priests of Baghdád became aroused as her words began to woo away their own followers. She was emptying their classes. Many rose up against her, so she challenged them publicly. Through the governor she invited them all to meet her in a great public discussion upon the truth or falsehood of the Báb's Faith. They refused, made excuses, and instead complained to the government about the revolution she was stirring up.

The following story is told of a Jewish physician, Hakím Masih, who in the company of the king, passed through Baghdád on his way to Karbilá. One day he came upon a large group of people, mostly priests, listening to a lecture by a woman who was sitting veiled from their sight behind a curtain. He went in to listen. As soon as she finished, they began arguing with her. Her speech was so logical and convincing that the doctor was very much attracted. The priests were unable to answer her proofs. He was very astonished and soon he became convinced that this woman was right. He thought that this magic speaker must be the Promised One of Whom everyone was speaking. He attended her lectures and learned of the Message of the Báb, and believed in Him. Thus, a Jew who had passed by the wonderful message of both Christ and Muhammad was won over to the Faith of the Báb by the eloquence and logic of Táhirih. Now he believed in both Christ and Muhammad, and all the messengers of God.[9]

One day a delegation of the ablest religious leaders of Baghdád came to see Táhirih. Her popularity had grown so astonishingly that they became alarmed at the effect she might have upon their people and united against her. This delegation had representatives from the two leading sects of Islám, and from the Jewish and Christian communities as well. Their mission was to silence her.

"We have come," they informed her, "to convince you of the folly of your actions, and to turn you from your purpose."

Prior to this meeting, these religious leaders had thought of Táhirih as a gifted woman whose enthusiasm for something new had overleaped the bounds of moderation. Her popularity, they felt sure, was based on novelty, but once she came face to face with a group of such eminent religious leaders, she would be subdued and once more resume her humble place as a woman. They were unprepared for her reckless indifference to their combined wisdom and her cool appraisal of their motives. Following that meeting they looked upon her as a dangerous and powerful adversary. Táhirih was able to silence every protest. She astounded them with the force of her argument and the depth of her knowledge. She was not lowly and submissive before them as they expected. Instead, she was aflame with the love of God and she burned away their flimsy reasoning with the fire of her words. "She is no mere woman," they said. They were embarrassed at their inability to subdue her. Disillusioned at their complete failure, they withdrew. Such victories increased her fame and their anger.[10]

So great was the influence which Táhirih exerted upon the people, so intense became the excitement caused by her teaching, that she was seized by the authorities and placed in the house of the chief-lawyer, by order of the governor of Baghdád. She was kept there under virtual arrest until the governor could receive instructions about her from the central Turkish government in Constantinople.[11]

During her imprisonment there, Táhirih defended her Faith and her own character before the chief-lawyer with great ability. Before she left his home, he told her sincerely, "I share your belief, but I am apprehensive of the swords of the ruling family of Turkey."

With so many powerful local leaders pitted against her, the government felt the question had to be settled quickly as to whether or not she should be permitted to continue her teaching. Her case was submitted first to the governor of Baghdád, and finally to the authorities in Constantinople.[12]

That same lawyer later wrote a book in Arabic in which he spoke of Táhirih's stay in his home. He said that every morning in the early hours of dawn she would arise to pray and meditate. She fasted frequently. He stated that he had never seen a woman more virtuous, more devoted, nor had he seen any man more learned or more courageous than she.[13]

One evening the chief-lawyer's father came to call upon his son. He did not even greet Táhirih. Instead, in her presence, he began to rebuke his son for his kindness to her and cursed her as an enemy of religion. The father said with grim satisfaction that a message had just arrived from Constantinople. The Sultán of Turkey had given Táhirih her life and her freedom, but she was commanded to leave Turkish territory immediately.

"Make preparations to leave Iraq tomorrow," the father told her bluntly, the only words he spoke to her, then he departed.

The chief-lawyer was ashamed of his father's behavior. He apologized to Táhirih. After she had left his home, he confided to his friends: "I see in her such knowledge, education, politeness and good character as I have not seen in any great man of this century."

Táhirih crossed the Turkish-Persian border and entered the city of Kirmánsháh. Here, unlike Baghdád, she was given an enthusiastic welcome. The priests, the government officials and people all came out to welcome so famous a figure. They were impressed by her eloquence and fearlessness. She translated one of the writings of the Báb and had it read publicly in Kirmánsháh. The governor and his family acknowledged the truth of the Cause of the Báb during her presence. They showed their great admiration and love for Táhirih.

In the village of Karand, Táhirih remained and taught for three days. Openly she proclaimed the teachings of the Báb, and was successful in awakening an interest among all classes of people. Twelve hundred persons are reported to have accepted the Faith.[14]

In the small village of Sahnih she stayed for two days. Her reception there outshone even that of Karand. Upon her departure the inhabitants of the village begged to be allowed to gather together the members of their community and come with her. They were prepared to leave everything behind and join her in the spread and promotion of the Faith of the Báb. Táhirih, however, advised them to remain where they were and to teach among their own people.[15]

Táhirih went next to Hamadán. There the city was divided in its attitude toward her. Some tried to arouse the people against her, while others loudly praised her.

One of the leading priests of Hamadán deeply resented her fame, and wished to kill her. He would have openly urged the people to attack her except for his fear of reprisal from her friends.

Táhirih knew of the priest's desire, and she wrote him a long letter explaining carefully the teachings of the Báb. She sent it to him by a faithful friend, Mullá Ibráhím. He arrived with this letter just at an hour when several of these unfriendly priests were meeting to decide what steps they could take against Táhirih to silence her. They considered the letter impudent. It enraged them. They all fell upon Mullá Ibráhím and beat him until he was unconscious. When he was carried back to Táhirih, still unconscious, she did not weep at the sight of him as those about her had expected her to do. She astonished them all by saying: "Get up, Mullá Ibráhím! Praised be God you have suffered in the path of your Beloved. Now rise up, and continue to work for Him!"

When Mullá Ibráhím opened his eyes, Táhirih smiled at him.

"O Mullá Ibráhím," she said. "For one small beating you became unconscious. This is the time we are ready to give our lives. Did not the disciples of Christ do it, and the disciples of Muhammad?"

And Mullá Ibráhím actually arose from his faint and departed from her presence, and began to teach.[16]

From Hamadán Táhirih planned to go to Tihrán to try and meet his Majesty, Muhammad Sháh, so that she could tell the king about these new teachings. However, one of the priests who had refused to meet her in open debate when she was in Kirmánsháh had secretly written to her father in Qazvín. He told him that his daughter was disgracing the reputation of all the clergy, let alone her family.

Her father at once sent his son with a strong party of relatives to Hamadán to intercept Táhirih, and to urge her to return home. Some time before they arrived from Qazvín, Táhirih said to her companions, "They are coming for us from Qazvín. We shall go out to meet them before they arrive here." She gave up her visit to Tihrán, and returned to her home with her escort.

That first night when Táhirih arrived in Qazvín, there was a family council. Her father and her uncle strongly reproached her for her behavior.

"What can I do with you," her father complained, "when you choose to follow this Shírází lad?"

Her uncle Taqí cursed the Báb and His Faith. In his violent anger he struck Táhirih several blows. With her quick intuition of the avenging hand of God, Táhirih uttered fatal words of foresight.

"O uncle," she cried out, "I see your mouth fill with blood!"

These words so infuriated him that he threatened to have her branded with hot irons. The council broke up in anger. Next day the family tried to persuade her to return to her husband, hoping this would keep her under restraint.

"We have been separated for three years," she said. "He has rejected the religion of God. He is ashamed of me. There can never be anything in common between us."

Her husband, who considered himself to be one of the great religious leaders of Persia, sent a stern message to Táhirih to transfer her residence at once to his house. She replied: "Neither in this world or in the next can I ever be associated with him. I have cast him out of my life forever."

Her husband in a burst of fury pronounced her a heretic and strove to undermine her position and sully her fame; in anger he divorced her three weeks later.[17]

Her father and her brothers still hoped that by having Táhirih at home they could diminish her influence and slowly win her back to the old ways. However, the opposite proved true. Her fearlessness, her organizing ability, her skill, and her unquenchable enthusiasm won many new victories for the Báb.

Táhirih's uncle, Taqí, was murdered one Friday in the Mosque. He was stabbed in the throat. Although the evidence clearly showed that the murderer was not a follower of the Báb, still Táhirih was accused of the slaying. Her family recalled those prophetic words spoken on the night of her return: "O uncle! I see your mouth fill with blood!"

The entire city was aroused. The mobs were encouraged to seek revenge by arresting, robbing and killing, and plundering the houses of anyone suspected of being a follower of the Báb.

Táhirih herself was placed in strict confinement. Out of respect for her father, an eminent Islamic jurist, the authorities permitted him to save her life and imprison Táhirih in the cellar of his home, but the women who were assigned to watch her were told never to let her out of their sight. She must not escape.

A member of Táhirih's family, one day years later while showing visitors the prison cellar in which she had been confined, said: "Táhirih's father truly loved his gifted daughter even though he clashed violently with her in religious beliefs. He imprisoned her in his home trying to protect her from the savagery of those who were ready to brand her with irons because she belonged to the despised. [Faith of the Báb], but even her father could not save her. They came and carried her away to the city prison."[18]

In a spirit of revenge, although well aware of her innocence, Táhirih's husband persuaded the governor to put her on trial for the murder of her uncle, Taqí. Her father refused to let her leave his house, but she was taken from him by force and brought to the government house. They also arrested her servant Káfiyih whom they hoped to influence to testify against her.

Hour after hour they questioned them, trying to get them to confess to the murder. To each question, Táhirih replied calmly: "We know nothing of this deed. It was done without our knowledge."

Her husband, seething with hatred, fearful she would go free, kept pleading with the governor to inflict some harsh punishment upon Táhirih. "Something severe," he said, "something very severe."

Acting on this hint, the governor gave the executioner orders to bring in the irons for branding.

In order to terrorize Táhirih and perhaps secure a false confession by torture, they placed the hands of Káfiyih under a sliding door, intending to brand her hands from the other side.

Táhirih knew that she was helpless. Her only refuge was Almighty God. She uncovered her face and turned toward the prison of the Báb at Máh-Kú and began to pray. The hot irons were brought forward and the hands of Káfiyih were prepared for the burning. At that terrifying moment, a town crier's voice could be heard shouting in the street outside: "The murderer is found! The murderer is found!" [19]

The murderer had confessed. He came by himself to government house, rather than let innocent people suffer. Táhirih and Káfiyih were freed. Táhirih was returned to her father's house, still a prisoner. Her husband made another unsuccessful attempt on her life by trying to poison her, but in spite of all this opposition Táhirih continued to teach many people.

She profoundly affected the city of Qazvín. Although it prided itself that no fewer than a hundred of the highest religious leaders of Islám dwelt within its gates, though she was a prisoner for much of her stay, Táhirih's triumphs were greater in Qazvín than any she had yet won.[20]

The *Journal Asiatique* in a study of this period frankly asks the question: "How, . . . in a city like Qazvín, where the clergy possessed so great an influence, . . . how could it be there . . . a woman could have organized so strong a group of heretics?" This study concludes: "There lies a question which puzzles even the Persian historian, Sipihr, for such an occurrence was without precedent." [21]

The Prime Minister, Mírzá Taqí Khán, took no action against those who without reason had plundered and killed the followers of the Báb in Qazvín. He closed his eyes to the mistake, secretly pleased. This encouraged the clergy and people of Qazvín to turn once more against Táhirih. They were determined that she should be slain, quietly if necessary, but as quickly as possible. She must never leave Qazvín alive.

When word of this new plot reached her, she was unafraid. She wrote a bold letter to her former husband, now the chief priest of Qazvín. She dared him to take her life, saying: "If my Cause is the Cause of Truth, the Lord will deliver me from the yoke of your tyranny before nine days have passed. Should He fail to rescue me, you are free to do with me as you wish." [22]

From that moment on, Táhirih was watched more closely than ever, but in spite of all their efforts, on the ninth day she escaped quietly in the night. Her sudden and mysterious removal filled her foes with fear and her friends with concern. The authorities immediately entered every house in Qazvín and searched all night for her. They were both angered and baffled by her disappearance, and the fulfillment of the prediction she had uttered.

Meanwhile Táhirih was in the capital, Tihrán. She spent many happy days there, teaching and meeting the followers of the Báb from other parts of Persia. These carefree days ended when word came that the Báb's followers were gathering at the village of Badasht in Khurásán. Táhirih left at once to join the group. Her enemies were still on the watch for her everywhere along the road, but she escaped from Tihrán in disguise and journeyed to Badasht. It was early in the summer, 1848.

Eighty-one of the leading followers of the Báb gathered at that village to meet in consultation. Quddús was among those present, since this was before the days of the fort of Tabarsí. The purpose of the gathering was two-fold. First, to decide upon the steps to be taken so that the Faith of the Báb would no longer be looked upon as a sect of Islám, but rather as a new, independent Faith with its own Prophet and Writings. Second, to consider the means of freeing the Báb from His cruel imprisonment in Chiríq. The gathering succeeded in the first goal, but failed in the second.

The followers of the Báb were eager to make a complete break from the outmoded religious laws, priesthood, traditions and ritual of the past. Táhirih, herself, was an instrument of that separation. She became its outward symbol, when one day she appeared without her veil. She had cast aside this emblem of women's inferior station.

The effect was electric. Even her fellow-believers were shocked. They stood aghast at this unexpected and unprecedented sight. Happiness and triumph shone from her face. Dignified and confident that a new day had dawned, Táhirih arose from her seat. She was completely indifferent to the tumult which her unveiled appearance had caused. It was indecent for men to look upon her uncovered face.

Táhirih, however, was universal in her vision. She knew that the

Báb's Teaching had wiped out all the limiting traditions of the past. The injustice and slavery practiced against both men and women were soon to be ended. She stood before them radiant with an inward and an outward beauty.

"I am the blast of the trumpet!" she cried out. "I am the call of the bugle!"

Gone are the days of dread and subjection for any of the creatures of God, her words called out. Exultant with joy, she then delivered a fervent and eloquent appeal to that assembly. Some on that day recalled the words of the prophecy which foretold that in the day of the Promised One, Fátimih, herself, would appear unveiled before them. Others may have remembered the sound of the "bugle" and the "stunning trumpet blast" promised in their own holy Book for the "last days." [23]

Táhirih finished her appeal by inviting all who were present to celebrate this great occasion befittingly.

"This is the day of festivity and of universal rejoicing," she said. "The day on which the fetters of the past are burst asunder. Let those who have shared in this great achievement arise and embrace each other." [24]

The conference ended after several days, and the followers of the Báb scattered in all directions to announce the new day. Each carried with him to his own area the exciting news of these momentous happenings at Badasht.

Táhirih was on her way back to Tihrán when she was intercepted by a party of searchers. Her captors sent her under escort to the capital where she was brought into the presence of the king. He commented upon seeing her, "I like her looks. Leave her, and let her be."

She was then taken as a prisoner to the home of the mayor of Tihrán, Mahmúd Khán. The king sent a letter to Táhirih at the mayor's house. He urged her to deny the Báb and again become a true Muslim. He promised her that if she would do this, he would give her an exalted position as the guardian of the ladies of his household, he would even make her his bride. She replied on the back of his letter in verse, saying that the kingdom and crown were for him, but wandering and calamity were for her. The king, reading the reply, was deeply moved. He spoke of her spirit and courage. He said, "So far, history has not shown such a woman to us." [25]

Táhirih was given considerable freedom during her imprisonment in the mayor's house, and she was able to continue her teaching. She was still alive with the fire and fervor of Badasht. It was during this period in Tihrán that Táhirih reached the height of her popularity and fame. She openly denounced polygamy, the veil, and all the restraints which had so unjustly shackled her sex for so many centuries in the East. She aroused the women by pointing out to them the abject roles they had been given by their past beliefs, and she won them over by showing them the freedom, respect and dignity which the Faith of the Báb would bestow upon them.

Sir Francis Younghusband who wrote of Táhirih's life, says: "So strong in her faith did she become that although she was both rich and noble, she gave up wealth, child, name and position for her Master's service and set herself to proclaim and establish his doctrine." He adds in yet another place: "The beauty of her speech was such as to draw guests away from a marriage feast rather than listen to music provided by the host." 26

Comte de Gobineau writes of her: "Many who have known her and heard her at different times have stated that, for a person so learned and so well read, the outstanding characteristic of her discourse was an amazing simplicity, and still, when she spoke, her audience was deeply stirred and filled with admiration, often in tears." 27

Táhirih stirred up the entire capital city to such an extent that finally the authorities took action against her. The government sent a special delegation to question her about her Faith. They held seven conferences with her in which she offered proofs showing that the Báb was the expected Messenger of God. She quoted from their own holy Book to convince them. During the last of these conferences, Táhirih became exasperated with their obstinate refusal to accept anything but the most literal interpretation of sacred scripture, and especially certain prophecies.

"How long will you cling to these follies and lies? When will you lift your eyes toward the Sun of Truth?" she exclaimed.

Her accusers were shocked by her attitude. They returned to their homes, wrote out a denunciation of Táhirih, saying that she refused to give up her faith, and upon the recommendation of this delegation, Táhirih was sentenced to death.28

Táhirih was now placed in strict confinement in a single room in the house of the Mayor of Tihrán, Mahmúd Khán. The wife of

the mayor, while not a follower of the Báb, became very attached
to her. Before Táhirih was taken away to be slain, this woman
became a devoted friend. She has left the following account:

"One night I went to her room and found her dressed in a gown
of snow-white silk. I expressed my surprise.

"She said: 'I am preparing to meet my Beloved, and I wish to
free you from the cares and anxieties of my imprisonment.'

"I was much startled at first and began to weep at the thought
of separation from her.

"She comforted me, saying: 'Weep not. The hour when I shall
be condemned to suffer martyrdom is fast approaching. It is my
wish that my body shall be thrown into a pit, and the pit be filled
with earth and stones.

"'My last request is that you permit no one to enter my chamber.
Until the time I shall be summoned to leave this house, let no one
be allowed to disturb my devotions. I intend to fast, a fast which
I shall not break until I am brought face to face with my Beloved.'

"With these words, she bade me lock the door of her chamber
and not to open it until the hour of departure should strike.

"I locked her door, and retired to my room in a state of un-
controllable sorrow. I lay sleepless and disconsolate upon my bed.
The thought of her approaching martyrdom was more than I could
bear. Unable to contain myself, several times I arose and stole
quietly to the threshold of her room. I was enchanted by the melody
of her voice as she intoned the praise of her Beloved." [29]

Táhirih prayed throughout the night that she might be worthy
of meeting Almighty God in Whose service she longed to give her
life.

The hour of her death is recalled by the mayor's wife in the
following words: "Four hours after sunset, I heard a knocking at the
door. I hastened to my son and told him of the last wishes of
Táhirih. He pledged his word that he would fulfill every instruction.
My son opened the door. He told me that the attendants of 'Azíz
Khán-i-Sardár, who was to execute her, were standing at the gate,
demanding that Táhirih be delivered into their hands.

"I was struck with terror at the news, and as I tottered to her
door and with trembling hands, unlocked it, I found her veiled
and ready to leave her apartment. As soon as she saw me, she came
and kissed me. She placed in my hand the key to her chest, in which

she had left for me a few trivial things as a remembrance of her stay in my house.

"'Whenever you open this chest,' she said, 'and behold the things it contains, I hope you will remember me and rejoice in my gladness.'

"With these words she bade me her last farewell. What pangs of anguish I felt that moment as I beheld her beauteous form fade away in the distance. She mounted the steed which 'Azíz Khán-i-Sardár had sent for her, and with my son and a number of attendants on each side, rode away."

They led Táhirih to a garden outside of the gates of Tihrán. 'Azíz Khán-i-Sardár and his lieutenants were in the midst of a drunken brawl when they arrived. Flushed with wine and roaring with laughter, they were unaware of Táhirih's approach.

Táhirih dismounted and turned to the mayor's son who had accompanied her as a friend. She asked him to act as an intermediary with 'Azíz Khán-i-Sardár.

"They will wish to strangle me," she said. "I set aside, long ago, a silken handkerchief which I hoped would be used for this purpose. I deliver it into your hands. I am disinclined to address my slayers in the midst of their revelry."

The mayor's son approached 'Azíz Khán-i-Sardár. As the boy came up to him, he waved him aside.

"Do not interrupt the gaiety of our festival!" he cried. Then he laughed uproariously and turned back to his party. "Let that miserable wretch be strangled," he mouthed to his attendants, "and throw her body into a pit."

The boy gave the attendants the kerchief. This young man has, himself, given an eye-witness account of that fateful moment.

"They consented to grant her request," he reported. "That same kerchief was wound round her neck and was made the instrument of her martyrdom. I hastened immediately afterwards to the gardener and asked him whether he could suggest a place where I could conceal the body. He directed me to a well that had been dug recently and left unfinished. With the help of a few others, I lowered Táhirih into her grave and filled the well up with earth and stones in the manner she herself requested. Those who saw her in those last moments were profoundly affected."

Dr. Jakob Polak, Austrian physician to the king, in a book written in 1856, states that he was an eye-witness of Táhirih's last hours. She endured her death with "super-human fortitude," he said.[30]

The son returned to tell his mother what had happened.

"I wept hot tears," she recalled later, "as my son unfolded to me that tragic tale." As she stood before the chest Táhirih had given her, she wondered what it was that could have induced so great a woman to forsake all the riches and honors with which she had been surrounded, and to identify herself with the Cause of an obscure youth from Shíráz. What could have been the secret of that power that tore her away from home and kindred, that sustained her to her grave. Could the hand of the Almighty have guided her?

Thus ended the life of Táhirih. She was one of the greatest of the disciples of the Báb. She was the first woman-suffrage martyr as well. As the hour of her death approached, she turned to the one into whose custody she had been placed, and declared boldly: "You can kill me as soon as you like, but you cannot stop the emancipation of woman!" [31]

Her career was dazzling, brief, tragic, and eventful. The fame of Táhirih spread with the same remarkable swiftness as that of the Báb, Who was the direct source of all her inspiration.

Lord Curzon in his book on Persia states bluntly: "Of no small account, then, must be the tenets of a creed that can awaken in its followers so rare and beautiful a spirit of self-sacrifice." [32]

Sarah Bernhart the famous actress, requested the playwright Catulle Mendes to write a dramatized version of Táhirih's life. The playwright himself called her the "Persian Joan of Arc." [33]

A noted commentator on the life of the Báb and His disciples has paid Táhirih the tribute of calling her "a miracle of science and a miracle of beauty."

"The heroism of the lovely but ill-fated poetess," testifies Lord Curzon, "is one of the most affecting episodes in modern history."

The British orientalist, Professor E. G. Browne, said that if the Faith of the Báb had no other claim to greatness than that it had produced a heroine like Táhirih, it would be sufficient. "The appearance of such a woman, . . ." he wrote, "is, in any country and any age, a rare phenomenon, but in such a country as Persia it is a prodigy—nay, almost a miracle."

The French diplomat, Comte de Gobineau, writes, "She was held with every justification to be a prodigy."

"This noble woman, . . ." writes Dr. T. K. Cheyne, a renowned

English clergyman, "has the credit of opening the catalogue of social reforms in Persia."

"No memory," writes Sir Valentine Chirol, "is more deeply venerated or kindles greater enthusiasm than hers, and the influence she wielded in her lifetime still inures to her sex."

The famous Turkish poet, Sulaymán Nazím Bey, exclaims: "O Táhirih! You are worth a thousand Násiri'd-Dín Sháhs!"

Marianna Hainisch, the mother of one of Austria's presidents says: "The greatest ideal of womanhood has been Táhirih."

One of the most penetrating comments of those historians who followed her life was this: "Looking back on the short career [of Táhirih] one is chiefly struck by her fiery enthusiasm and by her absolute unworldliness. This world was, in fact, to her . . . a mere handful of dust." 34

Táhirih was faithful to the Cause of the Báb from the first moment of her acceptance until the last hour of her death. Not for an instant did she swerve from that confident belief expressed in her message sent to Him in those beginning days in Shíráz: "Then speak the word, 'Am I not your Lord?' and: '. . . Thou art!' we will all reply."

Táhirih lived and died by the words she had spoken so boldly to another great disciple of the Báb one evening in Tihrán, so long ago. She had been listening with some of the other believers to a brilliant and eloquent discourse upon the Faith of the Báb, given by Vahíd, himself. He spoke of the signs and proofs of the coming of the Báb. Táhirih listened patiently for some time, then suddenly she interrupted his words.

"Let deeds, not words, testify to your faith," she cried out, "if thou art a man of true learning. Cease idly repeating the traditions of the past, for the day of service, of steadfast action, is come. Now is the time to promote the Word of God, and to sacrifice ourselves in His path. Let deeds, not words, be our adorning." 35

Táhirih had now justified those words by her death in a garden in the shadow of Persia's greatest city.

The same inevitable retribution which had remorselessly struck down the enemies of the Faith of Shíráz, Isfáhán, Tabríz, and Tabarsí, again made itself felt against the persecutors of Táhirih.

The king, who knew that she was innocent and might have saved her, was to feel the most punishing blow of all at a later date. Her uncle, Taqí, who had so brutally struck her, was slain by an assassin. The mayor of Tihrán, Mahmúd Khán, who kept her imprisoned for nearly three years, and who aided the Prime Minister in her execution, suffered a death similar to that which he had permitted to befall Táhirih.

The king ordered his slaying. He called upon the executioner to prepare some ropes and then commanded that these ropes be twisted about the neck of Mahmúd Khán until he was strangled. The king ordered the mayor's body to be hung on the gallows as a warning.[36]

Táhirih was at the height of her beauty and power when she was slain in August 1852. She was thirty-six. Siyyid Kázim had called her Qurratu'l-'Ayn—"Consolation of the Eyes." Others had called her Zarrín-Táj—one "Crowned of Gold." But the name by which she lives forever in the hearts of her people is Táhirih—the Pure One.

THE DEATH OF
THE WISEST PERSIAN

Vahíd, who had been sent by the king as his personal representative to investigate the truth of the Báb's mission, was the next to fall in this nation-wide wave of persecutions.

In the early days of the siege of Tabarsí, Vahíd hurried to Tihrán to make the necessary preparations for joining Mullá Husayn and Quddús inside the fort. He was about to leave Tihrán when he was told that it was too late, that his friends had already been captured or slain.

During this visit to Tihrán, Vahíd met a companion who wrote down his recollection of that meeting: "I observed in his (Vahíd's) august countenance the signs of a glory and power which I had not noticed during my first journey with him to the capital, nor on the other occasions of meeting . . . he said several times during the course of conversation: 'This is my last journey, and henceforth you will see me no more.' . . . Sometimes when we were together and the conversation took an appropriate turn, he would remark: 'I swear by that loved One in the grasp of Whose power my soul lies, that I know and could tell where and how I shall be slain, and who it is that shall slay me. And how glorious and blessed a thing it is that my blood shall be shed for the uplifting of the Word of Truth!' " [1]

Following his last visit to Tihrán, Vahíd journeyed to Táhirih's native town of Qazvín, and from there he went to Qum, Káshán, Isfáhán, Ardistán, and Ardikán. In each of these places he met his fellow believers and was able to stimulate their enthusiasm and reinforce their efforts.

In every city he would explain the fundamental teachings of the Báb with zest and fearlessness. He succeeded in winning a considerable number of the most able and notable citizens to His Cause. Thus, Vahíd became an important target for the Prime Minister and all other enemies of the Báb.

The story of Vahíd's investigation of the Báb, undertaken on behalf of the former king and Prime Minister, was well known to the people. That these two had agreed to abide by Vahíd's findings was also well known, as was the fact that they had broken their pledge when they heard that Vahíd had become a follower of the Báb.

Vahíd was a man of great influence, a man of wealth and fame. In addition to his beautiful house in Yazd where his wife and four sons lived, he also had a home in Dáráb, and still another in Nayríz. These homes were noted for their elegance and their superb furnishings.

Vahíd visited his home in Yazd on the feast of the New Year. It coincided with the anniversary of the Báb's declaration of His mission. The most important religious leaders and notables came out to meet him. The Navváb-i-Raduví, who was the most bitter of Vahíd's enemies, was also present. He resented the splendor of Vahíd's reception, and hinted maliciously it was not really the New Year Feast that Vahíd was celebrating.

"The king's royal banquets," he said, "can scarcely hope to rival this sumptuous repast. I suspect that in addition to the national festival which we are celebrating, you are commemorating another one beside it."

Vahíd's bold and sarcastic retort provoked the laughter of those present. They all applauded Vahíd's stinging rebuke because they were aware of the stinginess and wickedness of the Navváb. This ridicule enraged the Navváb. He promised himself that if it lay in his power, Vahíd would die violently because of it.

Vahíd seized this occasion to proclaim without reserve the principles of the Báb's Faith. Some were irresistibly attracted. Others, unable to challenge successfully the defense which Vahíd made for his new Faith, denounced it in their hearts. They joined forces with the Navváb and made plans to overthrow Vahíd without delay.

Nicolas in his history of those days writes: "'To love and conceal one's secret is impossible,' says the poet; so . . . [Vahíd] began to preach openly in the mosques, in the streets, in the bazaars, in the public squares, in a word, wherever he could find listeners. Such an enthusiasm brought forth fruit and the conversions were numerous and sincere. The Mullás [priests] deeply troubled, violently denounced the sacrilege to the governor of the city." [2]

The priests were agreed on one vital point: The life of Vahíd must be destroyed. They spread the report of that New Year's day banquet, saying: "Though his listeners ranked among the most illustrious doctors of law in Yazd, not one raised a word of protest against his proclamation of the Faith of the Báb. This silence has been responsible for the wave of enthusiasm which has swept over this city. Already half of the inhabitants have been brought to his feet, while the remainder are fast being attracted."

This report raced like a grass fire through all the surrounding districts. It caused hatred to flare up, but, at the same time, it brought crowds of interested people from distant towns and villages. They flocked to Vahíd's home to hear the message of the Báb. A great many embraced the Faith.

"What shall we do next?" they asked Vahíd. "How can we demonstrate the depth and sincerity of our faith?"

Each day from early morning until late night, Vahíd was absorbed in teaching them, answering their questions, and inspiring them to return home where they could teach in their own villages.

For forty days this feverish teaching activity continued. Vahíd's home became a rallying point for both men and women. The Navváb finally convinced the governor of Yazd that if Vahíd was not restrained, the city would soon revolt from the government of the king, and that he, the governor, would be to blame. The governor was new, young and inexperienced. The Navváb entreated him day after day to send a force of armed men to surround Vahíd's home and put an end to this teaching. After all, the Navváb told the governor, hadn't the Prime Minister himself encouraged everyone to use the harshest means against the followers of the Báb? Was Vahíd so prominent, so famous, so noble that he did not fall into this class? Was he not really the most flagrant offender of all? The governor at last succumbed to the Navváb's entreaties, and ordered out a detachment of soldiers.

The Navváb quickly sent his personal instructions to a degraded element of the people he had been keeping ready for just such an opportunity. Gleefully, he informed them that the governor had fallen into his trap, and that Vahíd was now under attack. He urged these people to rush to Vahíd's home and do all they could to add to his humiliation.

"There is no longer any need to restrain your indignation and righteous feelings of anger," he told them. He implied that Vahíd's death would be a welcome thing in the eyes of God.

Vahíd was standing at a window on the upper floor of his home speaking to a large gathering of his friends in the yard below when a regiment of soldiers accompanied by a huge multitude of people arrived. They completely surrounded his house.

Vahíd's friends were alarmed at the sight of the soldiers and the great mob of infuriated townspeople. They turned to Vahíd in their distress, asking for instructions. His servant, Hasan, quickly saddled Vahíd's horse and brought it into the courtyard below his window so that he might flee for safety. Vahíd called upon his friends to be calm.

"Do not fear," he told them. "In but a short time, all those who have now encircled us will have been scattered."

Vahíd pointed down at the horse standing below him in the courtyard. "That very steed," he said, "is the one which the late king gave me that I might ride upon it to undertake my mission of conducting an impartial investigation into the nature of the Faith proclaimed by the Báb. The king asked me to report to him personally the results of my inquiry, for he said I was the only one among the religious leaders in Tihrán in whom he had complete confidence.

"I undertook that mission riding upon that very horse. I was determined to refute everything the Báb said, and to prove my superiority. I planned to crush Him with my superior knowledge, force Him to acknowledge my leadership, and then conduct Him with me to Tihrán as a witness to my total triumph.

"When I came into His presence and heard His words, the opposite of what I imagined took place. In my first audience, I was humbled; by the end of the second, I felt helpless and ignorant;

the third found me as lowly as the dust beneath His feet. He became to me what He truly was: the Promised One, the living embodiment of the Holy Spirit."

Vahíd looked with indifference upon the enemies who were closing in around him. Of what importance could any of the happenings of this world be to him ever again, whether they were delights or disasters.

"Ever since that day," he told his friends, "I have yearned to lay down my life for His sake. I rejoice that the day which I have longed to witness is fast approaching." [3]

Vahíd's friends became frightened. They thought he was speaking of that very day and hour, for the soldiers and the mob were preparing to assault them. Seeing the agitation which had seized them, Vahíd urged them to be calm and patient.

"Rest assured," he said, "that God, the Avenger, will soon with His invisible hand inflict a crushing defeat upon these forces arrayed against us."

Shortly after Vahíd had uttered these words, the news came that a great number of friendly companions were approaching Vahíd's home to save him. This rescue party flung themselves upon the attackers. Their valor and reckless indifference to death was of a nature to alarm and scatter the entire detachment of soldiers and people. The soldiers abandoned their arms and fled for shelter. The mob, crying for help, scattered in all directions. Vahíd sent a messenger through the streets with the warning that he would not attack anyone but that he would defend himself and his home. After another skirmish, in which even the governor's troops were routed, Vahíd directed his companions to disperse to safety. He knew that the hour for his own departure from Yazd had come. He called his wife to him and told her to take the children and all of their belongings and go to the house of her father for safety. He instructed her to leave all of his own personal possessions in the house.

"I have built this palatial residence," he told her, "with the sole intention that it should be demolished eventually in the path of the Cause of God. The stately furnishings with which I have adorned it have been purchased with the hope that one day I should be able to sacrifice them all for the sake of my Beloved." Vahíd tried to make his wife understand, saying: "In that day friend and foe alike will realize that he who owned this house possessed another treasure so priceless that an earthly mansion, however magnificent, had no worth in his eyes; that it had sunk to nothing more than a heap of bones which only the dogs of the earth could desire."

Vahíd said farewell to his dear wife and bade a tender goodbye to his children.

In the middle of that night he collected the writings of the Báb which were in his possession, and gave them to his servant, Hasan, with the order to take them and await his arrival outside the gate of the city. He told Hasan which route to take so that he would be safe. "Do not disregard my instructions," he warned, "or we shall never meet again."

Hasan mounted his horse and prepared to leave. He heard the cries of the patroling sentinels who were keeping a night watch over the city. He was afraid they might capture him and seize the manuscripts, so he took what he thought to be a safer route to the gates of the city. As he was passing through one section of town, he was recognized by the sentinels.

"There goes Vahíd's servant!" they cried out.

They opened fire upon Hasan, shot down his horse, and captured him alive.

Vahíd, meanwhile, followed the route he had told Hasan to take and was soon safely outside the city. The moment Vahíd left Yazd, his enemies, under the leadership of the Navváb, rushed to his house to plunder his possessions. They carried away all of the furnishings, then demolished the house completely.

Vahíd set out at once for his home in Nayríz. That first night he walked twenty miles until he at last approached a village in which his brother lived. Vahíd did not enter his brother's house, instead, he encamped in a near-by mountain. His brother, hearing of his presence there, sent out horses and provisions which he felt Vahíd would need for his journey to Nayríz.

A body of the governor's troops was sent out from Yazd in pursuit of Vahíd. They followed his trail to the village of his brother. They searched the house where they suspected he was concealed. Not finding him, they appeased their anger and disappointment by seizing as much of his brother's property as they could carry away. They searched the neighborhood further, but did not find Vahíd's mountain camp. Disappointed, they returned to Yazd.

The Navváb was still not satisfied. Vahíd's teaching had stopped, but Vahíd had escaped. He did not pursue Vahíd himself. He left that to the governor. Instead, in concert with the leading priests of Yazd, he took a far more gratifying step.

Nicolas reports the Navváb's actions after Vahíd's departure as follows: ". . . he [the Navváb] gave a sigh of relief. Besides, he felt that to pursue the fugitive would involve some peril and that, therefore, it would be infinitely more practical, more beneficial, more profitable and less dangerous to torture the [followers of the Báb], or those presumed to be—provided that they were wealthy— who had remained in the city. He sought out the most prosperous, ordered their execution, and confiscated their possessions, avenging thus his outraged religion, a matter of perhaps little concern to him, and filling his coffers, which pleased him immensely." [4]

Having failed in their plans to capture and slay Vahíd, the authorities had to content themselves with the torture of his servant, Hasan. They led him out to a loaded cannon. They thought they might frighten Hasan into pleading for mercy and thus force him to renounce his Faith. After all, he was only a servant. Vahíd was a man of great nobility and wisdom, and he might be expected to know what he was doing; but this ignorant servant would certainly save his own life now that his master was gone. If they could make him cry for mercy, they could publicize his recantation. This would at least be a small way of humiliating Vahíd. The officer gave the instruction which was calculated to bring Hasan to his knees.

"Bind him with his back to the mouth of the cannon," he commanded.

"No," Hasan entreated them. "Do not do that to me."

The officer smiled, gratified by the expected words. His pleasure turned to wrath as Hasan continued his entreaty.

"Do not bind me with my back to the cannon," Hasan pleaded with the soldiers. "Rather bind me with my face to the gun so that I may see it fired."

The gunners and those who looked on were astonished at Hasan's composure and cheerfulness. To themselves they said: "One who can be cheerful in such a plight must needs have great faith and fortitude." [5]

All along the road to Nayríz, Vahíd continued his teaching. Wherever he made camp, his first action was to go immediately to the neighboring village or town. He would gather all the people together, then he would announce to them the "glad tidings" of the

Báb's appearance. In the mountain village of Bavánát, the high-priest of the village, Hájí Siyyid Ismá'íl, accepted the Faith.

Vahíd was utterly indifferent to fatigue. In whatever place he succeeded in attracting souls to the Faith of the Báb, he would stay the night so that he could deepen them in their understanding and prepare them to continue the work of teaching after his departure. If none arose to accept or to inquire further, Vahíd would leave that village at once.

"Through whichever village I pass," he told his companions, "and fail to inhale from its inhabitants the fragrance of belief, its food and drink are distasteful to me." [6]

When the news of Vahíd's approach to Nayríz became known, there was an exodus from the city to greet him. The governor forbade it, warning the people of the danger to their lives and possessions. Therefore, the majority of them set out at night to meet Vahíd under cover of darkness.

The governor was informed of their secret departure. He sent a special messenger to overtake them.

"You will be put to death," he warned them, "if you show allegiance to Vahíd. I will not permit his victories of Yazd to be repeated in Nayríz!"

Not one of the people heeded this warning. They continued on their way. The governor was dismayed when his messenger reported their disdainful neglect of his warning. He decided he must take some strong action to maintain his prestige.

The very first thing Vahíd did upon reaching Nayríz, even before going to his own home, was to enter the place of worship and address the congregation of his friends that had gathered there. He called upon them to embrace the Faith of the Báb. The Promised One of God has appeared, he told them. Still wearing his dust-laden garments, Vahíd ascended the pulpit and spoke with such convincing eloquence that the whole audience was electrified by his appeal. When the first flush of excitement subsided, Vahíd continued speaking.

"My sole purpose in coming to Nayríz," he explained, "is to proclaim the Cause of God. I thank and glorify Him for having enabled me to touch your hearts with His Message."

No less than a thousand persons from his own area, and five hundred from other sections of Nayríz, spontaneously responded to his appeal and accepted the Faith.

"There is no need for me to remain any longer in your midst,"
Vahíd told the crowd. "My work is done, and if I prolong my stay,
I fear that the governor will ill-treat you because of me."

The people assured Vahíd of their faith, saying: "We are resigned
to the Will of God. May He grant us strength to withstand the
calamities that may befall us. But we cannot, however, reconcile
ourselves to so abrupt and hasty a separation from you."

Vahíd submitted to their wishes, and agreed to remain a few days
longer in Nayríz. At this news a crowd of men and women gathered
around him and with cheers and praise they escorted him to the
very entrance of his house.

The governor was terrified to hear that such an avalanche of
victories could be won by Vahíd in such an astonishingly short
time. The finest citizens from all fields were accepting the Faith of
the Báb. This number included the governor's own nephew.[7]

The governor felt that he must destroy this influence before it
undermined his own position with the king and Prime Minister.
He recruited a thousand soldiers, both cavalry and infantry. He
supplied them with ammunition and ordered them to make a
sudden attack upon Vahíd.

"Seize him and bring him here as a prisoner!"

Vahíd was informed of this secret attack. He and his companions
followed the pattern of their fellow-believers at Tabarsí and
sought refuge. The prince, who was governor at Shíráz, joined
forces against Vahíd and his companions. He gave the same instructions which had been given at Tarbarsí: "Exterminate all of them!"
Vahíd and his friends had taken refuge in Fort Khájih where they
were besieged in the same manner in which Quddús and Mullá
Husayn had been besieged at Tabarsí. They were deprived of
water and food. Finally, by the same treachery used at Tabarsí,
they were betrayed into coming out from their sheltered protection.

The governor of Nayríz, failing time after time to win by force,
resorted to deceit, contrary to the pure spirit of Muhammad's
teaching. A Qur'án was sent to Vahíd with the following solemn
promise:

"This Qur'án is the witness of the integrity of our purpose. Let
this holy Book decide whether the claim you make for your Faith
is true or false. Emerge from the fort and meet us in the camp.
If you prove able to demonstrate the truth of your Faith, we, too,

will readily embrace it. The malediction of God be upon us if we should attempt to deceive you."

Vahíd received the book with reverence.

"Our appointed hour has struck," he said. "Though I am well aware of their intention, I feel it my duty to accept their call and once again take the opportunity of telling them about our beloved Faith."

With five companions, Vahíd left the fort and entered the camp of the governor. For three days he spoke to them of the Báb. Though outwardly they appeared to listen, inwardly they were secretly plotting how they could get the rest of his friends out of the fort so that they could all be destroyed.

A plot to persuade Vahíd's friends to leave their fort to join Vahíd at the camp of the soldiers was conceived and proved successful. This was the beginning of the slaughter. Vahíd's companions were seized and arrested the moment they set foot outside the fort. When the news of their capture reached the governor and his staff, they immediately began to take their revenge upon Vahíd. They consulted upon the best way in which they could evade fulfilling the oath which they had sent with the Qur'án into the fort.

Their scheme was simple. A man notorious for his ruthlessness and cruelty volunteered to proceed with the killing of Vahíd without conscience pangs, because he had not taken the oath.

"If you are troubled by this oath," he assured the governor and his staff, "forget your worries. I am ready to do whatever you would like to have done. I am ready to put to death those you deem guilty of having violated the laws of the land."

He summoned all the relatives of those people who had perished in the long struggle to conquer the fort in which Vahíd and his friends had been sheltered. He had them all pronounce the sentence of death against Vahíd, thus relieving, in his own mind, both the governor and himself of any responsibility for their deaths. He offered to three men in particular the privilege and pleasure of striking the first blows at the person of Vahíd before turning him over to the mob. He knew these three men would be without mercy.

Nayríz echoed to the sound of drums and cymbals as Vahíd was brought before the people. The eager crowd was held back while the three men took their turns. The first, Mullá Ridá, snatched Vahíd's turban from his head, uncoiled it, then wound it about

Vahíd's neck and dragged him to the ground. Vahíd was then tied
to the saddle of a horse. Then the horse was whipped so that it
would drag Vahíd through the streets of the city. The second, Safar,
as well as the third, 'Aqá Khán, struck and beat Vahíd at will and
with such ferocity that the onlookers were afraid there might be
no sport left for them.

In the midst of his agony, Vahíd called out: "Thou knowest, O
my Beloved, that I have abandoned the world for Thy sake, and
have placed my trust in Thee alone. I am impatient to hasten to
Thee."

The mob screamed with anger at Vahíd's radiant acceptance of
his fate. They were determined that he would show some sign of
fear and be forced to plead for mercy. They fell upon him in a
great wave. Their fists and weapons pounded him into insensibility
and tore his flesh. Horsemen scattered the crowd so that they could
have their turn. Women danced around the corpse rejoicing, to
the increased beat of the drums and cymbals.

A. L. M. Nicolas in his history writes that the multitude "aroused
by the scene, stoned and beat to death the unfortunate man. They
then severed the head, tore off the skin, stuffed it with straw and
sent that trophy to Shíráz!" [8]

The frenzied crowd did the same to the heads of Vahíd's companions and sent them as a gift to the prince in Shíráz who had
called for the extermination of Vahíd and his friends. They were
to be proof to him of the thorough execution of his commands.

The prince was feasting when the caravan bearing these awesome trophies arrived.

It was a festival day in Shíráz. "The bazaars were adorned with
flags—joy was general. Suddenly, there was absolute silence. They
saw coming thirty-two camels, each carrying an unfortunate prisoner, a woman or child, bound and thrown crosswise over the
saddle like a bundle. All around them were soldiers carrying long
lances and upon each lance was impaled the head of a follower
of the Báb who had been slain at Nayríz . . . the sight deeply
affected the holiday population of Shíráz, and they returned
saddened to their dwellings.

"The horrible caravan passed through the bazaars and continued
to the palace of the governor. This personage was in his garden
where he had gathered . . . the rich, the eminent citizens of Shíráz.
The music ceased, the dancing stopped." [9]

Mihr 'Alí Khán stepped toward the prince bearing his trophies. He told the prince of his own brave deeds in the assault upon Vahíd and his companions. Mihr 'Alí Khán then named all the prisoners who had been brought, men, women, and children. He received congratulations from the prince for his great victory. Special favors were bestowed upon Mihr 'Alí Khán and his fellow leaders for this gift of severed heads.

These events literally fulfilled the well-known prophecy of the coming of the Promised One, saying: "In Him [shall be] the perfection of Moses, the preciousness of Jesus, and the patience of Job. His saints shall be abased in His time, and their heads shall be exchanged as presents; they shall be slain and burnèd; the earth shall be dyed with their blood, and lamentation and wailing shall prevail amongst their women; these are my saints indeed." [10]

The governor of Nayríz was still not satisfied. He hungered for even greater revenge upon those who had survived his betrayal. He planned for their annihilation so that none might live to tell the tale of his treachery.

Nicholas writes: "His hatred knew no bounds and it was to last as long as he lived. It was actually the very poor that had been sent to Shíráz, the rich had been kept back. [The governor] had entrusted them to a guard who was ordered to walk them through the city beating them as they went. The people of Nayríz were greatly entertained that time." [11]

The end of Vahíd's noble life was the signal for the out-break of a fierce wave of violence in Nayríz that lasted long beyond that day of betrayal. The fort in which Vahíd and his friends had sought refuge was burned to the ground. Their property was seized, their houses destroyed, many were thrown into dungeons before being subjected to a final fiendish torture. The greedy officials made certain that the prisoners had nothing of value left before they were slain. During that black period, many were crucified.

The fate that befell the betrayers of Tabarsí struck almost at once against one of the most treacherous leaders of the Nayríz upheaval. Mihr 'Alí Khán, who had escorted those trophies of severed heads to the prince at Shíráz, whose lips had sung loud praises of his own valor, was suddenly struck dumb. He was no longer able to boast of his victorious march with his gruesome prize to the palace of the prince. Mihr 'Alí Khán fell ill shortly after that march. His lips could form words, but no sound would come out. He remained mute and speechless until the very day of his death. On that last day, as he was about to expire, those who stood around him saw from the movement of lips that he was whispering something. They leaned down to catch his last words and heard the only sound that had issued from his lips since he had been stricken. Three times he whispered faintly the words, "Followers of the Báb!" Then he fell back dead.[12]

In *A Traveller's Narrative*, it is reported that "of those chiefly responsible for these cruelties not one but came to a bad end and died overwhelmed with calamity."

Another great figure among the followers of the Báb had fallen, a man who has been called "that unique and peerless figure of his age." [13] The illustrious Vahíd, described by the king and Prime Minister "the wisest of the Persians," had surrendered all that men hold dear for the privilege of laying down his life in the path of God. The day of Vahíd's martyrdom was but ten days before that of his Beloved One, the Báb.

THE SEVEN HEROES OF TIHRÁN

THE DEATH OF VAHÍD came as an added blow to the heart of the Báb. He was already in great sorrow because of the suffering at Tabarsí, when He was told of the betrayal at Nayríz. Yet even these tragedies were not the final troubles to becloud the remaining days of His fast-ebbing life. The Báb's beloved uncle, Hájí Mírzá Siyyid 'Alí, who had reared Him from childhood and who had so faithfully served His Cause, was soon to be engulfed in this same wave of persecution.

The Báb's uncle had just visited Him in the castle of Chiríq. The Báb had sent him forth from that prison-city to obtain the crown of martyrdom, saying: "I Myself will follow you, together with one of My loyal disciples, and will join you in the realm of eternity."

When the Báb's uncle entered Tihrán, his friends warned him of the grave danger of his presence there.

"Why fear for my safety?" he confidently replied. "I, too, am anxious to share in the banquet which the hand of God is spreading for His chosen ones throughout the land."

Shortly after this a traitor who pretended to be interested in the Faith of the Báb attended classes, and thus secured a list of fifty names which he turned over to Mahmud Khán, the mayor of the city. The mayor immediately ordered the arrest of the fifty. Fourteen were seized and brought before the authorities. One of these fourteen was the Báb's uncle. They were all placed in confinement in the home of the mayor. It was on the upper floor of this same house that Táhirih was also held prisoner.

Every kind of ill-treatment was inflicted upon these fourteen captives to induce them to reveal the names and addresses of the other believers in the city. The Prime Minister, Mírzá Táqí Khán, was informed of their capture. According to historical record, this arch-enemy of the Báb was the son of the head cook of a former Prime Minister. He had risen in a few short years from the kitchen to become chief advisor to the king through a policy of self-advancement and ruthlessness. He immediately issued an order threatening with execution whoever among the fourteen was unwilling to deny his Faith.

Seven were compelled to yield to the pressure he exerted, and were released at once. The remaining seven who remained steadfast became known as the "Seven Martyrs of Tihrán." The Báb's uncle was one of the seven.

His business friends urged him to deny his Faith and save his life. God winks His eyes at such things, they said. Several rich merchants offered to pay a ransom to free him, but the Báb's uncle rejected their offer. Finally, he was brought before the Prime Minister.

"A number of prominent people have interceded in your behalf," the Prime Minister told him. "Wealthy merchants from Shíráz and Tihrán are willing, nay eager, to pay your ransom. A word of denial from you will set you free, and we shall return you to your native city with honors."

The Bab's uncle boldly replied to these words. "Your Excellency," he said, "my rejection of the truths which are given in this Revelation would be the same as rejecting all the Revelations that have preceded it. If I refuse to acknowledge the mission of the Báb, I must also deny the divine character of the message which Muhammad, Jesus, Moses and all the Prophets of the past have revealed."

The Prime Minister did not try to hide his impatience as the Báb's uncle continued. "God knows that whatever I have heard and read concerning the lives of these past Messengers of God, the same have I been privileged to witness from this Youth, this beloved Kinsman of mine, from His earliest boyhood to this, the thirtieth year of His life. I only request that you allow me to be the first to lay down my life in His path."

The Prime Minister was stupefied by such an answer. Without uttering a word, he motioned that the Báb's uncle should be taken out and beheaded.

As he was being conducted to his death, the Báb's uncle called out to the crowd that swarmed around him.

"For over a thousand years you have prayed that the Promised One appear. Now that He *has* come, you have driven Him to a hopeless exile in a remote corner of the land. With my last breath I pray that the Almighty may enable you to awaken from your sleep of heedlessness."

The executioner was shaken by those words. He pretended that the sword he had been holding in readiness needed to be sharpened. He hurried away and never returned. He told the story of that moving event many times expressing his repentance of the act he had been compelled to perpetrate. Whenever he spoke of the Báb's uncle, he could not repress the tears which bore witness to the depth to which he had been stirred.[1]

The second to fall beneath the headman's axe was Mírzá Qurbán 'Alí. He was a close friend of many of the notables of the city. So greatly was he esteemed that when he visited Karbilá, a vast concourse of people lined the road all along his route in order to pay tribute to him. The mother of the king was a great admirer of Qurbán 'Alí. Because of her close friendship and admiration for him, she told her son, the king, that Qurbán 'Alí was being branded with lies.

"He is no follower of the Báb," she insisted. "He has been falsely accused."

So they sent for Qurbán 'Alí. The Prime Minister brought him to the palace under guard. His arrest had already caused a commotion such as Tihrán rarely experienced. Huge crowds followed Qurbán 'Alí as he was led through the streets. Some cried out encouragement to him. Some, bewildered, asked, "What has he done? What harm can be found in this great man?" The people packed the approaches to the government headquarters anxious to hear some word about his fate.

At first Qurbán 'Alí was treated with great respect. The authorities assured him of their confidence in him, and expressed concern that so grave an injustice should have been done to him.

"We know you do not belong to these misguided followers of the Báb," they assured him. "A false charge has been made against you. We know that you have not accepted him as a Prophet."

Qurbán 'Alí replied simply: "I know not whether He has accepted me, but I have accepted Him. I reckon myself as one of the followers and servants of the Báb."

They tried to persuade him to give up this foolishness.[2] He was far too intelligent to be anyone's servant, they said, far too important to lower himself in the eyes of his fellowmen. They promised Qurbán 'Alí a permanent salary and a generous pension if he would accompany them to the street and announce now to the public that he had denied this false Faith.

Qurbán 'Alí waited patiently until they were finished. Then he spoke with quiet conviction. "This life and these drops of blood of mine are of but small account. But if the entire earth were mine, and if I had a thousand lives, I would freely cast them all at the feet of the humblest of the Báb's friends."

The Prime Minister himself then tried to show Qurbán 'Alí the foolishness of such a stubborn attitude.

"Since last night," he said, "I have been swamped by all classes of state officials. They are all vigorously speaking in your defense. From what I learn of the position you occupy and the influence your words exercise, I cannot understand your attitude. If you had claimed such leadership for yourself, it would have been better for you. Far better than declaring your allegiance to one who is obviously inferior to you in knowledge."

Qurbán 'Alí shook his head. "That is not so," he told him. "All of the knowledge which I have acquired has led me to recognize Him and bow down before Him. I have judged Him fairly. If the Báb is false, then every Prophet from the beginning of time until this very day is false." *

The king and his mother each in turn tried to sway Qurbán 'Alí from his belief, but neither the sweetness of bribes nor the threat of death had any effect. The treasure which the Báb offered him, he told them was of a matchless kind. Seeing their astonishment at his refusal to accept honors and riches in place of death, he tried to explain.

"I have over a thousand admirers who are influenced by my

* See Appendix, Note Two.

words, yet I am powerless to change the heart of the least among them. The Báb, however, has proved Himself capable of uplifting and changing the most degraded among His fellowmen. He has exerted such an influence over our hearts, that we consider it a most inadequate sacrifice when we lay down our lives for His sake."

The Prime Minister hesitated. "I do not know whether your words are of God or not. But I am reluctant to pronounce the sentence of death against one of your exalted rank and station."

"Why hesitate?" burst forth Qurbán 'Alí. "For this I was born. By this I shall prove I am worthy of the knowledge God has given to me. This is the day on which I shall seal with my life-blood my faith in His Cause."

Seeing the Prime Minister's uncertainty, Qurbán 'Alí added, "Be not reluctant. Rest assured that I shall never blame you for your act. The sooner you strike off my head, the greater will be my gratitude to you."

The Prime Minister became angry. "Take him away from this place!" he cried. "Another minute and he will have cast his spell over me!"

Qurbán 'Alí smiled gently. "No," he said, "you are proof against that magic. It is a magic that can captivate only the pure in heart."

Infuriated, the Prime Minister arose from his seat. His face was mottled and his whole frame shook with anger. He shouted aloud: "Nothing but the edge of the sword can silence the voice of this deluded people!" He turned to the executioner. "It is enough! No need to bring any more members of this hateful people before me. Words are powerless to overcome their unswerving obstinacy. Whomever you are able to induce to deny his Faith, release him. As for the rest, strike off their heads! I will face no more of them!"

As Qurbán 'Alí was led to the scene of his death, he spoke with exultation. "Hasten to slay me," he cried, "for by this death you will have offered me the cup of everlasting life. In exchange for this withered breath which you now extinguish, my Beloved will reward me with a life such as no mortal heart can conceive."

A great crowd pressed in about him. Qurbán 'Alí addressed them in these words: "The Promised One has risen from Shíráz in the person of His Holiness the Báb." The people shouted at him, deaf to his call. Their mocking cries drowned out his words. His friends had now withdrawn, unable to look upon the tragic sight. The mob, seeing a great one fallen, was now eager for his finish.

"Strike him!" they cried out. "Slay the enemy of God!"

Qurbán 'Alí sighed sadly. "Oh the blindness of this generation! My soul is filled with ecstasy, but alas, I can find no heart to share with me its charm, and no mind to understand its glory."

He approached the spot where the Báb's uncle had been slain. When Qurbán 'Alí saw that broken body, he gathered it up tenderly into his arms. He looked out over that sea of hatred, then summoned the executioner.

"Approach," he told him, "and strike your blow. My faithful comrade is unwilling to release himself from my embrace. He calls me to hasten with him to the Kingdom of God."

The blow was struck. Sounds of distress and sorrow stirred even through that hostile crowd as the two were united for all time.[3]

The next of the seven martyrs was Hájí Mullá Ismá'íl. Like Qurbán 'Alí, he had planned to go to the fort at Tabarsí to join Mullá Husayn and Quddús, but had been stricken with illness. When he recovered he was told that the siege was over and his friends massacred. He began to teach the Faith with renewed energy in order to try to make up for the tragic loss which the Cause of the Báb had suffered at Tabarsí.

Mullá Ismá'íl was arrested in Tihrán with the others. He was told that if he would renounce the Báb's Faith and speak evil of its Author, he would be released, otherwise he would suffer death.

"Renounce my Faith?" he cried. "Never! I am determined to confess my faith openly and to lay down my life for the Báb." He explained the importance of his feelings to the other prisoners. "If we fail to proclaim the coming of the Promised One, who else will proclaim it? If we fail to direct men into the right way, to arouse them from the slumber of death, who else will do it? We are the instruments of God. Let everyone who is able, come forth in all steadfastness and bear me company."

As Mullá Ismá'íl was being led to the place appointed for his death, one of the surrounding crowd called out.

"He is one of them! There goes a follower of the Báb!"

Mullá Ismá'íl turned and laughed. He said, "Yes, I am a follower of the Báb, and I am going to die for you."

As he passed through the crowd, they cursed him and threw stones at him.

"Followers of the Báb," they mocked, "and madmen!"

Mullá Ismá'íl answered. "Followers of the Báb we are, but mad-

men we are not. By God, O people, it is to awaken such as you
that we have forsaken wealth, wife, child and life. We have shut
our eyes to the world and all that dwell therein in the hope that
you may at last be led to make an inquiry into this Faith. We are
willing to die so that you may understand that the Messenger of
God has come, and be no longer blind."

Even at the headsman's block a few personal friends broke
through the crowd and tried to persuade Mullá Ismá'íl to deny the
Báb. They pleaded with him.

"It is such a little thing," they said. "Just to say, 'I don't believe.' "

"For thirty years I have yearned to witness this blessed day,"
he replied. "I was fearful lest I should carry this wish with me
unfilled to my grave."

Mullá Ismá'íl turned away from them and looked toward those
two martyrs who had preceded him. They were still entwined in
each other's embrace.

"Well done, my beloved companions," he cried. "You have turned
Tihrán into a paradise. Would that I had preceded you." He removed his turban from his head and turned to the executioner.

Then Mullá Ismá'íl lifted his eyes toward heaven.

"Accept me, O my God, unworthy though I be."

The executioner cut short his prayer.[4]

The death of the other four martyrs of Tihrán followed in swift
succession. For three days and three nights the bodies of these
heroic men remained abandoned in the public square adjoining the
imperial palace. Thousands gathered round their corpses, kicked
them with their feet, and spat in their faces. They were pelted
with stones, cursed and mocked by the angry multitude. Heaps of
refuse were flung upon the remains. Not one hand was raised to
halt the atrocities. The ferocious fanaticism even broke out in
"insults to the mortal remains of those whose spirits had now
passed beyond the power of their malice."[5]

The religious authorities refused to permit the bodies to be
buried. They were cast into a pit outside the gate of the city,
where, in a common grave, they remained as united in body as
they had been in spirit when they kneeled at the headsman's feet.

Professor Browne points out one of the most significant things
about these seven martyrs of Tihrán.

"They were men representing all the more important classes in
Persia—divines, dervishes, merchants, shopkeepers, and government

officials; they were men who had enjoyed the respect and consideration of all; they died fearlessly, willingly, almost eagerly." [6]

Browne further states: "This eventful day brought to the Báb more secret followers than many sermons could have done. I have just said that the impression created by the prodigious endurance of the martyrs was deep and lasting. I have often heard repeated the story of that day by eye-witnesses, by men close to the government, some even important officials. From their accounts, one might easily have believed that they were all [followers of the Báb], so great was the admiration they felt . . . and so high was the esteem they entertained for the resourcefulness, the hopes and the chances of success of the new doctrine."

Thus closes the tragic story of the lives of all but one or two of the chief disciples of the Báb. A relentless foe had struck down in swift succession Mullá Husayn, Quddús, Vahíd, and the Báb's uncle. This same wave of hatred swept to destruction Táhirih, Qurbán 'Alí and Mullá Ismá'íl. The wind of death now changed direction and blew its breath toward the Báb's prison-castle in Chiríq.

THE DAWN AND THE SUN

THE PRIME MINISTER, Mírzá Táqí Khán, despatched orders to Chiríq for the Báb to be brought from the prison to Tabríz. He vowed to himself that this would be the last journey the Báb ever made on this earth.

Forty days before the arrival of an officer and his soldiers at Chiríq, the Báb collected all the documents and writings in His possession. He placed them in a special box along with His pen-case, His seals, and His rings. He entrusted the box to Mullá Báqir, one of His disciples. The Báb also wrote a letter which he addressed to Mírzá Ahmad, who for a long time had served faithfully as His secretary. He put the key to the box in Mírzá Ahmad's letter, and instructed Mullá Báqir to take the utmost care of the box and letter. He emphasized the sacred character of the box and told Mullá Báqir to conceal its contents from everyone except Mírzá Ahmad.

Mullá Báqir found Mírzá Ahmad in Qum, where he delivered the letter and the box to Mírzá Ahmad. Mírzá Ahmad read the letter and was deeply moved. He told his friends that he must leave at once for Tihrán to deliver his trust. They all feared that the end of the Báb's earthly life was nearing, and they were eager to know what was in that treasured box. They overwhelmed Mírzá Ahmad with their entreaties until he agreed to disclose a little something of what it contained. Nabíl, the historian, was present at the time Mullá Báqir arrived in Qum. He was an eye-witness to the opening of that beautiful box.

"We marveled when we beheld, among the things which that box contained," he said, "a scroll of blue paper, of most delicate texture, on which the Báb, in His own exquisite handwriting, had penned, in the form of a pentacle, about five hundred verses, all consisting of derivatives of the word 'Bahá.' " [1]

The sight of this beautiful document caused great excitement among the followers of the Báb. They knew how often the Báb had told them to expect Someone far greater than Himself soon after His passing. Was the praise of this name "Bahá" yet another indication in which direction they must turn their eyes, they asked each other. They knew the word Bahá to be one of the titles of Husayn 'Alí, a distinguished nobleman of Tihrán, a follower of the Báb at this time, later known as Bahá'u'lláh.

Nabíl continued his account: "We were overcome with admiration as we gazed upon a masterpiece which no calligraphist, we believed, could rival. That scroll was replaced in the box and handed back to Mírzá Ahmad, who, on the very day he received it, proceeded to Tihrán. Ere he departed, he informed us that all he could divulge of that letter (from the Báb) was the injunction that the trust was to be delivered into the hands of [Bahá'u'lláh] in Tihrán."

Now that the shadow of death was hovering over Him, the Báb knew He must make clear once and for all the link that bound him to His Successor. As disaster struck on all sides, He sought to keep alive the fading hopes of those whom He would soon leave behind.

From that very first night when he had disclosed His Mission to Mullá Husayn, the Báb constantly referred to the One Who would come after Him. He alluded to this great event in nearly all of His writings. The Báb frequently told His followers that He, Himself, was merely "the channel of grace from some great Person still behind the veil of glory." [2]

The Báb warned His followers against the mistake made by the Jews in refusing to accept Christ because of the Old Testament, the Christians refusing Muhammad because of the New Testament, and the Moslems denying Himself because of the Qur'án. "Beware, beware," He cautioned them, "that the words sent down in the Bayán [the Báb's Book] shut thee not out as by a veil from Him."

"My sole purpose is to awaken you to the coming of His day," He assured them on yet another occasion. "I, Myself, am, verily, but a ring upon the hand of Him . . . If He were to appear at this moment, I would be the first to bow down before Him." [3]

"The Bayán deriveth all of its glory from 'Him Whom God shall make manifest,'" the Báb declared. "The Bayán and such as are believers therein yearn more ardently after Him than the yearning of any lover after his beloved."

Although this great Figure was still hidden from their eyes, the Báb promised His followers that the One Who was to come would grow from a seed into a mighty tree. This Tree, He told them, would shelter all humanity. The germ that holds within itself the potentialities of the Revelation that is to come, He said, is endowed with a potency superior to the combined forces of all those who follow Me. [4]

Now, on a special scroll, written in His own hand, the Báb had paid a final tribute of great love and respect for Bahá'u'lláh. It was no longer a vague reference, or a concealed intimation. The Báb knew that the hour of death was upon Him.

Dr. T. K. Cheyne in his book points out how plainly the lives of the Báb and Bahá'u'lláh were woven together during those days for anyone who had "eyes to see."

"The end of the Báb's earthly Manifestation is now close upon us," Dr. Cheyne wrote. "He knew it himself before the event, and was not displeased at the presentiment. He had already 'set his house in order,' as regards the spiritual affairs of [His] community, which he had, if I mistake not, confided to the intuitive wisdom of Bahá'u'lláh." [5]

The following pages are written to show the Báb's deep awareness of Bahá'u'lláh's coming. They show how the Báb carefully prepared certain souls to know, recognize, love and accept Bahá'u'lláh after His own martyrdom, so that the Faith of God might go on to fulfill it's destiny.

During those earliest days when students of scripture in America, Europe, Asia and Africa were expecting the Promised One, Shaykh Ahmad and Siyyid Kázim both repeatedly told their followers that the hour for His coming was now at hand. There would be twin Messengers in this day, they said. They would both appear in Persia. They would follow each other in rapid succession exactly as foretold in the holy Scriptures. They would be the two succes-

sive "trumpet blasts" mentioned in the Qur'án for the "last days";
the return of Elijah followed by the Lord of Hosts foretold in the
Old Testament; the "second woe" and the "third woe" that would
follow quickly, as promised in the Book of Revelation for the day
when the Lord would come "quickly into His temple." The Báb
Himself emphasized the brief time that would separate His own
Mission from the One to come after Him: "O My God! Bear Thou
witness," He wrote, "that through this Book, I have covenanted
with all created things concerning the Mission of Him Whom Thou
shalt make manifest, ere the covenant concerning My own Mission
had been established." [6]

Shaykh Ahmad and Siyyid Kázim promised their followers that
some of them would live to see both of these Messengers of God.
After the Dawn [the Báb], they were told, they would see the
promised Sun [Bahá'u'lláh].

Shaykh Ahmad was in Tihrán when Bahá'u'lláh was born. The
following historical account of his visit has been preserved:

"Shaykh Ahmad, who recognized in its full measure the meaning
of this auspicious event [birth of Bahá'u'lláh], yearned to spend
the remaining days of his life within the precincts of the court of
this divine, this new-born King. But this was not to be. His . . .
yearning unsatisfied, he felt compelled to submit to God's irrevocable decree," and turned his face away from the city.

"Ere his departure from that city he breathed a prayer that this
hidden Treasure of God, now born amongst his countrymen, might
be preserved and cherished by them, that they might recognize
the full measure of His blessedness and glory, and might be enabled
to proclaim His excellence to all nations and peoples." [7]

Shaykh Ahmad considered this moment of Bahá'u'lláh's birth to
be the hour foretold in the prophecy: "Ere long shall ye behold the
countenance of your Lord resplendent as the moon in its full glory.
Yet shall ye fail to unite in acknowledging His truth and embracing
His Faith."

Shaykh Ahmad also believed this to be the hour of fulfillment for
those prophetic words: "One of the most mighty signs that shall
signalize the advent of the promised Hour is this: 'A woman shall
give birth to One Who shall be her Lord.'"

The following similar words had been written in the Book of
Isaiah for the time of the end when the promised Saviour would

appear: "For Thy Maker is thine husband; the Lord of Hosts is His name; the God of the whole earth shall He be called." [8]

Shaykh Ahmad repeatedly impressed upon the minds of his followers the certainty of the appearance of twin Messengers. Mírzá Mahmúd, a follower of Shaykh Ahmad, recalls in this eye-witness account some of the excitement of those days of expectancy:

"At the hour of dawn," he said, "I found him fallen upon his face, . . . in wrapt devotion . . . To my great surprise, he turned to me and said mysteriously: 'That which I have been announcing unto you is now revealed. O Mahmúd, verily I say, you shall live to behold that Day of days.'

"Sometime afterwards, whilst conversing with the followers of the Báb, I was informed that the birthday of the Báb fell on [October 20th, 1819]. I realized that the day to which [my friend] had referred did not correspond with this date, that there was actually a difference of two years . . . This sorely perplexed me."

Long afterwards, he met a friend who told him of the Mission of Bahá'u'lláh and shared with him some of His writings. He was moved to the depths of his soul.

"I asked him the date of Bahá'u'lláh's birth," Mírzá Mahmúd said.

"He replied, 'He was born at dawn on the 12th of November, 1817.' *

"It was the very day and hour! Instinctively I fell prostrate upon the ground and exclaimed: 'Glorified art Thou, O my God, for having enabled me to attain unto this promised day.'" [9]

The hour of Bahá'u'lláh's birth marked the fulfillment of still another prophecy which spoke of the twin Messengers Who would appear at the time of the end. It was foretold that the Herald in that day would say of Him Who was yet to come: "I am two years younger than My Lord." [10]

Siyyid Kázim, who succeeded Shaykh Ahmad, continued to prepare his followers for that same approaching day.

"Verily I say," he told them, "that after the Qá'im [the Báb], the Qayyúm [Bahá'u'lláh] will be made manifest. For when the star of the Former [the Báb] has set, the Sun of the beauty of Husayn [Bahá'u'lláh] will rise and illuminate the whole world."

There is yet another proof of the unique oneness which linked the Mission of the Báb with that of Bahá'u'lláh. According to the

* See Appendix, Note Three.

solar calendar of the West, the Báb was born October 20, 1819 and Bahá'u'lláh was born November 12, 1817. However, according to the lunar calendar of the East (in Iran, the land of Their birth), the Báb was born on the first day of the month of Muharram and Bahá'u'lláh was born on the second day of Muharram. These twin successive holy days are celebrated as one great joyous Festival.

Siyyid Kázim told his followers: "What stress Shaykh Ahmad laid upon all those verses as foreshadowing the advent of twin Messengers Who are to follow Each Other in rapid succession, and Each of Whom is destined to suffuse the world with glory! How many times did he exclaim: 'Well is it with him who will recognize Their significance and behold Their splendor!'

"How often, addressing me," Siyyid Kázim concluded, "did he remark: 'Neither of us shall live to gaze upon Their glory. But many of the faithful among your disciples shall witness the Day which we, alas, can never hope to behold.'" [11]

When the Báb was on His way to Tihrán to meet the Sháh, the Prime Minister gave word that He was to be turned back and sent to imprisonment in Máh-Kú. Thus, within sight of a great victory, within thirty miles of the capital, the Báb was denied the opportunity of meeting the king. In that hour of keen disappointment, a letter was delivered to the Báb at the village of Kulayn. The letter came from Bahá'u'lláh.

Nabíl, the historian, records that episode as follows: Mullá Muhammad had been commissioned by Bahá'u'lláh to present to the Báb a sealed letter together with certain gifts, which as soon as they were delivered into His hands, provoked in His soul sentiments of unusual delight. His face glowed with joy as He overwhelmed the bearer with marks of His gratitude and favor.

"That message," Nabíl continues, "received at an hour of uncertainty and suspense, imparted solace and strength to the Báb. It imbued His soul with the certainty of victory. The cry, 'Beloved, My Well Beloved!' which in His bitter grief and loneliness the Báb would often utter, gave way to expressions of thanksgiving and praise, of hope and triumph. The exultation which glowed upon His face never forsook Him until the day of the news of the great disaster which befell the heroes of Shaykh Tabarsí." [12]

'Abdu'l-Karím, one of the devoted followers of the Báb, gives the following eye-witness account of an episode which took place one night during the Báb's stay at Kulayn:

"My companions and I were fast asleep in the vicinity of the
tent of the Báb, when the tramping of horsemen suddenly awakened
us. We were informed that the tent of the Báb was vacant, and
that those who had gone in search of Him had failed to find Him.

"We heard Muhammad Big [the Captain of the Báb's escort]
calming the soldiers. 'Why worry?' he told them. 'Are not the
Báb's trustworthiness and nobility sufficiently established in your
eyes to convince you that He will never embarrass you for the sake
of His own safety? No doubt He has retired in the silence of this
moonlit night to a place where He can seek undisturbed com-
munion with God. Be confident that He will unquestionably return
to His tent. He will never desert us.'

"In his eagerness to assure his colleagues, Muhammad Big set
out on foot along the road leading to Tihrán. I, too, with my companions, followed him. Shortly after, the rest of the guards on
horseback were marching behind us.

"We had covered about a mile when, by the dim light of the
early dawn, we saw in the distance the lonely figure of the Báb.
He was coming toward us from the direction of Tihrán.

"'Did you believe Me to have escaped?' He said to Muhammad Big as He approached him.

"'Far be it from me to entertain such thoughts,' Muhammad Big
assured Him.

"Muhammad Big bowed down at the feet of the Báb. He was so
awed by the serene majesty which that radiant face revealed that
morning, he could not utter another word.

"A look of confidence had settled upon the Báb's countenance.
His words were invested with such a transcendent power that a
feeling of profound reverence seized our souls. None dared to question Him as to the cause of so remarkable a change in His speech
and demeanor. Nor did He Himself choose to allay our curiosity
and wonder." [13]

Nabíl in his history records yet another time when Bahá'u'lláh
wrote to the Báb. The letter was sent from Tihrán to the Báb in
His prison at Chiríq. "Shortly after," Nabíl states, "a reply penned
in the Báb's own handwriting was received." [14]

The Báb made specific promises to certain of His followers that
they would meet the One Whose coming He had foretold. Some
of them He carefully prepared for that meeting.[15] Mullá Báqir, one
of the Letters of the Living, received a letter from the Báb in which

He prophesied that Mullá Báqir would meet the Promised One face to face. To Sayyáh, another disciple, He made the same verbal promise. To 'Azím the Báb wrote a special tablet in which He gave the name as well as foretold the approaching advent of this One Whom they were all awaiting. All of His promises were fulfilled.

Shaykh Sultán was also one of the followers who received such a promise. He journeyed to Shíráz with a friend, Shaykh Hasan. They were both eager to meet the Báb, but Shaykh Sultán fell ill before his wish was fulfilled. One night he received a message saying that the Báb had heard of his illness and would visit him after dark. Shaykh Sultán describes that visit in his own words:

"The Báb, Who had bidden me extinguish the lamp in my room ere He arrived, came straight to my bedside. In the midst of the darkness, I held fast to His garment and entreated Him to let me sacrifice myself for His Cause.

"He replied: 'O Shaykh! it behooves us both to cling to the garment of the Best-Beloved and to seek from Him the joy and glory of martyrdom in His path. Rest assured I will, in your behalf, supplicate the Almighty to enable you to attain His presence. Remember Me on that Day, a Day such as the world has never seen before.'

"The allusion of the Báb to His 'Best-Beloved' excited my wonder and curiosity. I was perplexed and unable to unravel this mystery. When I reached Karbilá and attained the presence of Bahá'u'lláh, I became firmly convinced that He alone could claim such affection from the Báb; that He, and only He, could be worthy of such adoration." [16]

Shaykh Sultán's companion on that trip to Shíráz, Shaykh Hasan, was given the same promise by the Báb. He has testified to that promise in the following account:

"Addressing me one day, the Báb said, 'You should proceed to Karbilá and should abide in that holy city inasmuch as you are destined to behold, with your own eyes, the beauteous countenance of the Promised [One]. As you gaze upon that radiant face, do also remember Me. Convey to Him the expressions of My loving devotion.' He again emphatically added the words: 'Verily, I say, I have entrusted you with a great mission. Beware lest your heart grow faint, lest you forget the glory with which I have invested you.'

"Soon after I journeyed to Karbilá. I lived as bidden in that holy city. What afflictions befell me at the hands of those followers of

Shaykh Ahmad who had still not recognized the Báb! Patiently I submitted to their indignities. For two years I lived in that city.

"One day while passing the gate of a Shrine, my eyes fell for the first time upon Bahá'u'lláh. What shall I recount regarding the countenance which I beheld? The beauty of that face, those exquisite features which no pen or brush can describe, His penetrating glance, His kindly face, the majesty of His bearing, the sweetness of His smile—all left an indelible impression upon my soul.

"How lovingly He advanced towards me! He took me by the hand and addressed me in a tone of great power and beauty. He walked with me all along the market-street, and in the end He said: 'Praise be to God that you have remained in Karbilá, and have beheld with your own eyes the countenance of the Promised [One].'

"I recalled instantly the promise I had been given by the Báb, a secret which I had not shared with anyone. These words of Bahá'u'lláh's moved me to the depths of my being. I felt impelled to proclaim to a heedless people, at that very moment and with all my soul and power, the appearance of the One promised by the Báb.

"He [Bahá'u'lláh] bade me, however, repress my feelings and conceal my emotions. 'Not yet,' He cautioned. 'The appointed Hour is approaching. It has not yet struck. Rest assured and be patient.'

"From that moment on my sorrows vanished. My soul was flooded with joy. In those days I was so poor that most of the time I hungered for food. Now I felt so rich that all the treasures of the earth melted away into nothingness when compared with that which I already possessed." [17]

From that day [in August, 1851] Shaykh Hasan became magnetized by the charm of his newly found Master, and, but for the restraint of Bahá'u'lláh, would have proclaimed to all that the One promised by the Báb had already appeared, and that they should now shed the agonizing sorrow they felt because of the Báb's departure.

In the city of Baghdád, but a short distance away from Karbilá, Bahá'u'lláh was soon to make the same public declaration to His followers that the Báb had made to His disciples in Shíráz. This was the meaning hidden in that prophecy quoted to Mullá Husayn by the Báb Himself on the roof of the prison-castle of Máh-Kú: "Shíráz will be thrown into a tumult; a Youth of sugar-tongue will appear. I fear lest the breath of His mouth should agitate and upset Baghdád." [18]

There was a constant link between the Báb and Bahá'u'lláh through the Báb's disciples, especially those whose tragic story has been told in the preceding chapters. Bahá'u'lláh played a vital and moving part in the tale of Tabarsí, Nayríz, Tihrán and Badasht, as well as in the lives of Mullá Husayn, Quddús, Vahíd and Táhirih.

When the Báb bade Mullá Husayn farewell in Shíráz before leaving for Mecca to announce His Mission, He spoke these words to him:

"Follow the course of your journey towards the north, and visit . . . Tihrán. Beseech almighty Providence that He may graciously enable you to attain, in that capital, the seat of true sovereignty, and to enter the mansion of the Beloved. A secret lies hidden in that city. When made manifest, it shall turn the earth into a paradise. My hope is that you may partake of its grace and recognize its splendor."

To soften the blow of disappointment for Mullá Husayn at being left behind, the Báb once again emphasized the importance of Tihrán and Mullá Husayn's visit there, thus alluding to the birthplace of both Bahá'u'lláh and Himself.

"Grieve not that you have not been chosen to accompany Me . . . I shall, instead, direct your steps to that city which enshrines a Mystery of such transcendent holiness . . . as Shíráz cannot hope to rival." [19]

Mullá Husayn reached Tihrán. He spent the daylight hours teaching the Faith of the Báb, but from sunset to dawn he remained alone in his room in prayer and meditation, beseeching God to disclose to him this holy "Mystery" of which the Báb had spoken, and to lead him to the "mansion" of the Báb's Beloved.

Mullá Husayn met Mullá Muhammad of Núr at this time. Mullá Husayn asked him if he knew any person who was distinguished above others, someone renowned for his character.

"Yes, there is one," Mullá Muhammad told him.

"What is his occupation?" Mullá Husayn asked.

"He cheers the disconsolate and feeds the hungry."

"What of his rank and position?"

"He has none apart from befriending the poor and the stranger."

"What is his name?" Mullá Husayn asked.

"It is Husayn 'Alí."

"His age?"

"Eight and twenty."

"The eagerness with which Mullá Husayn questioned me, and the sense of delight with which he welcomed every particular I gave him, greatly surprised me. Turning to me with a face beaming with satisfaction and joy, he once more inquired: 'I presume you meet him often?'

" 'Frequently I visit his home.'

" 'Will you deliver into his hands a trust from me?' "

Mullá Husayn then gave Mullá Muhammad a scroll of the Báb's writings.

"Should He deign to answer me," Mullá Husayn added, "will you be kind enough to acquaint me with His reply?"

Mullá Muhammad took the scroll at once to Bahá'u'lláh. Bahá-'u'lláh accepted it and bade Mullá Muhammad be seated. He un-folded the scroll, glanced at its contents, and began reading it aloud to those who were present. He stopped reading and turned to His friends.

"Verily," He said, "I say, whoso believes in the Qur'án . . . and yet hesitates, though it be for a moment, to admit that these soul-stirring words are endowed with the same regenerating power, has assuredly erred in his judgment and strayed far from the paths of Justice."

Bahá'u'lláh gave a gift to Mullá Muhammad to bring to Mullá Husayn. It was a small gift of sugar and tea. He asked that His appreciation and love be conveyed to Mullá Husayn along with the gift.

"With what joy and exultation Mullá Husayn received them," Mullá Muhammad reported. "Words fail me to describe the in-tensity of his emotion. He started to his feet, received with bowed head the gift from my hand, and fervently kissed it."

Mullá Husayn embraced Mullá Muhammad and kissed his eyes which had so recently gazed upon Bahá'u'lláh.

"May God fill your heart with gladness," he told him, "even as you have rejoiced mine."

Mullá Muhammad was puzzled. He said to himself: "What can be the nature of the bond that unites these two souls? What could have kindled such a fellowship between strangers? Why should Mullá Husayn, who considers riches and fame as the merest trifles, have shown such gladness at the sight of this tiny gift from the hands of Bahá'u'lláh?"

A few days later Mullá Husayn left for Khurásán. As he said farewell to Mullá Muhammad, he warned him: "Do not breathe to anyone what you have heard and witnessed. Let this be a secret within your breast. Divulge not His name, for they who envy His position will arise to harm Him. Pray that God may protect Him until such a day as He may exalt the downtrodden, enrich the poor, and redeem the fallen. The secret of this thing is still concealed from our eyes. Ours is now the duty to raise the call of the New Day and prepare men's hearts, and proclaim this Divine Message unto all people.

"Many a pure soul," Mullá Husayn concluded, "will shed his blood in this city. That blood will water the Tree of God, and will cause it to flourish until it overshadows all mankind." [20]

With these parting words, Mullá Husayn left Tihrán. He wrote a report to the Báb, telling Him of his teaching work, and describing to Him his experience with Bahá'u'lláh in Tihrán. Quddús and the Báb's uncle were both with the Báb when that letter from Mullá Husayn arrived. The Báb's uncle has left an account of that moment:

"That night," he said, "I saw such evidences of joy and gladness on the faces of the Báb and Quddús as I am unable to recount. I often heard the Báb in those days exultantly repeat the words: 'How marvelous, how exceedingly marvelous, is that which occurred between the months of Jamádí and Rajab!'

"As He was reading the letter from Mullá Husayn, He turned to Quddús and, showing him certain passages, explained the reason for His joyous expressions."

The Báb's uncle told his fellow-companions what he had witnessed that night. He also mentioned the Báb's reference to the wonder of the days between Jamádí and Rajab. This impressed Mírzá Ahmad who waited until Mullá Husayn returned to Shíráz, then asked him what had happened at that particular time.

Mullá Husayn smiled and said, "Between the months of Jamádí and Rajab, I chanced to be in Tihrán."

He would give no further explanation. "This was sufficient to convince me that in the city of Tihrán there lay hidden a Mystery which, when revealed to the world, would bring unspeakable joy to the heart of the Báb." [21]

Mullá Husayn met Bahá'u'lláh a second time just before he began his journey on foot to the Báb's prison in Máh-Kú. He was ushered with secrecy into the presence of Bahá'u'lláh, and shortly after this interview, Mullá Husayn set out for his last visit with the Báb. From Máh-Kú, he returned yet another time to the presence of Bahá'u'lláh. Their last meeting was inside the fort of Tabarsí.

Quddús also knew the joy of meeting Bahá'u'lláh. When the Báb and Quddús returned from Medina to Bushihr, the Báb sent Quddús to Shíráz. He said to him in parting: "In the streets of Shíráz indignities will be heaped upon you . . . you will survive, . . . and will attain the presence of Him Who is the object of our adoration and love. In His presence you will forget all the harm and disgrace that shall have befallen you."

Quddús suffered greatly in Shíráz, from there he went to Tihrán where he was admitted into the presence of Bahá'u'lláh, and all of the Báb's promises came true.

Quddús and Bahá'u'lláh met again at the conference of Badasht. When Bahá'u'lláh was informed of the arrival of Quddús at a town near Badasht, He set out on horseback to meet him. They returned to Badasht together the next morning at sunrise.[22]

Shortly after this conference when Quddús and a party of the followers of the Báb were being ruthlessly attacked, Bahá'u'lláh came to their rescue. He immediately gave His protection to Quddús. He clothed Quddús in His own garments to disguise him so that he would not be recognized, then He escorted him to a place of safety.

When Quddús was imprisoned in Sárí by Muhammad Táqí, it was Báha'u'lláh Who secured his release so that Quddús might join Mullá Husayn at the fort of Tabarsí. Bahá'u'lláh, Himself, then visited them there.[23]

The night preceding the arrival of Mullá Husayn and his party at Tabarsí, the guardian of the shrine dreamed that a holy man and a large company of his friends came and fought valiantly and triumphantly. He dreamed that the Prophet of God, Himself, came one night and visited that blessed company.

Soon after this Bahá'u'lláh arrived at a nearby village. He sent word to Mullá Husayn that he and all his companions were to be His guests that night, and that He would join them at Tabarsí that very afternoon. The following is an eye-witness account of that meeting:

"The tidings imparted an indefinable joy to the heart of Mullá Husayn. He bade his companions bestir themselves for the reception of Bahá'u'lláh. He himself joined them in sweeping, cleaning, and sprinkling with water the dusty entrances for the arrival of the beloved Visitor. As soon as he saw Him approaching, he rushed forward and embraced Him tenderly, and conducted Him to the place of honor. We were too blind in those days to recognize the glory of Him Whom our leader had introduced with such reverence and love into our midst. What Mullá Husayn had perceived, our dull vision was yet unable to recognize. We, too, were soon made to feel the charm of His utterance. Mullá Husayn was so filled with delight, so lost in admiration that he was utterly oblivious of us all. It was Bahá'u'lláh, Himself, Who finally bade us be seated."

Bahá'u'lláh examined the fort, then assisted the companions with suggestions on how to strengthen their defenses to help protect their lives. He dispelled their fears and raised their determination to sacrifice all for God.

Bahá'u'lláh said, "The one thing this fort and company require to render it complete is the presence of Quddús." He instructed Mullá Husayn to send six friends to Sárí to demand that Muhammad Táqí deliver Quddús into their hands. Mullá Husayn and his companions were surprised, knowing that Quddús was being held prisoner. Bahá'u'lláh assured them, "The fear of God and the dread of His punishment will prompt him to surrender unhesitatingly his captive."

Before Bahá'u'lláh left Tabarsí, He told the friends to be patient and resigned to the Will of God. "If it be His will, We shall once again visit you at this same spot and shall lend you Our assistance."

Mullá Husayn sent six of his companions to Sárí with Bahá'u'lláh's message. Muhammad Táqí released Quddús at once, to the astonishment of all.

Mullá Husayn's companions were deeply moved by the effect of Bahá'u'lláh's presence upon them all. One of them has left this memory of Mullá Husayn's reaction to that visit:

"I can still remember him [Mullá Husayn] as he advanced towards me in the stillness of those dark and lonely hours which I devoted to prayer and meditation. 'Banish from your mind,' he told me, 'these perplexities. Arise, and seek with me to drink of the cup of martyrdom. Then you will be able to comprehend, as the year [1863] [the year of Bahá'u'lláh's Declaration] dawns upon the world the secret of the things which now lie hidden from you.'"

Bahá'u'lláh was also the moving Figure behind the conference of Badasht at which so many of the outstanding followers of the Báb were present.[24]

Nabíl, the historian, relates, "It was the beginning of summer. Upon His arrival at Badasht, Bahá'u'lláh rented three gardens, one of which he assigned to Quddús, another to Táhirih, and a third for Himself. All of those who gathered at Badasht were the guests of Bahá'u'lláh from the time of their arrival until the day of their departure. Upon each of the followers of the Báb, Bahá'u'lláh bestowed a new name. It was He Who gave the name 'Quddús' to the last of the Báb's chosen disciples. He also gave the name 'Táhirih' to that great woman." He Himself was henceforth designated by the name "Bahá."

The close relationship of spirit between the Báb and Bahá'u'lláh is nowhere better demonstrated than at Badasht. None of those companions knew the Source of the bold, defiant and far-reaching changes in the old laws and traditions which took place there, and no one suspected that it was Bahá'u'lláh's hand which steadily and unerringly steered the course of that conference.

"To each of those who had convened at Badasht," Nabíl continues, "a special letter was written by the Báb. He addressed each one by the name which Bahá'u'lláh had conferred upon him." From that time on, they were known only by those names.

When some of the followers complained about the boldness of Táhirih, saying that she had been indiscreet to cast aside the veil, the Báb replied in these stirring words: "What am I to say regarding her whom the Tongue of Power and Glory [Bahá'u'lláh], has named Táhirih, ['the Pure One']?"

At that same conference, Táhirih concluded one of her eloquent addresses by glancing toward Bahá'u'lláh and quoting a prophetic verse: "Verily, amid gardens and rivers shall the pious dwell in the seat of Truth, in the presence of the Potent King."

Then Táhirih declared that she was the blast of the bugle that annulled the past ages. Dr. T. K. Cheyne writes of this, stating, "It is said, too, that this short speech of the brave woman was followed by a recitation by Bahá'u'lláh of the Súrih [Chapter] of Resurrection ... the inner meaning of this was that mankind was about to pass into a new cosmic cycle, for which a new set of laws and customs would be indispensable." [25]

Bahá'u'lláh arranged for the departure of the friends from Badasht, just as He had arranged for their arrival. On their way home, Táhirih composed an ode each day which she shared with her companions. These verses told of the obsolete conventions, rituals and traditions which had chained the consciences of men and women in the past, and how these fetters had at last been boldly challenged and fearlessly swept away by the meeting held at Badasht. The companions memorized the odes and chanted them in unison as they walked along together. Mountain and valley echoed with the shouts of that enthusiastic band as they hailed the extinction of the old and the birth of the new Day.[26]

Bahá'u'lláh's guiding hand constantly reached out to assist the companions of the Báb. Táhirih, more than any other disciple, was indebted to Him for His protection and kindness.[27]

When she was imprisoned in Qazvín and threatened with hot irons, she boldy declared to her captor: "If my Cause be the Cause of Truth, if the Lord Whom I worship be none other than the One True God, He will, ere nine days have elapsed, deliver me from the yoke of your tyranny."

It was Bahá'u'lláh Who rescued Táhirih from her prison in Qazvín. When He heard of her captivity, He dispatched a woman, disguised as a begger, to the home where Táhirih was confined. He instructed that she deliver a letter to Táhirih who would then of her own will, unmolested by her captors, walk out free from that prison-house. The begger-woman was instructed to await Táhirih's appearance at the entrance.

"As soon as Táhirih has joined you," Bahá'u'lláh informed this messenger, "start immediately for Tihrán. This very night, I shall dispatch to the neighborhood of the gate of Qazvín an attendant with three horses that you will take with you and station at a place outside the walls. . . . You will conduct Táhirih to that spot, will mount the horses, and will, by an unfrequented route, endeavor to reach at daybreak the outskirts of the capital. As soon as the gates of the city are opened, you must enter the city and proceed immediately to My house. You should exercise the utmost caution lest her identity by disclosed."

Bahá'u'lláh reassured the worried messenger, who felt that such a delivery would require a miracle. "The Almighty will assuredly

guide your steps," He said, "and will surround you with His un-
failing protection."

Nabíl writes, "The hour which Táhirih had fixed for her deliverance found her already securely established under the sheltering shadow of Bahá'u'lláh. She knew full well into Whose presence
she had been admitted; she was profoundly aware of the sacredness
of the hospitality she had been so graciously accorded. She [per-
ceived] through her own intuitive knowledge the future glory of
Bahá'u'lláh."

"I have myself been shown," Nabíl affirms, "the verses which she,
in her own handwriting, had penned, every letter of which bore
eloquent testimony to her faith in the exalted Missions of both
the Báb and Bahá'u'lláh."

Bahá'u'lláh rescued Táhirih another time immediately following
the conference of Badasht. On the way to their homes, the party
had assembled in the village of Níyálá. They were all resting at
the foot of a mountain, when suddenly at the hour of dawn, they
were awakened by a shower of stones. The people of the village
were hurling rocks at them from the top of the mountain. The
attack was unexpected and fierce. The cries of the mob, the sound
of the rolling rocks and showering stones, alarmed the friends and
they fled for safety.

Bahá'u'lláh found Táhirih in grave danger. She and one believer
from Shíráz had been unable to escape. The enemy had demolished
the camp and was plundering the property. The follower from
Shíráz was defending what remained of the companion's possessions. He was already badly wounded.

Bahá'u'lláh walked into the crowd of attackers armed only with
the sword of His tongue. He convinced them of the cruelty and
shamefulness of their behavior. He induced them to restore the
property which they had not yet carried off. He rescued Táhirih
from their hands and escorted her to a place of safety.

Nabíl writes of these frequent victories which Bahá'u'lláh won
by His word alone. "All classes of men marveled at His miraculous
success in emerging unscathed from the most perilous encounters.
Nothing short of Divine protection, they thought, could have assured His safety on such occasions." [28]

Bahá'u'lláh also lent His strength and assistance to Vahíd. The
following is an historical account of their friendship:

"[Vahíd] hastened to the capital where he undertook the necessary preparations for his journey to the fort of Tabarsí. He was preparing to leave, when Bahá'u'lláh arrived from Mázindarán and informed him of the impossibility of joining his brethren. He was greatly saddened at the news, and his only consolation in those days was to visit Bahá'u'lláh frequently, and to obtain the benefit of His wise and priceless counsel." [29]

It was following these visits with Bahá'u'lláh that Mírzá Jání, Vahíd's friend, wrote: "I observed in his [Vahíd's] august countenance the signs of a glory and power which I had not noticed during my first journey with him to the capital, nor on other occasions of meeting." [30]

The messenger, Sayyáh, whom the Báb commissioned to go to Tabarsí and Bárfurúsh on His behalf, and to bring back some of the holy earth that covered the remains of Mullá Husayn and Quddús, visited Bahá'u'lláh before returning to the Báb's prison of Chiríq. Vahíd was an honored guest of Bahá'u'lláh at the time of Sayyáh's coming.

Sayyáh appeared at Bahá'u'lláh's door in the bitter cold of winter. He was barefooted, poorly clad, and dishevelled. Vahíd was told of Sayyáh's arrival from Tabarsí. Completely oblivious of the dignity and honor to which a man of his position and fame was accustomed, Vahíd rushed forward to meet him and threw himself at Sayyáh's feet. He embraced those legs which were covered to the knees with mud from the earth of Tabarsí.

It was to this same Sayyáh that Bahá'u'lláh gave a letter to take to the Báb at Chiríq. Shortly afterward a reply came from the prison in the Báb's own handwriting.

Bahá'u'lláh overwhelmed Sayyáh with His kindness during this visit, and showered the same love upon Vahíd. The brother of Bahá'u'lláh has said: "I was amazed at the many evidences of loving solicitude which Bahá'u'lláh evinced toward Vahíd. He showered him with such favors as I had never seen Him extend to anyone. The manner of His conversation left no doubt in me that this same Vahíd would, ere long, distinguish himself by deeds no less remarkable than those which had immortalized the defenders of Tabarsí." [31]

Following this final visit to Bahá'u'lláh's home, Vahíd set out on his last journey to Yazd and Nayríz where he laid down his life for his Faith.

The same love and encouragement which Bahá'u'lláh gave to

Vahíd was bestowed upon Hujjat of Zanján as well. Hujjat was the hero of the most violent upheaval of all. In the village of Zanján, nearly two thousand followers of the Báb, including Hujjat, gave up their lives. When the Báb had passed through Zanján on His way to prison, He foretold this disaster: "This town will be thrown into a great tumult, and its streets will run with blood." [32]

His prediction came true, and His much loved Hujjat, along with many of his companions, was besieged by a host of soldiers in Zanján. The governor of Zanján sent a crier through the streets saying, "All who throw in their lot with Hujjat will be destroyed, and their wives and children exposed to misery and shame!"

This warning divided the city into two camps. There were pathetic sights of families being separated by their belief or disbelief in the Báb. Fathers turned away from their sons, women from their husbands, children from their mothers. Every tie of worldly affection seemed to be dissolved on that day. Zanján became a city of panic. Men ran frantically to and fro trying to collect their wives and children and to persuade them to stand with them. Families divided their belongings and their children. Many wept over what they had to abandon. Whole houses were deserted. When a man, a woman, or a child would tear itself from its family or friends and rush to the support of Hujjat, a cry of joy would go up from one camp, and a moan of despair from the other.

It was such a day as foretold by Christ for the days of the end when "brother shall deliver up brother to death, and the father the child: and the children shall rise up against their parents and cause them to be put to death." [33]

This was the day prophesied also by Muhammad, the day on which man shall fly from his brother, and his mother and his father, and his wife and his children." [34]

One night during the struggle, the followers of the Báb carried out His instructions to repeat the following praises of the Almighty:
"God the Great!"
"God the Most Great!"
"God the Most Beauteous!"
"God the Most Glorious!"
"God the Most Pure!"

In unison they repeated the phrases over and over. "So loud and compelling was the reply," historical account states, "that the enemy was rudely awakened from sleep, abandoned the camp in horror, and, hurrying to the environs of the governor's residence, sought shelter. A few were so shocked they dropped dead."

Part of the soldier's camp was in the midst of noisy revelry. Their boisterous party was suddenly interrupted by the shouts of those voices raised in praise of God. Officers who were holding their wine glasses in their hands, dropped them instantly. Men and women rushed headlong from the building as if stunned by the outcry. Gambling tables were overturned in the disorder that followed. Half dressed, a number ran out into the wilderness. Others fled to the homes of the religious leaders.

As soon as the camp discovered that it was not a dreadful attack being launched against them, but words of praise raised to the glory of God, they returned to their posts and pleasures, reassured, though greatly humiliated by this experience.[35]

Hujjat had boldly testified in the presence of the king and the Prime Minister and the assembled priests and other religious leaders that the Báb was the Promised One.

"It is my firm and unalterable conviction," he told them, "That the Báb is the very One Whose coming you yourself, with all the peoples of the world, are eagerly awaiting. He is our Lord, our promised Deliverer. If He were to entrust me with the meanest service in His household, I would deem it an honor such as the highest favors of my King could never hope to surpass." [36]

Hujjat returned to his home urging everyone to accept the Báb. "The goal for which the world has been striving is now here," he told them. "The Sun of Truth has risen. Fix your eyes upon the Báb, not upon me, the least of His slaves. My wisdom compared to His is as an unlighted candle to the sun at midday." [37]

Shortly before his death, Hujjat was grievously wounded. His wife and child were slain before his eyes. Though filled with the greatest grief, he refused to yield to complete sorrow. He would not permit himself to become one who begs for this world's favors. He cried out in his pain:

"O my God, on the day when I found Thy Beloved One, I foresaw the woes I should suffer for Thee. Great as have been my sufferings, they cannot compare to the agonies I would willingly suffer in Thy name.

"How can this miserable life of mine, and even the loss of my dear wife and child, and the sacrifices of my kindred and companions, compare to the blessings which the recognition of Thy

Messenger can bestow both in this world and in the next. I only wish that a multitude of lives were mine, and that I possessed the riches of the whole earth, so that I might freely and joyously resign them all in Thy path!" [38]

Gobineau in his account says, "I have seen at Zanján the ruins of that fierce encounter; whole sections of the city have not yet been rebuilt and probably never will be." [39]

Nicolas testifies that the entire affair was settled by the same treachery resorted to at Tabarsí and Nayríz. He portrays the attitude of the enemies of Hujjat as follows: "Why not resort to deceit? Why not make the most sacred promises, even though it might later become necessary to massacre those gullibles who had put their trust in them?" [40]

No wonder that the Báb was to give Zanján the title: "That exalted spot." [41]

When, at Chiríq in the summer of 1848, the Báb finished His letter "The Sermon of Wrath," in which He foretold the downfall of the Prime Minister, Hájí Mírza Áqásí, it was given to Hujjat to deliver. He instructed Hujjat to place it personally in the hands of that official.

Immediately after delivering that letter to Hájí Mírzá Áqásí, Hujjat went to the home of Bahá'u'lláh. He revealed the contents of that "Sermon of Wrath" and recited for Him and a few other believers the entire letter which he had memorized. Hujjat's sole comfort in those days was his close association with Bahá'u'lláh, from Whom he received the sustaining power that enabled him to distinguish himself by remarkable deeds in the days to come. [42]

From Bahá'u'lláh's home, Hujjat went to Zanján where he, like his illustrious companions Vahíd, Táhirih, Mullá Husayn, and Quddús, laid down his life for his Beloved.

From the very first moment when the Báb had revealed the commentary for Mullá Husayn on the eve of May 23, 1844, He linked His own Mission with that of Bahá'u'lláh. Nabíl states in his history: "Did not the Báb, in the earliest days of His Mission allude, in the opening passages of His commentary of the Súríh of Joseph, to the glory and significance of the Revelation of Bahá'u'lláh? Was it not His purpose, by dwelling upon the ingratitude and malice which characterized the treatment of Joseph by his brethren, to predict what Bahá'u'lláh was destined to suffer at the hands of His brother and kindred?" [43]

In His farewell address to His chosen disciples, the Báb stated
clearly that He was but the forerunner of a greater One yet to
come.

"I am preparing you for the advent of a mighty Day," He told
them in that parting message. "Scatter throughout the length and
breadth of this land, and, with steadfast feet and sanctified hearts,
prepare the way for *His* coming." [44]

The Báb also instructed His disciples to record the names of
all the believers who accepted the Faith.

"Of all these believers I shall make mention in the Tablet of
God," He told them, "so that upon each one of them the Beloved
of our hearts may, in the Day when He shall have ascended the
throne of glory, confer His inestimable blessing." [45]

It was from the names of these believers that the first followers
of Bahá'u'lláh came, and upon whom He conferred His special
blessing and love.

The Báb did everything in His power to assist His followers so
that they would know where to turn after His own martyrdom. He
clearly announced that He was the Promised One, but that He
"stood in relation to a succeeding and greater (Messenger) as did
John the Baptist to the Christ. He was the Forerunner of One
more mighty than Himself. He (the Bab) was to decrease; that
Mighty One was to increase. And as John the Baptist had been the
Herald or Gate of the Christ, so was (He) the Báb the Herald
or Gate of Bahá'u'lláh." [46]

"Consecrate thou, O My God, the whole of this Tree unto
Him . . . ," He wrote of Bahá'u'lláh. "I have not wished that this
Tree should ever bear any branch, leaf, or fruit that would fail to
bow down before Him on the day of His Revelation . . . And
shouldst Thou behold, O my God, any branch, leaf or fruit upon
Me that hath failed to bow down before Him on the day of His
Revelation, cut it off, O My God from that Tree, for it is not of
Me. . . ." [47]

"Ere nine [years] will have elapsed from the inception of this
Cause," the Báb wrote in another place, pointing out even the
exact hour of Báha'u'lláh's coming, "the realities of the created
things will not be made manifest. . . . Be patient until thou beholdest a new creation." "In the year nine ye will attain unto all
good." "In the year nine ye will attain unto the presence of God." [48]

Before nine years had elapsed, in fact during the ninth year

[1853], Bahá'u'lláh's Mission began, thus fulfilling not only the promise of the Báb and that of Shaykh Ahmad and Siyyid Kázim, but also the prophecy from the sacred writings of that land which said: "In the year [1844] the earth shall be illumined by His light. . . . If thou livest until the year [1853] thou shalt witness how the nations, the rulers, the peoples, and the Faith of God shall have been renewed." [49]

The Báb's challenging words written at Máh-Kú seal forever the bond that unites Him with Baha'u'lláh.

"Well is it with him who fixeth his gaze upon the Order of Bahá- 'u'lláh and rendereth thanks unto his Lord! For He will assuredly be made manifest." [50]

"I verily am a believer in Him," the Báb declares to the world, "and in His Faith, and in His Book. . . ." [51]

Bahá'u'lláh on His part had such a love for the Báb that He would not let Him suffer any pain, indignity, or humiliation in which He, Bahá'u'lláh, did not share.

The Báb was first confined in the house of the Chief Constable of Shíráz. Shortly after this Bahá'u'lláh was confined in the house of one of the religious leaders in Tihrán. The Báb's second imprisonment was in the castle of Máh-Kú; that of Bahá'u'lláh followed when He was imprisoned in the residence of the governor of 'Amul. The Báb was scourged in the prayer-house in Tabríz. The very same punishment was inflicted shortly after this upon Bahá'u'lláh in the prayer-house at 'Amul. The Báb's third imprisonment was in the castle of Chiríq; that of Bahá'u'lláh followed in the "Black Pit" prison of Tihrán. The Báb was struck in the face with missiles in the streets of Tabríz. Bahá'u'lláh was pelted with stones on the streets of 'Amul, and struck in the face with a rock on His way to prison in Tihrán. The Báb was slain in the public square of Tabríz. Bahá'u'lláh underwent nearly half a century of living martyrdom. He was exiled and imprisoned for forty years. He was poisoned in the "Black Pit." He was set upon by assassins in Baghdád. He was poisoned again in Adrianople. He was approached by yet another assassin in the prison of 'Akká. To His grave Bahá'u'lláh carried the scars of great prison-chains which had torn the flesh from His shoulders.

Nabíl recounts in his history: "The Báb, Whose trials and sufferings had preceded, in almost every case, those of Bahá'u'lláh, had offered Himself to ransom His Beloved from the perils that beset that precious life; whilst Bahá'u'lláh, on His part, unwilling that He Who so greatly loved Him should be the sole sufferer, shared at every turn the cup that had touched His [the Báb's] lips.

"Such love no eye has ever beheld, nor has mortal heart ever conceived such mutual devotion. If the branches of every tree were turned into pens, and all the seas into ink, and earth and heaven rolled into one parchment, the immensity of that love would still remain unexplored, and the depths of that devotion unfathomed." [52]

Their Missions were bound together for eternity.

Thus it was that the Báb was able to leave the prison of Chiríq in peace and with eagerness, and begin what He knew would be His last journey on this earth. He had fulfilled His task. He was the Dawn, and He had faithfully prepared His followers for the coming of the Sun itself.

"I, verily, have not fallen short of My duty to admonish that people, and devise means whereby they may turn towards God . . . ," He said. "If, on the day of His Revelation, all that are on earth bear Him allegiance, Mine inmost being will rejoice, inasmuch as all will have attained the summit of their existence, and will have been brought face to face with their Beloved . . . I truly have nurtured all things for this purpose. How then can anyone be veiled from Him?" [53] "I have educated all men, that they may recognize this Revelation."

The Báb's heart was turned toward Tihrán and Bahá'u'lláh when He wrote those moving words which foreshadowed the hours that were fast sweeping down upon Him:

"I have sacrificed Myself wholly for Thee; I have accepted curses for Thy sake, and have yearned for naught but martyrdom in the path of Thy love." [54]

The soldiers bearing the fatal edict from the Prime Minister which called for His execution were already at the gates of the prison-castle of Chiríq. The Báb, confident that He had expended every effort in the path of God, had already sent His writings, His pen-case, His seals, and His ring to Bahá'u'lláh, along with a beautiful scroll filled with the praises and glory of His name.

Now He calmly awaited His escort of death.

THE MARTYRDOM OF THE BÁB

A WAVE OF VIOLENCE unprecedented in its cruelty, its persistency, and its breadth swept the face of the entire land. From Khurásán on the eastern border of Persia to Tabríz on the west, from the northern cities of Zanján and Tihrán stretching as far south as Nayríz, the country was enveloped in darkness. Many recalled the prophecy of Shaykh Ahmad who spoke so glowingly of the Twin Revelations that were at hand. He had warned his followers to expect these days of suffering. "Pray God," he told them, "that you may not be present in (1) the day of the coming of the Prophet or (2) the day of His return, as there will be many civil wars. If any of you should be living at that time, he shall see strange things between the years 1844 and 1851." [1]

Nicolas in his account of those days says: "The anxious priests, feeling their flock quivering with impatience and ready to escape their control, redoubled their slanders . . .; the grossest lies, the most bloody fictions were spread among the bewildered populace, torn between terror and admiration." [2]

When the news of the death of His beloved uncle reached the Báb, and he heard the moving account of the tragic fate of the "seven martyrs of Tihrán," His heart was plunged in sorrow.

He wrote a special tribute in their honor which testified to the exalted position they occupied in His eyes. The Báb said that these

seven heroes were the "Seven Goats" spoken of in the prophecies
of Islám who on the Day of Judgement would "walk in front of the
Promised Qá'im [He who shall arise]." [3]

It was at this moment that the Prime Minister, Mírzá Táqí Khán,
issued the command that brought the Báb out of His prison-cell
in Chiríq. The Prime Minister had at last decided to strike at the
very head of the Faith. The forces of the Sháh and the members
of the clergy were suffering humiliating defeats all across the land.
Remove the Báb, the Prime Minister told himself, and the old
order could be restored. He called his counsellors together and
unfolded to them his plan.

This was a drastic change from the Prime Minister's original
plan. Up to now, Mírzá Táqí Khán had felt that the most effective
way of destroying the Báb's influence would be to ruin him morally
"to bring him out of his retreat in Chiríq where a halo of suffering,
holiness, science and eloquence made him radiate like a sun; to
show him to the people just as he was . . . a vulgar charlatan,
a weak dreamer who did not have courage enough to conceive,
still less to direct the daring enterprises" of Tabarsí, Nayríz and
Zanján, "or even take part in them." [4]

These counsellors pointed out that the Báb's conduct while He
was in prison gave no evidence that He was such a person as the
Prime Minister suggested. He bore all hardships without complaint.
He prayed and worked incessantly. Those who came near Him felt
the power of His personality. Did they not have the alarming
example of the two wardens of Máh-Kú and Chiríq? Both had
been bitter enemies of the Báb, but through His mere presence
among them, they had become enraptured friends.

Had not the authorities sent the greatest religious leader of them
all, Vahíd, to investigate and discredit the Báb? He, too, upon
meeting Him had forsaken the King, his own fame, and his very
life for this Prisoner. Was there any comfort to be found in this?
What about Manuchir Khán's conversion?

What about the reports of the spies near the prison of Chiríq?
They reported that the Báb spoke often of His death during these
days. It was said that He referred to His death as something not
only familiar, but pleasant. Suppose He should display an undaunted courage if exhibited in chains throughout the country?
Suppose He confused and bewildered the subtle doctors they chose
to debate against Him? Suppose they bowed down in belief before

Him as the wisest of all, Vahíd, had done? Suppose He became more of a hero and martyr than ever to the people as a result of this treatment? What then?

Gobineau himself in his history, says, "Those who came near him felt in spite of themselves the fascinating influence of his personality, of his manner and of his speech. His guards were not free from that weakness." [5]

The risk was too great. After weighing the matter with care, the counsellors of the Prime Minister decided against this plan. They dared not take the chance.

Now the Prime Minister insisted on more drastic action against the Báb. He cursed the laxity with which his predecessor, Hájí Mírzá Áqásí, had allowed so great a peril to grow. He was determined that this weak policy must cease at once. To allow the Báb to continue to gain in glory and prestige was unthinkable.

"Nothing," he told them, "short of his public execution can, to my mind, enable this distracted country to recover its tranquillity and peace!"

Seeing his wrath, not a single voice dared to speak against his plan. After a long silence, one quiet courageous voice arose in protest. It was that of the Minister of War who was later to succeed Mírzá Táqí Khán. He suggested a less violent course. The Prime Minister was very displeased. He put down this opposition at once.

"Nothing short of the remedy I advocate can uproot this evil and bring us the peace for which we long," he said.

Disregarding the advice of any who disagreed with him, the Prime Minister dispatched an order to the governor of Tabríz, commanding that the Báb be brought from Chiríq to Tabríz. The order requested that the Báb be imprisoned in this city where He would later be told of His fate. The Prime Minister was afraid to bring the Báb to Tihrán for an execution, lest His presence there set in motion forces which the Prime Minister would be powerless to control. Therefore, the Báb was to be done to death in Tabríz, in the north. [6]

Three days after the Báb was transferred from prison to Tabríz, a second order was sent to the governor. This order instructed him to execute the Báb. He refused.

"This is a task only for the most ignoble," he said indignantly. "Who am I to be called upon to slay an innocent descendent of our own Prophet?"

The Báb was descended from the family of Baní-Háshim, which was the family of Muhammad, and through Ismá'íl from Abraham, Himself, Whose "seed would inherit the earth."

The governor, as well as most of the people, was familiar with the prophecy in their Books which said that "should a youth from Baní-Háshim be made manifest and summon the people to a new book and to new laws, all should hasten to Him and embrace His Cause." [7]

The Prime Minister was very angry with the governor, but he was determined that nothing should stop this execution. He ordered his own brother, Mírzá Hasan Khán, to carry out his orders. The brother tried to inform the governor of these new instructions, but the governor refused to meet him, pretending to be ill. Mírzá Hasan Khán then personally took over the plans for the execution.

He ordered the immediate transfer of the Báb to a death cell in the city barracks. He had the Báb's turban and sash, the twin emblems of His noble lineage, ripped off. He ordered Sam Khán, the head of the execution regiment, to post ten special guards outside the door of the Báb's cell.

As the Báb was being led through the courtyard to His cell in the barracks, a young boy from Tabríz rushed forward from the crowd. He was but eighteen years old. His face was haggard, his feet were bare, his hair dishevelled. He forced his way through the mob, ignoring the peril to his own life which such an action involved. He flung himself at the feet of the Báb.

"Send me not from Thee, O Master," he implored. "Wherever Thou goest, suffer me to follow Thee."

The Báb smiled down upon him and spoke gently. "Muhammad-'Alí, arise," He told the young man, "and rest assured that you will be with Me. Tomorrow you will witness what God hath decreed." [8]

Dr. T. K. Cheyne writes: "It is no doubt a singular coincidence that both [the Báb] and Jesus Christ are reported to have addressed these words to a disciple: 'Today thou shalt be with Me in Paradise.'" [9]

The youth was arrested and cast into the same cell with the Báb and condemned to death with Him. Soon the story of this young man became known to everyone. He had learned of the Faith of the Báb when the Báb had first passed through Tabríz on His way to prison at Máh-Kú. At once he became an ardent believer.

He longed to visit the Báb in His prison and offer his life for the Faith. The boy's stepfather was one of the most illustrious citizens of Tabríz. He refused to let the boy leave the city. He feared that his son would shame the family by publicly admitting that he believed in the Báb, so he confined the boy to his room and put a strict watch over him. The young man began to sicken in this confinement until at length the stepfather became worried.

Shaykh Hasan, who was related to the stepfather, had just been sent to Tabríz by the Báb with a number of manuscripts. He gives the following eye-witness account of his meeting with that young man.

"Every day I visited him," Shaykh Hasan recalls, "and every day I witnessed the tears of sorrow that rained from his eyes. After the Báb had been scourged and returned to Chiríq, I visited him again. This time I was surprised to note the joy and gladness which had illumined his countenance. His handsome face was wreathed in smiles as he stepped forward to receive me.

" 'The eyes of my Beloved have beheld this face of mine,' he said, 'and these eyes have gazed upon his countenance.'

" 'Let me tell you the secret of my happiness,' he said. 'After the Báb had been taken back to Chiríq, one day as I lay confined in my cell, I turned my heart to Him and besought Him in these words: "Thou beholdest, O my Best-Beloved, my captivity and helplessness, and knowest how eagerly I yearn to look upon Thy face. Dispel the gloom that oppresses my heart, with the light of Thy countenance."

" 'I was so overcome with emotion that I seemed to lose consciousness. Suddenly I heard the voice of the Báb, and lo! He was calling me. He bade me: "Arise!" I beheld the majesty of His countenance as He appeared before me. He smiled as He looked into my eyes. I rushed forward and flung myself at His feet. "Rejoice," He said, "the hour is approaching when, in this very city, I shall be suspended before the eyes of the multitude and shall fall a victim to the fire of the enemy. I shall choose no one except you to share with Me the cup of martyrdom. Rest assured that this promise which I give you shall be fulfilled."

" 'I was entranced by the beauty of that vision. When I recovered, I found myself immersed in an ocean of joy, a joy the radiance of which all the sorrows of the world could never obscure. That voice keeps ringing in my ears. That vision haunts me both in the daytime and in the night season. The memory of that smile has removed all the loneliness of my confinement.

"'I am firmly convinced,' the young man told me, 'that the hour at which His pledge is to be fulfilled can no longer be delayed.'

"I urged him to be patient and to conceal his emotion. He promised not to divulge his secret and undertook to show the utmost forbearance and kindness toward his stepfather. I assured the stepfather of the boy's willingness to obey, and succeeded in obtaining his release from his confinement.

"That youth continued until the day of his martyrdom to associate in a state of complete serenity and joy with his parents and kinsmen. Such was his behavior towards his friends and relatives that, on the day he laid down his life for his Beloved, the people of Tabríz all wept and bewailed him." [10]

The young man's confidence in his vision never diminished, and the day came at last when he saw the Báb with his own eyes in the barracks courtyard. He flung himself at His feet, looked up at that wondrous smile he knew so well, and heard the Báb fulfill His promise with the words: "Arise, you shall be with Me."

On that last night in His barracks cell, the face of the Báb was aglow with a joy such as had never shone from His face before. Dr. T. K. Cheyne in his account of the Báb writes: "We learn that, at great points in his career . . . such radiance of might and majesty streamed from his countenance that none could bear to look upon the effulgence of his glory and beauty. Nor was it an uncommon occurrence for unbelievers to bow down in lowly obeisance on beholding His holiness." [11]

Siyyid Husayn has left the following eye-witness account of the Báb's last night on earth:

"Indifferent to the storm that raged about Him, He conversed with us with gaiety and cheerfulness. The sorrows that had weighed so heavily upon Him seemed to have completely vanished.

"'Tomorrow,' He said, 'will be the day of My martyrdom. Would that one of you might now arise and, with his own hands, end My life. I prefer to be slain by the hand of a friend than by that of the enemy.'

"We shrank, however, at the thought of taking away with our own hands so precious a life. We refused, and remained silent. The young boy suddenly sprang to his feet and announced himself ready to obey whatever the Báb might desire. 'This same youth, who has risen to comply with My wish,' the Báb declared, 'will together with Me suffer martyrdom. Him will I choose to share with Me its crown.' " [12]

Early the next morning, the chief-attendant came to the barracks to conduct the Báb into the presence of the leading doctors of law in Tabríz. They were to authorize His execution by signing a death-warrant, thus relieving the Prime Minister of the entire responsibility.

The Báb was engaged in a confidential conversation with Siyyid Husayn, one of His closest followers, who had been serving as His secretary. Husayn had been with the Báb throughout His imprisonment. The Báb was giving him last minute instructions.

"Confess not your Faith," the Báb advised Husayn. "Thereby you will be enabled, when the hour comes, to convey to those who are destined to hear you, the things of which you alone are aware."

The Báb was thus engaged when the chief-attendant arrived. He insisted upon the Báb's immediate departure. The Báb turned and rebuked the chief-attendant severely.

"Not until I have said to him all those things I wish to say," the Báb warned, "can any earthly power silence me. Though all the world be armed against Me, yet shall they be powerless to deter Me from fulfilling, to the last word, My intention."

The chief-attendant was amazed at such a bold speech on the part of a prisoner. However, he still insisted that the Báb accompany him with no further delay. The conversation with Husayn was left unfinished.

The Báb and the eighteen-year-old boy who was to die with Him were led, one by one, into the presence of each of three doctors of law. The guards made certain that the irons about the neck and wrists were secure. To the iron collar about the Báb's neck they tied a long cord which was held by another attendant. Then, so that everyone could see Him in His humiliation, they walked Him about the town. They led Him through the streets and the bazaars, overwhelming Him with blows and insults.[18] He was paraded publicly, as Christ had been, an object of derision.

To the people of Tabríz the Báb was no longer triumphant. He was to die. He was being humbled and degraded just as the Prime Minister had planned. The crowds packed the streets along which he was led. The people climbed upon each other's shoulders the better to see this Personage Who was so much talked about. What a pity He was so powerless, they said. Quite obviously this could not be a Man of God, and certainly not the Promised One.

The followers of the Báb who were in the crowd scattered in all directions. They were trying to arouse among the onlookers a feeling of pity or sympathy which might help them save their Master.

Jesus had entered Jerusalem hailed on all sides, with palm leaves strewn in His path, only to be mocked and reviled in that same Jerusalem within the week. In like manner the glory that had attended the Báb's first triumphant entry into Tabríz was now forgotten. This time the crowd, restless and excitable, flung insulting words at Him. They wanted to be entertained with miracles and signs of wonder, and the Báb was failing them. They pursued Him as He was led through the streets. They broke through the guards and struck Him in the face. When some missile hurled from the crowd would reach its mark, the guards and the crowd would burst into laughter.

The Báb was then brought before the priest who had previously incited the clergy to scourge Him. As soon as he saw the Báb approaching, he seized the death-warrant and thrust it at the attendant.

"No need to bring him into my presence," he cried. "This death-warrant I signed long ago, the very day I saw him at that gathering here in Tabríz. He is the same man I saw then, and has not since surrendered any of his claims. Take him away!"

The other priests in turn also refused to meet the Báb face to face. Their hatred of Him had increased since the day of His previous triumph over them.

"We are satisfied that it is right to pronounce the sentence of death," they said. "Do not bring him into our presence."

The chief-attendant, having secured the necessary death-warrants, delivered the Báb into the hands of Sam Khán, the leader of the regiment that was to execute Him.

Sam Khán found himself increasingly affected by the behavior of his Captive. He had placed a guard of ten soldiers about the Báb's cell door and had carefully supervised it himself. Throughout every step he felt an increasing attraction to this unusual Prisoner. He was in constant fear that his action in taking such a holy life might bring upon him the wrath of God. Finally, unable to bear this worry any longer, he approached the Báb and spoke to Him privately.

"I profess the Christian Faith," he said, "and entertain no ill-will against you. If your Cause be the Cause of Truth, then enable me to free myself from the obligation to shed your blood."

The Báb comforted him with these words: "Follow your instructions and if your intention be sincere, the Almighty is surely able to relieve you from your perplexity."

The hour for the execution could not be put off any longer. The crowds had been gathering for some time. They streamed into the public square. They came from all the neighboring villages.

Sam Khán ordered his men to drive a nail into the pillar between the doors of the barracks. To the nail they made fast the ropes by which the Báb and His young companion were to be separately suspended. Thus was fulfilled before the eyes of the people gazing upon the scene, the words of the prophecy in their own sacred Writings which foretold that when the Promised One was slain, He would be suspended like unto Christ before the gaze of the public. Muhammad-'Alí begged Sam Khán to allow him to be placed in such a manner that his own body would shield that of the Báb. He was eventually suspended so that his head rested upon the breast of the Báb.

The *Journal Asiatique's* account of that event states: "The Báb remained silent. His pale handsome face . . . his appearance and his refined manners, his white delicate hands, his simple but very neat garments—everything about him awakened sympathy and compassion." [14]

About ten thousand people had crowded into the public square. They were thronged on the roofs of the adjoining houses as well. All were eager to witness the spectacle. Yet each person was willing to change from an enemy into a friend at the least sign of power from the Báb. They were still hungry for drama, and He was disappointing them. Just as the crowd had stood on Golgotha, reviling Jesus, wagging their heads and saying, "Save thyself! If thou be the Son of God, come down from the cross!" so, too, did the people of Tabríz mock the Báb and jeer at His seeming impotence.

As soon as the Báb and His companion were fastened to the pillar, the regiment of soldiers arranged itself in three files, each file having two hundred and fifty men.

The leader of the regiment, Sam Khán, could delay the command no longer. The Báb had told him to do his duty; therefore, it was apparently the will of God that his regiment should take the life of the Báb. This was a source of great sorrow to him.

Reluctantly he gave the command, "Fire!"

In turn, each of the files opened fire upon the Báb and His companion until the entire regiment had discharged its volley of bullets.

There were over ten thousand eye-witnesses to the electrifying spectacle that followed. One of the historical accounts of that staggering moment states:

"The smoke of the firing of the seven hundred and fifty rifles was such as to turn the light of noonday sun into darkness.

"As soon as the cloud of smoke had cleared away, an astounded multitude looked upon a scene which their eyes could scarcely believe.

"There, standing before them, alive and unhurt, was the companion of the Báb, whilst He, Himself, had vanished from their sight. Though the cords with which they were suspended had been rent in pieces by the bullets, yet their bodies had miraculously escaped the volleys." [15]

Cries of astonishment, confusion and fear rang out from the bewildered multitude.

"The Báb has vanished!"

"He is freed!" they shrieked.

"It is a miracle! He was a man of God!"

"They are slaying a man of God!"

An intense clamor arose on all sides. The crowd was already dangerous. The public square became a bedlam as a frantic search for the Báb began.

M. C. Huart, a French author who wrote of this episode, says: "The soldiers in order to quiet the excitement of the crowd which, being extremely agitated, was quite ready to believe the claims of a religion which thus demonstrated its truth, showed the cords broken by the bullets, implying that no miracle had really taken place." [16]

"Look!" their actions implied. "The seven hundred and fifty musket-balls have shattered the ropes into fragments. This is what freed them. It is nothing more than this. It is no miracle."

Uproars and shouts continued on all sides. The people still were not certain themselves what really had happened.

M. C. Huart, giving his view of that astonishing event, states: "Amazing to believe, the bullets had not struck the condemned but, on the contrary, had broken the bonds and he was delivered. It was a real miracle."

A. L. M. Nicolas also wrote of this episode, saying: "An extraordinary thing happened, unique in the annals of the history of humanity: the bullets cut the cords that held the Báb and he fell on his feet without a scratch." [17]

The frenzied search by the authorities for the Báb came to an end within but a few feet of the execution post. They found Him back in His cell in the barracks, in the same room He had occupied the night before. He was completing His conversation with His secretary, Siyyid Husayn. He was giving to him those final instructions which had been interrupted that morning. An expression of unruffled calm was upon His face. His body, obviously, had emerged unscathed from the shower of bullets.

The Báb looked at the chief-attendant and smiled.

"I have finished My conversation," He said. "You may now proceed to fulfill your duty."

The chief-attendant was much too disturbed to resume his duties. He recalled vividly the words with which the Báb had rebuked him when he had interrupted that conversation: "Though all the world be armed against Me, yet shall they be powerless to deter Me from fulfilling, to the last word, My intention."

The chief-attendant refused to continue with any part of the execution. He left the scene of that barracks cell shaken to the core of his being. He resigned his post and cut himself off from the enemies of the Báb forever.

The head of the Christian regiment, Sam Khán, was likewise stunned by what had taken place. He, too, remembered clearly the words which the Báb had spoken to him: "If your intention be sincere, the Almighty is surely able to relieve you from your perplexity." Sam Khán had given the order to fire, yet the Báb had been freed. Surely the Lord had delivered him from the need to shed the blood of this Holy Man. He would not go on with the execution. Sam Khán ordered his regiment to leave the barracks square immediately. He told the authorities plainly that he was finished with this unjust act.

"I refuse," he said, "ever again to associate myself and my regiment with any act which involves the least injury to the Báb." As he marched his regiment out of the public square he swore before all of them: "I will never again resume this task even if it costs me my life."

After the departure of Sam Khán and his regiment, a colonel of the bodyguard volunteered to carry out the execution.

On that same wall and to that same nail, the Báb and His companion were lashed a second time. The new firing squad formed in line. As the regiment prepared to fire the final volley, the Báb spoke His last words to the gazing multitude.

"Had you believed in Me, O wayward generation," He said, "everyone of you would have followed the example of this youth who stood in rank above most of you, and willingly would have sacrificed himself in My path. The day will come when you will have recognized Me, but that day I shall have ceased to be with you."

A dread silence fell over the square. In the ominous hush, the only sound was the metallic click of rifles being readied to fire. The crowd stirred restlessly. The rifles were raised, the command given, and the rifles thundered. The bodies of the Báb and His youthful companion were shattered by the blast.

As Jesus had expired on the cross so that men might be called back to God, so did the Báb breathe His last against a barracks wall in the city of Tabríz, Persia.

The historian Nicolas in his account of those hours writes, "Christians believe that if Jesus had wished to come down from the cross he could have done so easily; he died of his own free will because it was written that he should and in order that the prophecies might be fulfilled. The same is true of the Báb so [His followers] say . . . He likewise died voluntarily because his death was to be the salvation of humanity. Who will ever tell us the words that the Báb uttered in the midst of the unprecedented turmoil which broke out. . . . who will ever know the memories which stirred his noble soul?" [18]

Christ in His agony in the garden of Gethsemane cried out, "Father! if Thou be willing, remove this cup from me: nevertheless, not my will, but Thine, be done." [19] The Báb in the frozen winter of Máh-Kú likewise called out to mankind that it was God's will and not His own that impelled Him to "throw Himself headlong into that ocean of superstition and hatred which was fatally to engulf Him." Both Christ and the Báb uttered the same words of warning, "O wayward generation!"

The martyrdom of the Báb took place at noon on Sunday, July 9, 1850, thirty years from the time of His birth in Shíráz.

An historical account of that second and final volley states: "This time the execution was effective. . . . But the crowd, vividly impressed by the spectacle they had witnessed, dispersed slowly, hardly convinced that the Báb was a criminal." [20]

On the evening of the day of His martyrdom, the mangled bodies of the Báb and His companion were removed from the courtyard of the public square. They were thrown at the edge of a moat outside the gate of the city. Four companies of ten sentinels each were posted to keep watch in turn over the remains so that none of His followers might claim them.

On the morning following the martyrdom, an official from one of the foreign consulates, accompanied by an artist, went to the moat and ordered that a sketch be made of the remains. Nabíl, in his history, gives the words of an eye-witness, "It was such a faithful portrait of the Báb! . . . No bullet had struck His forehead, His cheeks, or His lips. I gazed upon a smile which seemed to be still lingering upon his countenance." [21]

On the afternoon of the second day, Sulaymán Khán, a follower of the Báb, arrived from Tihrán. He had heard of the threat to the life of the Báb and had left Tihrán to try to rescue Him. To his dismay, he arrived too late. He resolved to rescue the bodies of the Báb and His companion in spite of the sentinels, and no matter what the risk to his own life.

In the middle of that same night, with the help of a friend, he succeeded in bearing away the bodies. The two friends watched the sentinels carefully. The hearts of the guards were not in the task of standing watch through a long night; so while they slept, Sulaymán Khán and his friend stole the sacred remains, and carried them from the edge of the moat to a silk factory owned by one of the believers. The remains were placed the next day in a specially constructed wooden case and were hidden in a place of safety.

The sentinels awakened, and finding their trust had been spirited away, sought to justify themselves by pretending that while they slept wild beasts had carried away the bodies. Their superiors also concealed the truth and did not report it to the authorities for fear of losing their own positions.

This pleased the followers of the Báb, who were anxious to prevent any further investigation which might take from them those blessed remains.

Meanwhile, from the pulpits of Tabríz, the religious leaders boastfully proclaimed that the Báb's remains had been devoured by wild animals.

"This proves us right and him false," they cried out. "For it is written in our prophecies that the holy body of the Promised One will be preserved from beasts of prey and from all creeping things."

Nicolas in his history says, "The most reliable testimony of the actual witnesses of the drama and of its actors does not leave me any doubt that the body of [the Báb] was carried away by pious hands and, at last . . . received a burial worthy of him." [22]

Sulaymán Khán reported the rescue of the remains of the Báb to Bahá'u'lláh in Tihrán. Bahá'u'lláh immediately sent a special messenger to Tabríz to arrange for the bodies to be transferred to the capital.

"This decision," Nabíl tells us, "was prompted by the wish of the Báb Himself."

In His own handwriting, the Báb had expressed the desire to be buried near His Loved One. In a letter written in the neighborhood of a shrine near Tihrán, Nabíl says that the Báb addressed the saint buried there in words such as these: "Well is it with you to have found your resting place . . . under the shadow of My Beloved. Would that I might be entombed within the precincts of that holy ground." [23]

Bahá'u'lláh respected that wish by having the remains of the Báb transferred to that very spot! * But the place remained secret until Bahá'u'lláh's departure from Persia.

The hand of the wrath of God began, almost at once, to strike down those primarily responsible for the martyrdom of the Báb. That same lack of mercy which had been shown to those who had injured Him throughout His life was now visited upon the last of His persecutors.

The governor of Shíráz, who first imprisoned the Báb, was hurled from power and abandoned by friend and foe alike. The high priest, or judge, who had scourged Him, was stricken with paralysis and died an agonizing death. The king, Muhammad Sháh, who had

* See Appendix, Note Five.

refused to meet the Báb, was struck down by illness and succumbed to a complication of maladies far before his time. His Prime Minister, Hájí Mírzá Áqásí, who had twice banished Him to prison, was toppled from power and died in poverty and exile.

The mayor of Tihrán, Mahmúd Khán, who held prisoner Táhirih and the seven martyrs of Tihrán and assisted in their deaths, was strangled and hanged from the gallows.

The new ruler, Nasiri'd-Dín Sháh, who permitted the slaying of the Báb, was awaiting a day of assassination which was to be far more dreadful and dramatic than that of his father.

His Prime Minister, Mírzá Táqí Khán, who ordered the Báb's execution, and who encouraged the wholesale slaughter of so many of His followers, was seized in the grip of this same relentless, punishing retribution. His greatest crime was the taking of the life of the Báb. His greatest massacre was that which took place in Zanján after the martyrdom of the Báb. Eighteen hundred were slain in Zanján village alone. Although the soldiers had promised on their honor to spare the followers of Hujjat who willingly came out of their shelters, they lined them up in rows, to the accompaniment of drums and trumpets, and pierced them with bayonets. Then the victorious army forced those of high standing who were left to march on foot before their horses all the way to Tihrán with chains about their necks and shackles on their feet. When they appeared before the Prime Minister, Mírzá Táqí Khán, he ordered that the veins of three leaders be slashed open. He would make an example of them, he said, as he had made of the Báb.

The victims did not betray the least fear or emotion. They told the Prime Minister that the lack of good faith which the authorities, the army, and himself had been guilty of was a crime which Almighty God would not be satisfied with punishing in an ordinary way. God would demand, they told him, a more impressive and striking retribution for the slayer of a Prophet and the persecutor of His people. They prophesied that the Prime Minister, himself, would very soon suffer the very same death which he, in his hatred, was now inflicting upon them.

Gobineau in his history says, "The only thing I can affirm . . . is that I was given assurance that the prophecy had really been made by the martyrs of Zanján." [24]

It happened precisely as those victims had foretold. Mírzá Táqí Khán fell from the favor of the king. Court intrigue and greed combined to complete his downfall. All the honors he had enjoyed were stripped from him. He had to flee in disgrace from the capital. Wherever he went he was pursued by royal hatred. Finally the hand of revenge caught up with him. The former Prime Minister's veins were slashed open. His blood stains the wall of that bath of the Palace of Fin to this very day, a witness to the atrocities his own hand had wrought.[25]

The wave of retributive justice was still not at an end. Mírzá Hasan Khán, the Prime Minister's brother, who carried out the execution of the Báb, was subjected to a dreadful punishment. No one would come to his aid. In despair, he succumbed and died.

The commander of the regiment that volunteered to replace that of Sam Khán lost his life during the bombardment of Muhammirih by the British. The regiment itself came to a dreadful end. In spite of the unaccountable failure of Sam Khán and his soldiers to destroy the life of the Báb, this regiment was willing to renew the attempt, and did eventually riddle His body with bullets. Two hundred and fifty of its members, that same year, with their officers, were crushed in a terrible earthquake. They were resting on a hot summer's day under the shadow of a wall, between Tabríz and Ardibíl. The structure suddenly collapsed and fell upon them, leaving not one survivor.[26]

The remaining five hundred members of the regiment suffered an ever more dramatic fate. They were executed by a firing squad. Thus they met the same indentical fate as that which their hands had inflicted upon the Báb. Three years after His martyrdom, that regiment mutinied. The authorities ordered that all of its members should be mercilessly shot. Significantly, there was not only one volley, but, as in the case of the Báb, a second volley was fired to make sure that none survived. Then their bodies were pierced with spears and lances. Their remains were left exposed to the gaze of the public as had been the bodies of the Báb and His companion.

This event caused much concern and whispering in Tabríz.

"Is this not the regiment that destroyed the Báb?" the people asked each other. "They have been overtaken by the same fate. Could it be the vengeance of God that has now brought the whole regiment to so dishonorable an end?"

When the leading lawyers overheard these misgivings and doubts they were alarmed. They issued a warning stating that all who expressed such thoughts would be severely punished. To demonstrate their anger they made an example of a few of the people. Some were fined and some were beaten. All were warned under threat of further punishment to cease such talk at once.

"It can only revive the memory of a terrible adversary," they were told.

History records that from the very hour that the volley of bullets was fired at the Báb, "a gale of exceptional severity arose and swept over the whole city. A whirlwind of dust of incredible density obscured the light of the sun and blinded the eyes of the people." The city of Tabríz remained wrapped in that fearful darkness from noon until night.

This was the hour promised in the Old Testament in the Book of Amos Who said: "And it shall come to pass in that day, saith the Lord God, that I will cause the sun to go down at noon, and I will darken the sky on a clear day." [27]

The "lamb" had been slain just as it was promised in the Revelation of St. John. The events that soon took place in the city of the Báb's birth were also foreshadowed in that Book: "And the same hour there was a great earthquake, and the tenth part of the city fell, and in the earthquake were slain men seven thousand."

A written account of the period following the execution of the Báb states:

"This earthquake occurred in Shíráz after the martyrdom of the Báb. The city was in a turmoil, and many people were destroyed. Great agitation also took place through diseases, cholera, dearth, scarcity, famine, and afflictions, the like of which had never been known." [28]

The prophecies and promises of Christ were fulfilled with the coming of the Báb, although the religious leaders turned to them a blind eye and a deaf ear. These religious authorities, as testified to by the introduction to the most authentic history of the Báb, "confidently expected that the promised Advent would not substitute a new and richer revelation for the old, but would endorse and fortify the system of which they were the functionaries. It would enhance incalculably their personal prestige, would extend their authority far and wide among the nations, and would win for them the reluctant but abject homage of mankind. When the Báb proclaimed a new code of religious law, and by precept and example instituted a profound moral and spiritual reform, the priests immediately scented mortal danger. They saw their monopoly undermined, their ambitions threatened, their own lives and conduct put to shame. They rose against Him in sanctimonious indignation."

"The cause of the rejection and persecution of the Báb," this historical analysis continues, "was in its essence the same as that of the rejection and persecution of the Christ. If Jesus had not brought a New Book, if He had not only reiterated the spiritual principles taught by Moses but had continued Moses' rules and regulations too, He might as merely a moral reformer have escaped the vengeance of the Scribes and Pharisees. But to claim that any part of the Mosaic law, even such material ordinances as those dealing with divorce and the keeping of the Sabbath, could be altered—and altered by an unordained preacher from the village of Nazareth—this was to threaten the interests of the Scribes and the Pharisees themselves, and since they were the representatives of Moses and of God, it was blasphemy against the Most High. As soon as the position of Jesus was understood, His persecution began. As He refused to desist, He was put to death.

"For reasons exactly parallel, the Báb was from the beginning opposed." [29]

There is but one parallel in all recorded history to the brief turbulent ministry of the Báb. It is the passion of Jesus Christ. There is a remarkable similarity in the distinguishing features of Their careers. Their youthfulness and meekness; the dramatic swiftness with which each ministry moved toward its climax; the boldness with which They challenged the time-honored conventions, laws, and rites of the religions into which They had been born; the role which the religious leaders played as chief instigators of the outrages They were made to suffer; the indignities heaped upon Them; the suddenness of Their arrest; the interrogations to which They were subjected; the scourgings inflicted upon Them; Their passing first in triumph, then in suffering through the streets of the city where They were to be slain; Their public parade through the streets on the way to the place of martyrdom; Their words of hope and promise to a companion who was also to die with Them; the darkness that enveloped the land in the hour of Their martyrdom; and finally Their ignominious suspension before the gaze of a hostile multitude.

"So momentous an event could hardly fail to arouse widespread and keen interest even beyond the confines of the land in which it occurred." [30]

One particularly moving document on the Báb points out: "This illustrious soul arose with such power that he shook the supports of the religion, of the morals, the conditions, the habits, and the customs of Persia, and instituted new rules, new laws, and a new religion. Though the great personages of State, nearly all of the clergy and the public men arose to destroy and annihilate him, he alone withstood them and moved the whole of Persia." [31]

"Many persons from all parts of the world," one writer states, "set out for Persia and began to investigate wholeheartedly the matter."

A noted French publicist testifies: "All Europe was stirred to pity and indignation." "Among the littérateurs of my generation in the Paris of 1890," he said, "the martyrdom of the Báb was still as fresh a topic as had been the first news of his death. We wrote poems about him. Sarah Bernhardt entreated Catulle Mendès for a play on the theme of this historic tragedy." [32]

A drama was published in 1903 entitled "The Báb" and was played in one of the leading theatres of St. Petersburg. The drama was publicized in London and was translated into French in Paris and into German by the poet Fiedler. [33]

M. J. Balteau in a lecture on the Faith of the Báb quotes M. Vambery's words spoken in the French Academy, words which testify to the depth and power of the Báb's teachings. The Báb, he states, "has expressed doctrines worthy of the greatest thinkers." [34]

The famous Cambridge scholar, Edward Granville Browne, wrote: "Who can fail to be attracted by the gentle spirit of [the Báb]? His sorrowful and persecuted life, his purity of conduct and youth; his courage and uncomplaining patience under misfortune . . . but most of all his tragic death, all serve to enlist our sympathies on behalf of the young Phophet of Shíráz." [35]

"That Jesus of the age . . . a prophet and more than a prophet," is the judgement passed by the distinguished English clergyman, Dr. T. K. Cheyne. "His combination of mildness and power is so rare," he states, "that we have to place him in a line with supernormal men." [36]

Sir Francis Younghusband in his book *The Gleam* has written: "The story of the Báb . . . was the story of spiritual heroism unsurpassed . . . The Báb's passionate sincerity could not be doubted, for he had given his life for his faith. And that there must be something in his message that appealed to men and satisfied their souls was witnessed to by the fact that thousands gave their lives in his cause and millions now follow him . . . his life must be one of those events in the last hundred years which is really worth study." [37]

The French historian, A. L. M. Nicolas, wrote: "His life is one of the most magnificent examples of courage which it has been the privilege of mankind to behold . . . He sacrificed himself for humanity, for it he gave his body and his soul, for it he endured privations, insults, torture and martyrdom. He sealed, with his very lifeblood, the covenant of universal brotherhood. Like Jesus, he paid with his life for the proclamation of a reign of concord, equity and brotherly love. More than anyone, he knew what dreadful dangers he was heaping upon himself . . . but all these considerations could not weaken his resolve. Fear had no hold upon his soul and, perfectly calm, never looking back, in full possession of all his powers, he walked into the furnace." [38]

At last the clergy and the state prided themselves on having crushed the life from the Cause they had battled so long. The Báb was no more. His chief disciples were destroyed. The mass of His followers throughout the land had been beaten, exhausted, and silenced.

The King and the Prime Minister rejoiced. If they were to believe their counsellors, they would never hear of the Báb again. His Faith was swiftly receding into oblivion and the wings of death were hovering over it. The combined forces which had engulfed it on every side had at last put out the light which the young Prince of Glory had kindled in His land.

Yet, at that very moment in a suburb of the capital, Bahá'u'lláh was receiving a visitor, a friend who was soon to be the new Prime Minister.

He told Bahá'u'lláh: "The Báb has been slain. He has been put to death in Tabríz. It is all over. At last the fire which I feared might engulf and destroy you has been extinguished."

Bahá'u'lláh replied: "If this be true, you can be certain that the flame that has been kindled will by this very act, blaze forth more fiercely than ever and will set up a conflagration such as the combined forces of the statesmen of this realm will be powerless to quench." [39]

Gobineau echoes this statement, recording in his history that "instead of appeasing the flames, it had fanned them into greater violence." [40]

Judged by the standards of the world, the life of Christ had been a catastrophic failure. Of His chosen disciples one had betrayed Him, another had denied Him, and only a handful stood at the foot of the cross. Centuries were to pass before the world ever heard of His name. Judged by the standards of the same world, the life of the ill-fated Youth of Shíráz appeared to be one of the saddest and most fruitless in history. The work He had so gloriously conceived and so heroically undertaken, seemed to have ended in a colossal disaster.

Swift as a meteor that short heroic career had flashed across the skies of Persia. Now death had plunged it into the darkness of despair. This was but the last in the series of heartbreaks which had beset His path from the beginning.

At the very outset of His career, the Báb went to Mecca, the heart of Islám, to proclaim publicly His Mission. He was treated to icy indifference. He planned to return to the city of Karbilá and establish His Cause. His arrest prevented it. The program He outlined for His chosen disciples was for the most part unfulfilled. The moderation He urged them to observe was forgotten in the first flush of enthusiasm that seized the early pioneers of His Faith. His only chance of meeting the king was dashed to the ground by the Prime Minister. His ablest disciples were struck down one after the other. The flower of His followers was slain in ruthless carnage all across the land. Then followed His own martyrdom. All these events, on the surface so humiliating, would seem to have marked the lowest depths to which His Cause had fallen. They seemed to threaten the virtual extinction of all His hopes.

Yet burning like a flame through the darkness of all these setbacks and sufferings was the Báb's constant promise that before the year nine would pass, the Promised One of all religions would appear.* There was never a moment of doubt in His teaching. He was only the Herald of a greater One to come. He knew that the

* See Appendix, Note Six.

seed had been firmly planted in the fields and meadows of human hearts. He was the Dawn, the Sun was yet to come.

Of all those great figures who loved Him so dearly not one soul was left alive save Bahá'u'lláh, Who with His family and a handful of devoted followers was driven destitute into exile and prison in a foreign land.[41] He was banished from place to place until He reached the "Mountain of God" in Israel, the Holy Land. Bahá'u'lláh was exiled, a prisoner, to the fortress situated on the plain of 'Akká, and those startling words of the prophecy given several hundred years before about the "last days" of the Twin Messengers were literally fulfilled: "All of them [the companions of the Herald] shall be slain except One Who shall reach the plain of 'Akká, the banquet Hall of God." [42]

Although the Faith of God had been crushed into the ground at an early age and rudely trampled upon, this very process would bring about its germination. Buried in the earth, warmed by the blood of Its martyrs, His Faith would blossom out in glory at a later date with the brightness of the sun, and would fulfill prophecy with the exactness of the stars.

The Dawn would give way to the Sun, and the era promised to the earth since the beginning of time, the Day of the "One fold and the One shepherd" * would be ushered in by the sacrifice of that gentle Youth from Shíráz: the Báb, the Gate of God.

* See Appendix, Note Seven.

APPENDIX

APPENDIX

NOTE ONE

The period in history from the years 1830 to 1850 was one of strange and troublesome events. Men stared in wonder and uneasiness at the great halo that circled the sun. They looked up in horror at the night sky where a giant comet with a fiery tail rushed through the darkness. It was whispered that the comet was racing toward mankind bringing the "end of the world."

In America, Europe, Asia and Africa, there were men warning the people to prepare for the return of Jesus, for the second coming of Christ.

Wolf in Asia, Sir Edward Irving in England, Mason in Scotland, Davis in South Carolina, William Miller in Pennsylvania, and many others throughout the world agreed that this was indeed the "time of the end." [1] Christ, they said, would soon appear. Leonard Heinrich Kelber and his fellow Christians in Germany confidently awaited the coming of Christ during this same period. This millennial zeal reached its climax in the year 1844.

An historical account of those days states: "A converted Jew in Palestine, Joseph Wolf, predicted the Advent for 1847. Harriet Livermore, an eloquent and arresting woman of the time, who figures in Whittier's *Snowbound,* preached the Second Coming everywhere, including the House of Representatives at Washington where crowds gathered to hear her. Lady Hester Stanhope, the valiant madwoman, niece of William Pitt, who turned her back on

London and power and fashion, made her home in Lebanon among the Arabs and Druses, in order to be ready and near to the scene of the Advent. She kept, it was reported, two white Arab steeds in her stable, one for the Messiah, one for herself! So real was the hope of the Advent (Christ's "coming"), people were actually taking almost violent measures for it. It was the nineteenth century, yet the shooting stars of the year 1833, and the parahelia, or halo-like rings, around the sun in 1843, were objects of the most awesome speculation and discussion. And the tail of the great comet of 1843 measured 108 million miles in length. . . . Whole families were engaged in making shrouds against that fateful day." [2]

Some of the more zealous went so far as to sell their possessions and to await Christ's descent upon the clouds. Their more practical neighbors pointed out that clouds did not descend but were vapors that rose up from the earth. Others quoted St. Augustine who had written an entire volume proving that there could not be anyone living on the other side of the earth because it would be impossible for such people to see Christ when He came down on the day of His return. Mathematicians tried to calculate how many hundreds of thousands of "solo" flights it would be necessary for the Messiah to make before all humanity could see Him due to the curvature of the earth. It was reported that shops in some of the eastern cities of America advertised special "ascension robes" for the coming event.

When the great comet streaked across the heavens in 1843, it was believed to be an omen for the hour of Christ's return. In that same year, the poet James Russell Lowell wrote:

> Once to every man and nation comes the moment to decide.
> Some great Cause, God's new Messiah . . .[3]

On May 24, 1844 in Washington D. C., Mr. Samuel F. B. Morse, the inventor of the telegraph, stepped to the keyboard of his new instrument. He was about to send the first official telegram in history flashing along the wires from Washington to Baltimore. The press had heralded this day as a modern miracle. By this invention the world would soon be united physically in the twinkling of an eye, they said.

The scholars of Scripture asked: Is this not still another proof that the hour has come for Christ's appearance? Is it not written in the Book of Job that only God can send "lightnings that they may go and say unto thee here we are!" [4] Was not this electric telegraph of

Morse the "lightnings" spoken of by which the "Word" would go?

Morse put his hand to the keyboard and tapped out the message. It was a message chosen from the Bible, from the Book of Numbers: "What hath God wrought?" [5]

The evening before, May 23, 1844 in Shíráz, Persia, the Bahá'í Faith began. The Báb proclaimed Himself to Mullá Husayn as the One foretold in all the holy Books of the past. This day, He said, was the beginning of the fulfillment of all the holy Scriptures.

The Báb arose in a Muslim country, whose people in their holy writings had the unmistakable prophecy which said that the Messenger of God would come when by "beating the iron upon the iron, you will hear the news from a far distance."

The Báb was a descendant of Abraham. He was of the "seed" which would "inherit the earth." The message of Morse had quoted only a part of the verse from Numbers. The full verse is: "According to this time it shall be said of Jacob and of Israel *what hath God wrought?*"

Why did so many Bible scholars from all parts of the world agree upon the years between 1843-1845 as the time for the return of Christ? Careful research makes it clear that they chose this time in history because of three very plain and specific promises given by Christ Himself foretelling the hour of His second coming.

Christ assured His disciples that He would return to earth when the following three things took place:

1. When His Gospel shall be preached throughout the world.
2. When the "times of the Gentiles" is fulfilled and the Jews return to Israel (Palestine).
3. When all mankind would see the "abomination of desolation" foretold by Daniel the Prophet.

FIRST PROMISE: When the Gospel of Christ is taught "in all the world," then He will return. This promise was made by Christ in direct reply to a question asked by His disciples: "Tell us, when shall these things be? and what shall be the sign of Thy coming, and of the end of the world?"

Christ gave His promise in the following words: "But he that shall endure unto the end, the same shall be saved. And this Gospel of the Kingdom shall be preached in all the world for a witness; then shall the end come." [6]

A study of the spread of Christianity made by these scholars of the 1840's convinced them that the message of Christ had already well-circled the globe. It was being taught in all the continents. By 1844 it was being taught not by solitary missionaries, but on a wide and organized scale, even in the interior of Africa. A commercial history of East Africa states: "Christian missions began their activities amongst the African people in 1844." [7]

The Gospel of Christ had now been "preached in all the world for a witness" and therefore, these scholars had reasoned, the hour of His coming was at hand.

Thus the first promise of Christ was fulfilled by the year 1844.

SECOND PROMISE: When the "times of the Gentiles" is fulfilled and the Jews return to Israel, Christ will come back to earth. Christ gave this promise in answer to the questions of His disciples. They asked Him: "When shall these things be? and what sign will there be when these things shall come to pass?" [8]

He gave them His promise in the following words: "And they shall fall by the edge of the sword, and shall be led away captive into all nations: and Jerusalem shall be trodden down of the Gentiles, until the times of the Gentiles be fulfilled . . . and then shall they see the Son of Man coming in a cloud with power and great glory." [9]

The meaning of the term "times of the Gentiles" was very clear to these scholars of Scripture. It denoted that period of time during which Jerusalem would be held by the power of aliens, non-Jews (Gentiles), and during which the Jews themselves would be banished from their homeland.

The "times of the Gentiles" would be fulfilled, therefore, when the Jews came back to their homeland following this banishment.

The first part of Christ's promise came true almost immediately. His words, "they shall be led away captive into all nations" began its fulfillment less than forty years after His crucifixion. Jerusalem was destroyed by the Roman Titus in 70 A.D. and the Jews were exiled.

The Jews tried to regain their freedom in 132 A.D. under Bar Kochba but were crushed by the armies of the Roman Emperor Hadrian. This time Jerusalem was devastated even more completely than it had been by Titus. The site of the city was ploughed under and a new city named in honor of Hadrian was built upon the ruins. The Jews were banished. Many of them, exactly as had been foretold by Christ, fell "by the edge of the sword." They fled, scattered, and were "led away captive into all nations." [10]

The Romans were the first aliens after the time of Christ to trample down the city of Jerusalem. Then came the Persians and the Muslims. The latter conquered Jerusalem in 637 A.D. During the period of occupation by the Muslims, the Jews were rigidly excluded from their homeland.

The famous Irish scholar and author, George Townshend, former Canon of St. Patrick's Cathedral, Dublin, and Archdeacon of Clonfert, writes: "The strict exclusion of the Jews from their own land enforced by the Muslims for some twelve centuries was at last relaxed by the Edict of Toleration and the 'times of the Gentiles' were fulfilled."

Townshend goes on to point out that this document, the Edict of Toleration, was issued by the governing authorities in the year 1844.[11] *

There is a strong confirmation to be found in the Bible itself that 1844 was the year intended for the fulfillment of Christ's promise concerning the "times of the Gentiles." This confirmation is given in the Book of Revelation, chapter eleven:

> "And the Holy City [Jerusalem] shall they trod under foot for forty and two months, until the times of the Gentiles is fulfilled." [12]

This period of forty-two months is expressed in the very next verse in the form: 1260 days. Bible scholars found this period of forty-two months or 1260 days to be identical with the year 1844. They arrived at this conclusion by the following process of reasoning:

1. In the study of biblical prophecy, the period called a "day" becomes a "year" when calculating the passing of time.
2. This theory is supported by the following prophecies:
   (A) Numbers 14:34—"Even forty days, each day for a year."
   (B) Ezekiel 4:6—"I have appointed thee each day for a year."

---

* This famous scholar discovered the Bahá'í Faith in his studies, and wrote saying that when "modern scholars and statesmen speak of World government, Social Security, an International language, International police force, the United Nations, etc., they are merely ringing the changes on truths set down by Bahá'u'lláh in everlasting language nearly a century ago."

James Henry Foreman in his compilation *The Story of Prophecy* writes: ". . . Biblical prophecy students, after a scrutiny of the entire problem of Bible chronology, deduce the following conclusions as virtually axiomatic—namely, that—(1) In symbolic prophecy a day is the symbol of a year." [13]

By using the accepted formula of a "day" for a "year," forty-two months or 1260 days become 1260 years. Therefore, the "times of the Gentiles" would last for 1260 years.

The Muslims conquered Jerusalem in the seventh century, and according to the promise of Christ, they would tread the city underfoot until the hour of His return, which would be 1260 years later by the measurement of prophecy.

A study of the calendar of the Muslims reveals that the year 1260 of their calendar is identical with the year 1844 of the Christian calendar.

Thus the second promise of Christ was fulfilled by the year 1844, when the "times of the Gentiles" was ended.

THIRD PROMISE: When mankind witnesses the "abomination of desolation" spoken of by Daniel the Prophet, this will be the hour of Christ's return.

Christ gave this promise to His disciples in direct answer to their questions: When will you come, what shall we look for?

His promise was given in these words: "When ye therefore shall see the abomination of desolation, spoken of by Daniel the Prophet, stand in the holy place (whoso readeth, let him understand)." [14]

This third promise of Christ concerning the "abomination of desolation" is the foundation-stone upon which the biblical scholars rested the structure of their belief in the return of Christ during the 1844 period.

The chapters of Daniel which deal with this subject are those from eight through twelve. These foretell clearly not only the *second* coming of Christ, but His *first* appearance as well. Therefore, this promise of Christ is considered to be the most important of the three.

In these chapters, Daniel prophesies that: From the issuing of the decree to rebuild Jerusalem, until the time when the Messiah shall be cut off (crucified) there are appointed 70 weeks (490 days).[15]

The decree would be issued, the city rebuilt, then Christ would be crucified. This is the clear meaning, foretelling Christ's first coming.

There were four decrees issued to rebuild Jerusalem:

1. Issued by Cyrus in the year 534 B.C. This is recorded in the first chapter of the Book of Ezra. It went unfulfilled.
2. Issued by Darius in the year 519 B.C. This is recorded in the sixth chapter of the Book of Ezra. It also went unfulfilled.
3. Issued by Artaxerxes in the seventh year of his reign in the year 457 B.C. This is recorded in the seventh chapter of the Book of Ezra. It was fulfilled by the fourth decree.
4. Issued by the same Artaxerxes in the year 444 B.C. This is recorded in the second chapter of Nehemiah.

The scholars of Scripture accepted the third decree of Artaxerxes as the one prophesied by Daniel inasmuch as the fourth decree was merely an extension of the third. Therefore, this prophecy of Daniel could now be stated thus:

From the issuing of the decree of Artaxerxes in the year 457 B.C. until the time of the crucifixion of Christ there would be appointed 70 weeks (or 490 days). 70 weeks equal 490 days. By the use of our measure of prophecy, a "day" for a "year," 490 days become 490 years. Therefore, from the issuing of the decree until the crucifixion on Calvary there would be 490 years according to Daniel's prophecy.

It has been clear to scholars that the time of the first coming of Christ was foretold by Daniel with amazing accuracy. No wonder Christ Himself was so emphatic about Daniel's prophecy. What of His second coming? Christ promised that He would return when Daniel's prophecy came to pass.

These are the words spoken by Daniel:

"How long shall be the vision concerning the daily sacrifice, and the abomination of desolation, to give the sanctuary and the host to be trodden under foot? And he said unto me, Unto two thousand three hundred days, then shall the sanctuary be cleansed." [16]

When would this take place? In 2300 days, says Daniel. These 2300 days in our prophetic measure become 2300 years. Using the same frame of reference as that used for Christ's first coming, the biblical scholars made their calculations.

Although many disputes arose as to the exact month, day, and hour, there was a basic agreement among all that Christ's return *must* take place between 1843 and 1845, with the year 1844 as the central point of reference.

One group of Christian scholars worked out Daniel's prophecy in the greatest detail. They even built a special chart to show that Christ would return in the middle of the year 1844.[17]

The Báb, the Herald of the Bahá'í Faith, made His declaration to the world well into the year 1844: May 23rd.* This hour marks the beginning of the Bahá'í Faith.

Thus the proofs were now complete. All three of the specific promises of Christ concerning the time of His return pointed to the exact same period:

1. The Gospel was preached around the world by 1844.
2. "The times of the Gentiles" was fulfilled in 1844.
3. The prophecy given by Daniel came to pass in 1844.

Christ told His disciples: When ye see these things, it will be the time of My coming, and the time of the end.

The words of Daniel, which told with such startling accuracy the story of both the *first* and *second* coming of Christ, were written by Daniel in Elam, a part of ancient Persia. It was in the capital of ancient Persia, Shushán, that Daniel gave his prophecy foretelling 1844 as the time for Christ's return. He not only gave the time, he also directed attention to the place in which he would appear, saying that "Elam" would be given as a place of "vision" in the latter days.[18]

The holy Bible of Christianity, as well as the sacred writings of the Jews, and the Scriptures of Islám *all* foretold that the Promised One would appear in the last days in Elam or Persia.

The Prophet Jeremiah, speaking of the time of the end, says: "And I will set my throne in Elam." [19]

In a prophecy of remarkable clarity, the sacred writings of Islám state: When the Promised One appears, "the upholders of His faith shall be of the people of Persia." [20]

With all these proofs to guide them, why did the people fail to recognize Christ in the day of His return in 1844? Why did over a century pass with no clear explanation of this great riddle?

The answer is simple. It was for the same reason that the people did not recognize Christ in the day of His *first* coming, until after the passing of centuries.

Those who were spiritually "alive" knew Him, but the great mass

---

* For a further explanation, see *Some Answered Questions*, pp. 43-52.

of mankind were spiritually "dead" and knew Him not. These were the people spoken of by Jeremiah:

> "O foolish people, and without understanding; which have eyes, and see not; which have ears and hear not." [21]

When Christ did not appear (the first time) in the magic, glorious way which the people expected of a Messiah, they denied Him. They called Him a false prophet and they slew Him. After all, He was born of a woman and walked among them. Surely, they said, this is not the manner in which our great Messiah will appear. Their eyes were closed.

The disciples of Jesus were greatly troubled because most of the people, especially the religious leaders and other influential persons, neither understood nor accepted His Message. They asked Jesus: "Why do they not believe?" Christ answered them:

> "Because it is given unto you to know the mysteries of the kingdom of heaven but unto them it is not given . . . their ears are dull of hearing, and their eyes they have closed . . . but blessed are your eyes, for they see: and your ears, for they hear." [22]

It was to be the same in the day of His return in 1844. It takes special "eyes" and "ears" to recognize and accept the Messiah *each* time He appears.

The great mass of mankind did not recognize Christ in the day of His *first* coming, nor would they recognize Him in the day of His *second* coming. For He would appear in the same manner: He would be born of a woman, and walk among them. He would have the same Christ-spirit, but He would have a new physical identity. Jesus Himself had explained this spiritual truth with the greatest care so that mankind would understand and not be misled.

The people said of Christ, "Why then say the scribes that Elias must come first?" [23]

The disciples found this question too difficult to answer because they, too, had been taught that Elias must come first. If so, where was he? They put the question to Christ. He told them that Elias had already come, but that no one understood this truth, since Elias had come in a manner they did not expect.

> "If ye will receive it," He said, "this [John the Baptist] is Elias, which was for to come. He that hath ears to hear, let him hear." [24]

John the Baptist was Elias, Christ told them. He added: "If ye will receive it." He meant: If you can understand this symbolic truth. He added: "He that hath ears to hear, let him hear." This clearly warned them that it would take spiritual ears to hear and accept this truth. It was to be understood inwardly, not outwardly, in the world of comprehension, not by the senses.

Only in this symbolical way could anyone accept the man John as Elias. Elias had returned in the spirit, not in the flesh of John. If they did not understand the significance of this inward truth, they would believe Him to be false. They must have the "eyes that see" and the "ears that hear"; otherwise, it would be impossible to understand or to accept.

This truth was confirmed by John the Baptist Himself. He was asked: "Art thou Elias?" He answered: "I am not." [25] He was not the return of Elias in the flesh. He was the return of the spirit of Elias. In the Book of Luke it is promised for this same John the Baptist:

> "He shall be filled with the Holy Ghost, even from his mother's womb. . . . And he shall go forth before him in the spirit and power of Elias." [26]

This was the inward truth that Christ was trying to convey. He emphasized this vital spiritual truth on more than one occasion. He demonstrated to His disciples that a Messenger of God does not return in the flesh. It is the Holy Spirit that returns; but, through another channel, in another age, and with another outward name.

> "And his disciples asked him, saying, Why then say the Scribes that Elias must first come? And Jesus answered and said unto them, Elias truly shall come first, and restore all things. But I say unto you, that Elias is come already, and they knew him not, but have done unto him whatsoever they listed. Likewise shall also the Son of man suffer of them. Then the disciples understood that he spoke unto them of John the Baptist." [27]

Elias had come but they knew him not because he came in a way they did not expect or understand. Christ likewise they knew not because He, too, came in an unexpected manner. Christ would be rejected and slain, as was John, because He came in a manner contrary to the expectations of the people.[28]

Elias came; he was John the Baptist. The Messiah came; He was Jesus of Nazareth. The prophecies were symbolical. Christ warned His disciples that the same conditions would also be true in the day of His second coming. Elias returned in John the Baptist and was rejected. "Likewise shall also the Son of Man [Himself] suffer of them," Christ warned. When He returned in the promised Messiah in 1844, He was also rejected in spite of the overwhelming proofs; in spite of His own direct promise of the hour of His coming and His warning that man would need to have spiritual "eyes that see."

"When ye shall see the abomination of desolation spoken of by Daniel the Prophet," Christ warned, "stand ye in the holy place (whoso readeth, let him understand)."

Christ's last words show that His return would not be clear to outward vision or understanding. He says: "Whoso readeth, let him understand." He will return in the Christ-spirit, but not as Jesus of Nazareth. Man must look for the same Holy Spirit in a new physical identity.

Christ is here once again repeating the warning about His own second coming which He gave to His disciples about the return of Elias in John the Baptist: "He that hath ears to hear, let him hear."

1. The three direct promises of Christ giving the time of His return, all pointed to the year 1844.
2. The holy Scripture of the Christians, Jews and Muslims gave the place: Persia.
3. Christ Himself unmistakably gave the manner of His return; not in the flesh, but in the spirit. But only Almighty God could give mankind the "eyes to see" and the "ears to hear."

These proofs which make it possible for everyone to understand the Holy Scripture could not have been given to mankind in such detail until the time of Christ's return. Until the hour of His appearance in 1844 in Elam (Persia) no one would be able to understand these inner mysteries of the holy Books. The way was closed. This was yet another prophecy from the pen of the same Prophet, Daniel. The words came to him in a vision.

"But thou, O Daniel, shut up the words and seal the book, even to the time of the end."

Daniel, still not satisfied, pressed for an answer to the meaning of his visions:

"Then said I, O my Lord, what shall be the end of these things? And He said, Go thy way, Daniel; for the words are closed up and sealed till the time of the end." [29]

This much was clear. No one would be able to discover the meaning of the words until after the return of the Spirit of Christ in the new Messiah in the last days. Isaiah reinforces this truth:

> "And the vision of all is become unto you as the words of the book that is sealed, which men deliver to one who is learned, saying, read this I pray thee: and he saith, I cannot for it is sealed." [30]

These seals would not be opened by Christ in His first coming, but only in His second. Leaders of the early Christians understood this:

> "Therefore judge nothing before the time, until the Lord come, who will bring to light the hidden things of darkness. . . ." [31]

The Apostle Peter left this clear warning about trying to interpret the prophecies before the day of Christ's return:

> "We have also a more sure word of prophecy . . . that no prophecy of the scripture is of any private interpretation. For the prophecy came not in old time by the will of man: but holy men of God spake as they were moved by the Holy Ghost." [32]

It was written of Bahá'u'lláh early in this century that His teachings "are the keys to all doors. Every hidden secret will become discovered and every hidden secret will become manifest and apparent." [33]

With the coming of the Bahá'í Faith in 1844, the Books were at last opened. Mankind was once again faced with that same great spiritual challenge: To accept or reject the Messiah. His "throne" had been set in "Elam" (Persia) in the very hour (1844) foretold by Christ Himself in three distinct prophetic promises. From the pen of the new Messiah were to come explanations of the hidden meanings of the prophecies in all the holy Scriptures of the world. This, too, had been foretold in the Revelation of St. John:

> "In the midst of the elders, stood a Lamb as it had been slain. . . . And they sung a new song, saying Thou art worthy to take the book and to open the seals thereof." [34]

Even Daniel, who said the books were sealed until the time of the end, saw another vision of the "last days" in which the books would be opened by the new Messiah:

> "Ten thousand times ten thousand stood before him: the judgment was set and the books were opened."

Speaking further of his great vision, following the opening of the books, Daniel says that he saw:

"The Ancient of Days . . . and there was given him dominion and glory, and a kingdom, that all people, nations, and languages, should serve him: his dominion is an everlasting dominion, which shall not pass away, and his kingdom that which shall not be destroyed." [35]

This is the story behind the great search for the promised One undertaken by Shaykh Ahmad, Siyyid Kázim, Mullá Husayn, Quddús, Táhirih, Vahíd, and those holy souls who were so much like the disciples of Christ in His day. Now at last the books were opened and the truth revealed:

1. Christ would appear in Elam (Persia).
2. Christ would return in the year 1844.
3. Christ would return not in the flesh, but with the same Holy Spirit in a new identity.

In order that this last truth of the three might never be misunderstood, repeated promises were given throughout the Bible that in the last day the Messiah would come with a "new name." It was also promised that His followers would be called by a "new name."

1. "Thou shalt be called by a new name."
2. "The Lord God shall . . . call his servants by another name." [36]
3. "To him that overcometh will I give to eat of the hidden manna and will give him a white stone, and in the stone a new name written, which no man knoweth saving he that receiveth it."

Only those that had the "eyes to see" and the "ears to hear" would receive the name and know it. In the very chapter in which Christ revealed to John, "If therefore thou shalt not watch, I will come on thee as a thief, and thou shalt not know what hour I come upon thee," a *new* name for His *new* followers is promised yet again.

Christ counsels His followers to be prepared to cast aside all they hold dear at the time of His second coming, just as they had been forced to cast it aside in the day of His first coming. He makes it plain that His second coming will not be according to the beliefs, standards, or expectations of any man. He warns each individual that he must search for himself, must be alert, must look with an "inner eye." In this final book of Christian Scripture (Revelation), Christ says: "Blessed is he that watcheth."

It is chapter eleven of this final book of Christian Scripture which so clearly prophesied that the "times of the Gentiles" would be fulfilled by the year 1844. This was the hour (1844) when Christ Himself promised: "Then shall they see the Son of man coming."

There is no subject spoken of with more frequency and more power in all the New Testament than that of the Return of Christ. It is mentioned repeatedly on innumerable occasions. Christ says clearly, time after time:

1. "I will not leave you comfortless: I will come to you."
2. "And behold I come quickly."
3. "For the Son of man shall come in the glory of the Father."
4. "I go away but come again unto you."
5. "And if I go to prepare a place for you, I will come again."

Because mankind has failed to understand the symbolical fulfill-ment of Christ's return, he has been forced to abandon it and con-sider it a mistake; and teach some other doctrine concerning His coming. Yet, it is easy to understand why such a millennial zeal should have held the world in its grasp when we realize that the following references are but some of Christ's own promises of His coming: Matthew, chapters 16, 24, 25 and 26. Mark, chapters 8 and 13. Luke, chapters 12 and 21. Acts, chapter 1. I Corinthians, chap-ters 4 and 15. I Thessalonians, chapters 1, 4 and 5. II Peter, chapters 1 and 3.

In the second and third chapters of Revelation, chapters filled with the promise of Christ's second coming, and laden with warn-ings that it will require a spiritual ear to hear and to understand the manner of His coming, the "new name" for His followers is mentioned for the final time in Christian Scripture.

In these chapters, Christ speaks of the *new* city, the *new* Jeru-salem, and the *new* name. All the things of the past will be swept away forever:

> "Him that overcometh will I make a pillar in the temple of my God, and he shall go no more out: and I will write upon him the name of my God, and the name of the city of my God, which is new Jerusalem, which cometh down out of heaven from my God: and I will write upon him my new name." [37]

He that hath an eye to see, let him see. He that hath an ear to hear, let him hear.

NOTE TWO

Every Prophet has been called false by his own generation. This was true of Jesus. He was considered a "false prophet."

"And there was much murmuring among the people concerning him: for some said he is a good man; others said, Nay; but *he deceiveth the people.*" [1]

A famous philosopher named Celsus in the second century compiled an entire volume filled with terrible libels about Christ and His followers. Porphyry, one of the greatest of the Platonic philosophers, wrote a large book against Christ and the Christians, quoting the many abusive attacks against Jesus which were prevalent among the leaders and the masses. The book was later burned by order of Sydocius and Dovalantius, two Christian emperors, who after the passing of time lauded and defended Christ Whom the people of that same land had once called false and had despised.

James Murdock in his *History of the Church* quotes one of the great scholar-emperors of Rome, Marc Antony, as saying, "You should not ask concerning Jesus of Nazareth from these poor Romans, none of whom has seen him, but whom baseness and indolence have caused to follow him." He called them unimportant people, slaves, men and women without praiseworthy qualities. The emperor Julian, who denied his faith in Christ, said the Christians were the "enemies of the world of humanity."

Even hundreds of years after His crucifixion, Christ was called a false prophet by the leaders and people of the world.

Most people could not believe that Jesus of Nazareth fulfilled the prophecies about the coming Messiah which said:

1. He (the Messiah) will sit upon the throne of David. (Where was his throne?)
2. Mount Zion will dance. (Who had yet seen this wonder?)
3. He will rule with a sword. (He didn't even have a staff, let alone a sword.)
4. He will come from an unknown place. (Did not this Jesus come from Nazareth, a place from which tradition promised that no "good" could come?)

How then could this (Jesus) be the Messiah?

When it was explained to the people of that time that all these prophecies had been fulfilled "inwardly" not "outwardly," symbolically and not literally, they refused to believe it.

Some of Christ's own followers denied Him because they couldn't fully accept His teachings. They turned away from Him and considered Him to be a "false prophet."

> "From that time many of his disciples went back, and walked no more with him." [2]

Whenever a Messenger of God appears, such as Krishna, Moses, Zoroaster, Buddha, Jesus, Muhammad, the Báb or Bahá'u'lláh, He is denounced as a "false prophet" by those who are not spiritually awake.

What satisfactory proof can be given to the spiritually awake that Bahá'u'lláh is not a false prophet? After all, Christ *did* warn His followers to beware of false prophets.

In the twenty fourth chapter of Matthew, in which Christ so clearly foretold His own return in 1844, we also find one of His strongest warnings about the *last days* and *false prophets*:

> "Then if any man shall say unto you, Lo, here is Christ, or there; believe it not. For there shall arise false Christs, and false prophets, and shall shew great signs and wonders; insomuch that, if it were possible, they shall deceive the very elect." [3]

Here Jesus prophesies the coming of not one, but of many false Christs and false prophets. He points out that they will work such astonishing wonders that they will deceive even the elect—His own followers, the Christians.

There are "false prophets" who deceive many of the "elect" in every age. These false prophets do not always appear in the guise of religion. There is the "false prophet" who teaches that there is no God at all—atheism.

The coming of this last "false prophet," disbelief in God, was plainly foretold in both the Old and the New Testament for the "time of the end":

1. "That day [the return of Christ] shall not come except there come a falling away first. . . ." [4]
2. "There shall be false teachers . . . who privily shall bring in damnable heresies, even denying the Lord that bought them. . . . And

many shall follow their pernicious ways; by reason of whom the way of truth shall be evil spoken of." [5]

The prophet Amos, who foretold with such startling clarity that the "sun would be darkened at noon," (in the hour of the Báb's martyrdom) also prophesied that it should be a day of disbelief in God and a day of great "falling away" from religion:

3. "Behold, the days come, saith the Lord God, that I will send a famine in the land, not a famine of bread, nor a thirst for water, but of hearing the words of the Lord. And they shall wander from sea to sea, and from the north even to the east, they shall run to and fro, to seek the Word of the Lord, and shall not find it." [6]

4. "Knowing this first, that there shall come in the last days, scoffers walking after their own lusts, And saying: Where is the promise of His coming?" [7]

In the hour of Christ's crucifixion, the "scoffers" who considered Him a "false prophet" were many, those who believed in Him were few. One of His chosen disciples had betrayed Him for money, another had denied Him three times. When His enemies came against Him in the garden of Gethsemane with swords and stones, His most trusted disciples deserted Him, fear overcoming their faith: "Then all the disciples forsook Him, and fled." No wonder Christ repeatedly warned His followers not to make this same mistake in the hour of His return.

"Watch ye therefore," He warned them, "for ye know not when the master of the house cometh, at even, or at midnight, or at the cockcrowing, or in the morning. Lest coming suddenly he find you sleeping." [8]

Thus, Jesus warned all future humanity through His followers: "And what I say unto you, I say unto all, Watch!" [9]

In the twenty-fourth chapter of Matthew where we hear Christ foretelling the hour of His return (1844), He once again cautions His followers not to misread the signs of His coming and thus be misled into error:

"But if that evil servant shall say in his heart My lord delayed His coming [and thus not expecting Him, shall deny Him], and shall begin to smite his fellow servants, and to eat and drink with the drunken [become material-minded]; the lord of that servant shall come in a day when he looketh not for him, and in an hour he is not aware of, and shall cut him asunder and appoint his portion with the hypocrites!" [10]

Christ Himself, Who warned His followers to beware of "false prophets," gave humanity a measuring rod by which it is possible to judge every prophet and thus be sure of the truth. He provided an unerring standard by which every person can determine for himself whether a prophet is "true" or "false." This standard is found in the seventh chapter of Matthew. We find that in this one chapter Christ gave both the warning to beware of false prophets, and supplied the method by which to judge them.

> "Beware of false prophets, which come to you in sheep's clothing, but inwardly they are ravening wolves.
> Ye shall know them by their fruits. Do men gather grapes of thorns, or figs of thistles?
> Even so every good tree bringeth forth good fruit; but a corrupt tree bringeth forth evil fruit. . . . Wherefore by their fruits ye shall know them." [11]

Judge the prophet by his fruits. This is a sound basis for judgement. It is the measure established by Christ Himself. Therefore, let us judge Bahá'u'lláh by the standard given by Christ. Let us test the fruits of Bahá'u'lláh's tree, for Christ has promised us that if the "fruit" is good, the tree is good, and the prophet true.

Bahá'u'lláh wrote over a hundred volumes. Here it is possible to mention but a few of His teachings, and in the briefest manner. It is like trying to catch the ocean in a cup.

The following are "fruits" from the tree of Bahá'u'lláh upon subjects which are nearest to the heart of every man, and most vital to his welfare: 1. his home and family, 2. his country, 3. his religion, and 4. his individual self.

The first "fruit" we shall test is that relating to man's home and family:

1. HOME AND FAMILY

Bahá'u'lláh calls upon all mankind to honor the sanctity of marriage. The bond between husband and wife must be upon a spiritual as well as a physical foundation. It must be a happy and lasting union, for the family is the basis of society.

The Bahá'í law on marriage is that man must have but one wife (monogamy). If a man already has more than one wife, he does not give up any, but he can take no more. Thus an injustice or upheaval will not be caused in those lands where plural marriages are acceptable, but gradually by the application of this law, monogamy will be the rule everywhere.

Bahá'u'lláh calls upon all men and women to marry so that children may be raised up who can honor the name of God and render service to mankind. It is obligatory to educate the children and they must be educated and given moral as well as scientific training.

2. MAN'S COUNTRY

Bahá'u'lláh's teachings state clearly that it is the "unquestioned duty of every one of His followers to demonstrate their loyalty and obedience to their respective governments."

His teachings say, even more specifically: "According to the direct and sacred command of God we are forbidden to utter slander, are commanded to show forth peace and amity, and are exhorted to rectitude of conduct, straightforwardness and harmony with all the kindreds and peoples of the world." [12]

Bahá'u'lláh's followers are instructed to consider disloyalty unto a just government as disloyalty to God Himself. It is the sacred obligation of Bahá'ís to "promote, in the most effective manner, the best interests of their government and people." [13]

This is another "fruit" from the tree of Bahá'u'lláh by which you may judge whether He is a true or false prophet.

3. MAN'S RELIGION

Bahá'u'lláh teaches that just as there is only one God, there is also only one religion. All the great Prophets have taught this same one religion.

There is no exclusive salvation for the Hindu, the Jew, the Zoroastrian, the Buddhist, the Christian, the Muslim, or the Bahá'í. All these pure and holy Faiths are part of the one eternal religion of God which goes on for ever. No religion is the one exclusive faith, or the final outpouring of truth from Almighty God. Each religion is true, is beautiful, is valid for the age in which it appears. It is the *only* truth for that particular age, yet it is but one part of the single, great, progressive, never-ending religion of God. The Word of God is one though the Speakers (Messengers) are many.

The Bahá'í teachings point out that the growth of religion is like the growth of a tree. In the teaching of Krishna we see the "seed," in that of Moses the "shoot," in that of Zoroaster the "trunk," in that of Buddha the "branches," in that of Jesus the "twigs," in that of Muhammad the "leaves," in that of the Báb the "blossoms," in that of Bahá'u'lláh the "fruit." Because men failed to recognize and understand this oneness, the great religions have developed an enmity for each other.

The Founders were united in love, but the followers became divided in hate. One step is not greater than another. All are necessary. Each stage is the fulfillment of the one that went before. No step is exclusive; no stage is final, not even the stage of the "fruit." The "fruit" is the fulfillment of the "seed"; it is the end of a cycle; but from that "fruit" will come the seed of another great cycle.

"The Religion of God," Bahá'u'lláh declares, "is for the sake of love and union; make it not the cause of enmity and conflict." [14]

Bahá'u'lláh was exiled like Abraham, stoned like Moses, and scourged like Jesus. For nearly half a century Bahá'u'lláh underwent imprisonment and exile, during which He was poisoned, beaten, chained in a dungeon, and subjected to the most brutal and continuous indignities. In the depths of His suffering, He again pointed out the oneness of His own Mission with that of Christ. Bahá'u'lláh called out to mankind: "If ye be intent on crucifying once again Jesus, the Spirit of God, put Me to death, for He hath once more, in My person, been made manifest unto you." [15]

Bahá'u'lláh commands His followers to "consort with the followers of all religions in a spirit of friendliness and fellowship." [16]

Bahá'u'lláh upholds the basic teachings of Christ, Moses, Muhammad, Krishna and all the prophets of the past. He speaks of them all with great love and beauty. In counselling His followers to mingle with the people of all Faiths with radiance and gladness, He says: "Ye are all the leaves of one tree and the drops of one ocean."

"Truly I say," Bahá'u'lláh tells us, "whatever lowers the lofty station of religion will increase heedlessness in the wicked. . . . O people of God! Be not occupied with yourselves. Be intent on the betterment of the world and the training of nations." [17]

This is yet another "fruit" taken from the tree of Bahá'u'lláh's teachings by which you may judge whether He is a true or a false prophet.

4. MAN'S INDIVIDUAL LIFE

The reason a Prophet (Messenger) comes to earth, Bahá'u'lláh says, is "to educate the souls of men, and to refine the character of every living man. . . ." [18]

"The essence of faith," Bahá'u'lláh counsels, "is fewness of words and abundance of deeds. . . ." "Beware, O people of Bahá, lest ye walk in the ways of them whose words differ from their deeds." "Let your acts be a guide to all mankind. . . . It is through your deeds that ye can distinguish yourselves from others. Through them the brightness of your light can be shed upon the whole earth."

"The most vital duty, in this day, is to purify your characters, to correct your manners, and improve your conduct," Bahá'u'lláh proclaims. "The beloved of the Merciful must show forth such character and conduct among His creatures, that the fragrance of their holiness may be shed upon the whole world. . . ."

"A good character is, verily, the best mantle for men. . . . The light of a good character surpasses the light of the sun. . . . Upon this the honor and glory of the world are based and are dependent. . . ." "Trustworthiness . . . is the door to the security and tranquility of mankind." [19]

Throughout Bahá'u'lláh's Teachings, such additional counsels on individual behavior as these are found:

"Do not be content with showing friendship in words alone, let your heart burn with loving kindness for all who may cross your path." [20]

". . . show the utmost kindness and compassion to the sick and suffering. This has greater effect than the remedy itself. You must always have this thought of love and affection when you visit the ailing and afflicted." [21]

Bahá'u'lláh has given the following standard of conduct for all His followers:

"Be generous in prosperity, and thankful in adversity. Be worthy of the trust of thy neighbor, and look upon him with a

bright and friendly face. Be a treasure to the poor, . . . an an-
swerer to the cry of the needy. . . . Be unjust to no man. . . . Be
as a lamp unto them that walk in darkness, a joy to the sorrowful,
a sea for the thirsty, a haven for the distressed, an upholder and
defender of the victim of oppression. . . . Be a home for the
stranger, a balm to the suffering, a tower of strength for the fugitive. Be eyes to the blind, and a guiding light unto the feet of
the erring. . . . a breath of life to the body of mankind. . . ." [22]

This is another "fruit" taken from the tree of Bahá'u'lláh. Christ
said "by their fruits ye will know them." These will help you to
decide whether Bahá'u'lláh is a true or a false prophet.

The following final "fruits" are but a few of the Teachings taken
from this vast reservoir which Bahá'u'lláh has left to humanity:

1. *Each individual shall make his own independent search after
truth.*

    The Teachings of Bahá'u'lláh say: "The greatest gift of God to
man is his intelligence."

    Each individual should investigate spiritual truth for himself.
He can, and should, learn from the knowledge and efforts of
others, but he should not accept their findings as the final truth
for himself without a personal investigation. Each person is in-
dividually responsible for the relationship between himself and
God. Only a sincere individual search can bring about a just
decision.

This is a "fruit" from the tree of Bahá'u'lláh's Teachings.

2. *Men and women should enjoy equal rights, privileges, education,
and opportunities throughout the world.*

    Bahá'u'lláh attached great importance to this principle. His
teachings emphasize the fact that since the mother is the teacher
of the child during its early and formative years, it is most necessary that she have a good education. The universal education
which Bahá'u'lláh advocates would give an equal position to
boys and girls, men and women.

    When the station of woman is elevated until it is co-equal to
that of man everywhere in the entire world, the stability and
wholesomeness of social affairs throughout the world will be
greatly improved.

This is also a "fruit" from Bahá'u'lláh's tree.

3. *Education must be made available to all.*

No one should be deprived of an opportunity for education, Bahá'u'lláh's teachings explain. Nor must anyone be permitted to deprive himself of an education. Education must be compulsory up to a certain age.

"To acquire knowledge is incumbent on all," Bahá'u'lláh declares, "but of those sciences which may profit the people of the earth. . . . The possessors of sciences and arts have a great right among the people of the world. . . . Indeed, the real treasury of man is his knowledge. Knowledge is the means of honor, prosperity, joy, gladness, happiness and exaltation." [23]

This is another "fruit."

4. *An International language must be taught throughout the world in addition to the mother-tongue.*

Bahá'u'lláh has instructed that a universal language must be fashioned or adopted from one of the existing languages. This will greatly aid commerce and will break down the barriers of misunderstanding among peoples.

This language would be an international auxiliary language. Each land would keep the beauty and charm of its own mother-tongue, but would learn in addition an international *auxiliary* language.

". . . my determination is to gather the nations. . . . For then will I turn to the people a *pure language* that they may all call upon the name of the Lord, to serve Him with one consent." [24]

This, too, is a "fruit" from the Teachings of Bahá'u'lláh.

5. *Religion must agree with science and reason.*

In a world society such as that foretold by Bahá'u'lláh, "science and religion, the two most potent forces in human life, will be reconciled, will coöperate, and will harmoniously develop." [25]

This is a "fruit" upon Bahá'u'lláh's tree.

6. *All men are the children of one Father, God, and are the brothers and sisters of one human family.*

However great the conqueror may be, he is finally entombed, possessionless. He keeps but one small plot of earth for his bones.

Thus every warrior is interred. The earth belongs to God, and
man is a tenant here for but a brief span. His greatest possession, next to love of God, is love for his fellow human beings.
Prejudices of all kinds must be banished from the earth. In order to eliminate racial prejudice, it is essential to eliminate racial
consciousness and to see all humanity as the children of one
Father.

"Lovers of mankind," His Teachings proclaim, "are the superior people, of whatever country, color or creed they may be."

This also is a "fruit" taken from Bahá'u'lláh's tree.

7. *The soul is the essential part of every human being, and lives
forever.*

The most vital belief any man can possess, Bahá'u'lláh assures
us, and one which man cherishes most of all at the moment of
death, is a belief in God and in the immortality of his own spirit.
Bahá'u'lláh repeatedly gives mankind comforting assurance upon
this essential truth.* After reading Bahá'u'lláh's words on this
subject, man has great confidence in that inner prompting which
tells him that he does indeed have an immortal soul.

Many of the great scientific minds of our day substantiate these
inner truths from their own research. They point out that matter
itself is indestructible and has a form of immortality; therefore,
how can the spirit be mortal?

The eminent biologist C. C. Hurst writes, "Recent genetical
research leads us to the inevitable conclusion that, in general,
living genes are relatively immortal.[26]

Arthur H. Compton, Nobel Prize Winner for his work in
physics, says: ". . . it is only fair to point out that science has
found no cogent reason for supposing that what is of importance
in a man can be buried in a grave."[27] Dr. Compton says in yet
another place, "Biologically speaking, life, whether it be an apple
seed or the germ cell of a man, is essentially continuous and
eternal . . . May we not also logically say that continuity of consciousness, mind or soul may be presumed from the essential
eternality of the germ cell?"[28]

---

* Read: *Gleanings from the Writings of Bahá'u'lláh, The Hidden Words,
Reality of Man, Life after Death, The Bahá'í World Faith, Some Answered
Questions.*

This is another "fruit" of Bahá'u'lláh by which you may judge Him.

8. *Prayer is both a blessing and an obligation.*

Prayer brings healing to the soul. It brings joy and happiness, and protects man from tests and difficulties. It is essential to the life of the spirit.

Just as the physical body must have food each day, so does the soul need food each day. Prayer is the spiritual food of the soul. A physical body which is not fed regularly becomes emaciated from malnutrition. It sickens and dies. The same is true of the soul of man. This spirit must be fed regularly and well, or it will suffer the same loss of power. It too, will sicken. While it never dies, it becomes so helpless that it exists in a form of death.

For example, if a man lets his arm hang at his side without ever using it, soon the power to move the arm vanishes. The arm has become atrophied and useless. A man's soul without the nourishment of regular prayer also becomes atrophied and useless.

Bahá'u'lláh has left a rich legacy of beautiful, uplifting prayers. However, His Faith instructs man to remember that prayer is by no means limited to the use of these prayers. Work itself, Bahá'u'lláh says, is worship. One's daily work when done in the spirit of service to mankind, and performed to the best of one's ability, is prayer of the finest kind.

"We have made this—your occupation—identical with the worship of God," Bahá'u'lláh has written.[29]

He teaches that one's whole life should be a prayer. Every thought, word or deed devoted to the good of one's fellow-man is a prayer in the truest sense of the word.

By means of these principles and laws, Bahá'u'lláh has laid the foundation for a united world, so that the prophecies of Scripture might be fulfilled and there might come that promised day of "one fold and one shepherd."

Nearly a century ago, Bahá'u'lláh proclaimed the essential need for the establishment of a universal House of Justice which would be dedicated to preserving the welfare of all men upon the planet. It would protect both great and small nations. It would guarantee the rights of individuals.

Bahá'u'lláh addressed the Rulers and Kings of the earth, warning them of the dire consequences which would follow if they failed to raise up such a structure. Without it, He told them, disaster would come upon the world.

This world organization envisioned by Bahá'u'lláh would have a world parliament which would be democratically elected. It would have a world metropolis, an international police force, and a world tribunal or court.

It would not be dedicated to the West or the East; it would not favor the light or the dark; it would not prefer the Jew or the Gentile. This world organization would be dedicated to one purpose only: the welfare of the entire human race.

This great universal body would establish a common system of weights and measures and a common currency. It would develop all of the world's natural resources and would regulate markets so that "have not" nations would no longer exist. It would eliminate the extremes of poverty and wealth without destroying the natural degrees of difference which talent and initiative create. It would harmonize capital and labor, protecting the rights of the laborer as well as those of the investor, to the advantage of both. It would foster an international auxiliary language. In short, it would take all the steps necessary to bring about a peace-loving, progressive, prosperous human family.

Professor Edward G. Browne of the University of Cambridge visited Bahá'u'lláh in 1890. He wrote of that moment as follows:

"The face of him on whom I gazed I can never forget, though I cannot describe it. Those piercing eyes seemed to read one's very soul; power and authority sat on that ample brow. . . . No need to ask in whose presence I stood, as I bowed myself before one who is the object of a devotion and love which kings might envy and emperors sigh for in vain!

"A mild dignified voice bade me be seated, and then continued: 'Thou hast come to see a prisoner and an exile. . . . We desire but the good of the world and the happiness of nations. . . . That all nations should become one in faith and all men as brothers; that the bonds of affection and unity between the sons of men should be strengthened; that diversity of religion should cease, and differences of race be annulled. . . . These strifes and this bloodshed and discord must cease, and all men be as one kindred and one family. . . .

Let not a man glory in this, that he loves his country; let him rather glory in this, that he loves his kind. . . .'

"Such, so far as I can recall them, were the words which, besides many others, I heard from Bahá. Let those who read them consider well with themselves whether such doctrines merit death and bonds, and whether the world is more likely to gain or lose by their diffusion." [30]

These are some of the "fruits" from the tree of Bahá'u'lláh. Christ said: "By their fruits shall ye know them." The responsibility of deciding whether or not Bahá'u'lláh is a true prophet now rests with you.

NOTE THREE

It is said in Scripture and Tradition that at the time of the birth or announcement of every Messenger of God, a star or a sign appears in the heavens.

Nimrod was warned of the star that told of the coming of Abraham. The soothsayers warned Pharaoh of the star in the heavens that foretold the coming of Moses. The Magi informed Herod of the new star that guided them to the throne of the "spiritual king," Jesus. The same legend is told of Buddha, Zoroaster, Muhammad and Krishna.

What were the signs in the heavens during the appearance of the Báb and Bahá'u'lláh? The holy Scriptures of all faiths had spoken of Twin-Revelations that would appear at the "time of the end." Now that the Báb and Bahá'u'lláh had appeared, fulfilling these prophecies, what were the signs in the heavens? Signs, not for one, but for *two* Messengers of God, Who would appear almost simultaneously?

Some of us know the story of the great comet of 1843 which foreshadowed the coming of the Báb.

Sir James Jeans, late British astronomer and mathematician, stated in his book *Through Space and Time*, "oddly enough, many of the most conspicuous appearances of comets seem to have coincided with, or perhaps just anticipated, important events in history." [1]

One of the most unique stories of a comet is that told of the period during which the Báb and Bahá'u'lláh were exchanging correspondence, and during which the Báb was preparing His followers for the appearance of Bahá'u'lláh. This story was told in the stars as well as on the earth.

In 1845 a comet appeared soon after the one in 1843. It was called Biela's comet. It seemed to be an ordinary comet, in a year in which some 300 comets had appeared, and it had appeared before many times in the past. In 1846 it was still visible. At this period in its history, it became one of the unique comets of all time. It was now entering into the last dramatic moments of its life.

The Encyclopedia Americana gives the following account of this event:

"It was found again late in November 1845, and in the following month an observation was made of one of the most remarkable phenomena in astronomical records, the division of the comet. It put forth no tail while this alteration was going on. Professor Challis, using the Northumberland telescope at Cambridge, on 15 Jan. 1846, was inclined to distrust his eyes or his glass when he beheld two comets where but one had been before. He would call it, he said, a binary (twin) comet if such a thing had ever been heard of before. His observations were soon verified, however." [2]

History shows that there had been other binary (twin comets) but Biela's was one of the most unusual. Sir James Jeans wrote of this same comet, saying: "The most interesting story is that of Biela's comet which broke in two while under observation in 1846."

The comet then disappeared. It returned in August, 1852. This was the very month and the very year in which Bahá'u'lláh was cast into an underground prison in Tihrán.

This was the year 1269 of the calendar of Islám. It was also exactly the ninth year after the Báb's Declaration to Mullá Husayn in the year 1260. The Báb had prophesied: "Ere nine years have elapsed" the Promised One of all ages and religions will come.

It was but a few weeks later, in that same prison, that Bahá'u'lláh's Mission began.

August, 1852, was the hour of the reappearance of the comet, the comet that had split in two to become twin-comets. Strangely enough, at the time of the reappearance of the twin-comets in 1852, one half had receded far into the background. The other half, though in a parallel orbit, now dominated the scene. Just so had the Báb, the Herald of the Bahá'í Faith, passed into history, and the

One Whose coming He had foretold, Bahá'u'lláh, had assumed His Mission.

The Americana record of this astronomical event states: "Late in August, 1852, the larger portion again came into view; and three weeks later the smaller one, now much fainter than its former companion was seen about 1,500,000 miles in the lead." Sir James Jeans confirms this: "Six years later [1852], when the comet's orbit again brought it near to the sun, two pieces were observed to be one and a half million miles apart."

Of that hour when the twin-comets rode the skies above His prison, Bahá'u'lláh has written: "I was but a man like others, asleep upon my couch, when lo, the breezes of the All Glorious [God] were wafted over Me and taught Me the knowledge of all that hath been. This is not from Me, but from One Who is Almighty and All-knowing." [3]

Following this twin-appearance, Sir James Jeans states, "neither of them has been seen in cometary form, but the place where they ought to be is occupied by a swarm of millions of meteors, known as the Andromedid meteors. Occasionally these meet the earth in its orbit, and make a grand meteoric display."

The two comets were no longer separate comets, but were mingled in one great shower of light, just as the Faith of the Báb and Bahá'u'lláh are not separate but one in the light which they shed upon the earth.

NOTE FOUR

The Báb was from the line of Bani-Háshim. Háshim was the great-grandfather of Muhammad.[1]

The Báb was also a descendant of Abraham through Abraham's second wife, Hagar. The Báb was of the seed of [Ismá'íl], and through him of the "seed of Abraham."

When Abraham, as is related in the book of Genesis, said unto God: "O that Ishmael might live before Thee," God replied: "And as for Ishmael, I have heard thee: Behold, I have blessed him, and will make him fruitful, and will multiply him exceedingly; twelve princes shall he beget, and I will make of him a great nation." [2]

Muhammad was a descendant of Ismá'íl. Through Muhammad the first concept of nationhood came into being. The first great "nation" was built upon His teachings. God's promise of Abraham that Ismá'íl would beget twelve princes was also fulfilled through Muhammad. These twelve princes were the twelve Imáms, the spiritual leaders of Shí'ah Islám.

In the holy traditions of Islám there is a prophecy which states that the twelfth of these princes (Imáms) disappeared in the year 260, and that he would reappear in a thousand years—in the year 1260 (1844). This is the very year of the Báb's announcement of His Mission.

Bahá'u'lláh also was descended from Abraham, through Abraham's third wife, Katurah. That historical record of the Bahá'í Faith, *God Passes By,* states: "He [Bahá'u'lláh] derived His descent . . . from Abraham (the Father of the Faithful) through his wife Katurah. . . ." [3]

Bahá'u'lláh was also descended from the great Prophet of Írán, Zoroaster, and in addition to the two Branches of Holiness mentioned above, Bahá'u'lláh was also a descendant of Jesse. He is the "Branch" that "shall grow out of his roots" as promised by Isaiah. Likewise, He is the "rod" and the "ensign."

"In that day there shall be a root of Jesse, which shall stand for an ensign of the people; to it shall the Gentiles seek: and his rest shall be glorious. . . . And he shall set up an ensign for the nations and shall assemble the outcasts of Israel, and gather together the dispersed of Judah from the four corners of the earth." [4]

This chapter of Isaiah refers to Bahá'u'lláh. He is the "Branch" of Jesse who will assemble the outcasts of Israel. The Jews were not dispersed until after the time of Christ; they were in his life still assembled in the Holy Land. They had not yet been banished to the four corners of the earth.

At the present time, however, the Jews have been returning from all parts of the earth to Israel. On the sides of Mount Carmel, the Bahá'í Shrines and holy places can be seen from the sea for miles. They stand within the shadow of the cave of Elijah where the feet of Bahá'u'lláh, of Christ, and of the Prophets of old once walked. From the arid waste of this mountain of rock has been carved a beautiful garden of paths, flowers, trees—indeed as Isaiah had promised, the place of "his rest shall be glorious."

The story in the Bible of the oneness of God began with Abraham, Father of the Faithful. Through the seed of Ismá'íl came the religion of Muhammad and of the Báb. Through the seed of Isaac came the religion of Moses and of Jesus.

Abraham talked with God in the land of Ur in the Chaldees in the valley of the Tigris and Euphrates rivers. He was then exiled to Syria. Bahá'u'lláh, of the seed of Abraham, made His open declaration to the world that He was the Promised One of all religions in this same valley of the Tigris and Euphrates rivers. He, too, was then exiled to Syria.

Descended from Abraham through his third wife, Katurah, Bahá'u'lláh extended one hand to the followers of Muhammad and the Báb, and the other hand to the followers of Moses and Christ and brought them together again as foretold for the day of the "one fold and one shepherd."

Thus Bahá'u'lláh fulfilled the words of Isaiah:

"And it shall come to pass in that day, that the Lord shall set his hand again the second time to recover the remnant of his people. . . ."[5]

NOTE FIVE

The remains of the Báb were destined to rest eternally within the shadow of His Beloved, Bahá'u'lláh.

Bahá'u'lláh was driven into exile far from His native land of Írán. He was sent to Baghdád, Constantinople, Adrianople, and finally He was banished to the prison-city of 'Akká across the bay of Haifa from Mount Carmel.

One day while resting on the side of this holy mountain, Bahá'u'lláh pointed out to His son, 'Abdu'l-Bahá, the exact spot where a Shrine should be built and where the sacred remains of the Báb should be entombed forever.

Those precious mangled bodies of the Báb and His fellow-martyr were rescued from the moat outside the city of Tabríz by Hájí Sulaymán Khán and were brought to a silk factory owned by one of the believers of Mílán. The next day they were laid in a wooden casket and carried to a place of safety. Bahá'u'lláh instructed that they be brought to Tihrán and be placed in the shrine of the Imám-

Zádih Ḥasan, where They would be, as the Báb Himself requested, "within the shadow of His Beloved."

But, Bahá'u'lláh was stoned, imprisoned and finally banished from Tihrán, and those sacred remains of the Báb were no longer within the shadow of Bahá'u'lláh, the One He loved.

Throughout every step of His enforced exile, Bahá'u'lláh knew the exact spot which held those holy remains.

They were later removed from the shrine to the house of Hájí Sulaymán Khán in the Sar-Chashmih quarter of Tihrán. They were then taken to the shrine of Imám-Zádih Ma'ṣúm, where they remained concealed until the year 1867-1868. A letter was received from Bahá'u'lláh in exile directing the friends to transfer them without delay to another spot. This was done immediately, and proved to be providential as shortly after this the shrine was reconstructed.

Two followers of Bahá'u'lláh continued to search for a safe suitable place. While they were on the road leading to Chashmih-'Alí, they came upon an abandoned and dilapidated school. That evening after dark they deposited their precious burden within one of its walls, having first re-wrapt the remains in a silken shroud brought by them for that purpose.

The next day they were alarmed to discover that their hiding place had been discovered. They were afraid that their sacred charge might fall into the hands of enemies, so they carried the casket secretly through the gate of the city of Tihrán to the house of a friend where it remained for fourteen months.

The long-guarded secret of its whereabouts became known to the believers, and soon they began to visit the house in large numbers. A letter was sent to Bahá'u'lláh begging for guidance. Word came instructing one of the followers to accept the Trust and to exercise the utmost secrecy as to its disposal.

The casket containing the remains was buried beneath the floor of the inner sanctuary of the shrine of Imám-Zádih Zayd. It remained there, undetected, until it was necessary to move it again. The friend commissioned to undertake this task was informed of the exact location through a chart forwarded to him by Bahá'u'lláh.

Under the instruction left by Bahá'u'lláh, those precious remains were moved from house to house, from hiding-place to hiding-place until the year 1899.

In that year, 'Abdu'l-Bahá instructed Mírzá Asadu'lláh, together with a number of other believers, to transport them by way of Isfá-hán, Kirmánsháh, Baghdád and Damascus, to Beirut. From there they came by sea to 'Akká, arriving at their destination on January 31, 1899.[1] Finally, in the year 1909, the Tomb of the Báb on the side of Mount Carmel was completed. 'Abdu'l-Bahá, following the instructions of Bahá'u'lláh, deposited, with His own hands, the wooden casket containing the sacred remains of the Báb and His companion within a waiting marble sarcophagus in the floor vault of this Shrine.

'Abdu'l-Bahá announced the news of this glorious victory to the followers of Bahá'u'lláh:

"The most joyful tidings is this, that the holy, the luminous body of the Báb . . . after having for sixty years been transferred from place to place . . . and having known neither rest nor tranquility has, through the mercy of the Abhá Beauty, been ceremoniously deposited on the day of Naw-Rúz [New Year], within the sacred casket, in the exalted Shrine on Mount Carmel." [2]

Today His beautiful Shrine and the terraces leading to it are illumined at night and can be seen for miles. The Báb was denied even a candle in the Mountain of Máh-Kú; now His Shrine of shining white, crowned with a dome of gold, on the side of its green throne on Mount Carmel, is a blaze of light.

When the famed Orientalist, A. L. M. Nicolas, heard that a Shrine had been raised to the glory of the Báb, he longed to see it. He had been very touched by the Christlike life of the Báb about Whom he had written so glowingly.

Shoghi Effendi Rabbani, the late Guardian of the Bahá'í Faith, sent M. Nicolas an artist's drawing of the Shrine as well as a copy of *The Dawn-Breakers,* Nabíl's history of those early days. Nicolas was so deeply moved that he kissed the bearer's hand.[3]

Thus, at last, the remains of the Báb were interred in Mount Carmel, the "vineyard of God," according to the direct instructions of Bahá'u'lláh. They rest near the cave of Elijah whose promised coming the Báb fulfilled, there on the side of God's holy mountain called the "nest of the prophets." The Shrine of the Báb faces directly toward the silver-city of 'Akká and toward the spot where Bahá'u'lláh Himself is enshrined.

Once again, and this time forever, the Báb was "within the shadow of His Beloved."

NOTE SIX

One of the most dramatic stories of the coming of Bahá'u'lláh, and His fulfillment of prophecy, is that told in the Book of Micah. Micah foretold: first, that the world would be disillusioned in that day, and that its only hope would be to await the coming of God's Messenger; second, that He would come from Babylon in the valley of the Tigris and Euphrates; third, that He would come to Israel and dwell in the midst of Carmel; and fourth, that He would fulfill specific prophecies on His journey to the Holy Land.

Of the condition of the world, Micah said:

"The good man is perished out of the earth; and there is none upright among them: they all lie in wait for blood; they hunt every man his brother with a net . . . they do evil with both hands. . . . the best of them is a brier; the most upright is sharper than a thorn hedge. . . ." [1]

That man's hope would lie in the coming of God's Messenger, he expressed in these words:

"Therefore I will look unto the Lord; I will wait for the God of my salvation: my God will hear me. . . . Then she that is my enemy shall see it, and shame shall cover her which said unto me, Where is the Lord thy God?" . . . "He will bring me forth to the light, and I shall behold His righteousness." [2]

Of the birth of the Mission of the Messiah in Babylon, Micah said:

"Be in pain, and labor to bring forth, O daughter of Zion, like a woman in travail: for now shalt thou go forth out of the city, and thou shalt dwell in the field, and thou shalt go even to Babylon, there shalt thou be delivered; there the Lord shall redeem thee from the hand of thine enemies." [3]

That the promised Redeemer would come and dwell in Israel in the "last days" and nourish humanity with His teachings, is promised in these words of Micah:

"Feed thy people with thy rod, the flock of thine heritage, which dwell solitarily in the wood in the midst of Carmel." [4]

The manner of His coming, and each step along His path to Israel, was set down in detail by Micah in the same chapter:

"In that day also he shall come even to thee from Assyria, and from the fortified cities, and from the fortress to the river, and from sea to sea, and from mountain to mountain." [5]

The exact number of years during which the Mission of the promised Messiah would last are also foretold by Micah:

"According to the days of thy coming out of the land of Egypt will I shew Him marvelous things." [6]

These startling and prophetic words were all fulfilled by Bahá'u'lláh in the following manner:

1. He was born in Persia, once part of the ancient kingdom of Assyria; thus He came from Assyria.

2. He was driven in exile to Baghdád, modern metropolis of Mesopotamia. It is near the site of the ancient capital, Babylon, which was queen of the region in Biblical times.

3. Bahá'u'lláh withdrew out of the city into the fields and mountains, as Christ had gone into the desert. After a period of prayer and meditation, He returned to Baghdád (successor of Babylon) to make His declaration that He was the promised Redeemer of mankind.

4. He came to the Holy Land and dwelt in the midst of Carmel; from there His flock was fed by the rod of His teachings, for Mount Carmel is the world center of His Faith, and the site of many of its holy places.

5. Bahá'u'lláh came from Assyria to Babylon. He was then marched over land as a prisoner, and finally shipped by sea to the fortified city of Constantinople. He was later exiled further, and came by sea to the fortified city of 'Akká. For two years He was confined in a cell in the fortress prison. After nine years within the prison walls of 'Akká, Bahá'u'lláh was at last permitted to leave the shadow of the fortress and go out to the river which flowed around an island in the garden of Riḍván. As a prisoner, he was shipped across the Black Sea to Constantinople, and via the Mediterranean Sea to Haifa and 'Akká. Bahá'u'lláh withdrew into the mountain of Sar Galu outside of Baghdád to pray before announcing His Mission, and in the last years of His life, He pitched His tent on the side of Mount Carmel, called by Isaiah the "mountain of God."

6. From the time Bahá'u'lláh's Mission began, until the day of His death in the Holy Land, exactly forty years elapsed, which was precisely "according to the days of thy [the Jews] coming out of the land of Egypt"; during these forty years Bahá'u'lláh poured out His teaching as Almighty God "shewed Him marvelous things."

Bahá'u'lláh had come to Israel "by way of the sea" as prophesied by Isaiah. He was sent as a prisoner to the great stone fortress in the valley of Achor, now called 'Akká, as foretold by the Book of Hosea:

> "And I will give her vineyard from thence, and the valley of Achor for a door of hope: and she shall sing there as in the days of her youth, and as in the day when she came up out of the land of Egypt." [7]

The Bahá'í House of Worship to be built upon Mount Carmel, and which will be open to the people of all nations and faiths, will look down upon both the plain of Sharon and the valley of 'Akká [Achor], as foreshadowed by the prophet Isaiah:

> "Sharon shall be a fold of flocks, and the valley of Achor a place for the herds to lie down in, for my people who have sought me." [8]

Bahá'u'lláh had been sent to the prison of 'Akká because it was believed by the religious leaders of Persia and Turkey that He would die there and be forgotten. The atmosphere was so foul that a proverb said of the spot: "If a bird flies over 'Akká, it dies!" His enemies did not realize that by driving Him there in exile, they were fulfilling the prophecies of sacred Scripture.

Soon the followers of Bahá'u'lláh came to this arid, desert land from far off places. They brought with them roses of every hue, flowers, plants, and fruit trees. It became a garden as the years passed, filled with colorful blossoms, the fragrance of orange and lemon trees, with the brilliance of the flaming pomegranate. Even as Isaiah had visualized:

> "It shall blossom abundantly and rejoice even with joy and singing: the glory of Lebanon shall be given unto it, the excellency of Carmel and Sharon, they shall see the glory of the Lord, and the excellency of our God." [9]

Thousands of visitors from all parts of the world now visit the magnificent Bahá'í gardens on the side of Mount Carmel and on the plain of 'Akká. Wherever the feet of Bahá'u'lláh walked, there are now lovely gardens and paths. Roses of every hue and description can be seen. White and red stone paths wind through beds of many-colored flowers of all shapes and shades. The rocky desolate side of Mount Carmel and the desert sand of 'Akká have been transformed into green lanes shaded by dark cedars of Lebanon, fir trees, pine trees, box trees, towering mulberry trees, and fruit trees of all varieties; it is a pageant of beauty. The words of Isaiah echo like a chorus through the mountainside:

1. "The wilderness and the solitary place shall be glad for them; and the desert shall blossom as the rose." [10]
2. "The glory of Lebanon shall come unto thee, the fir tree, the pine tree, and the box together to beautify the place of my sanctuary; and I will make the place of my feet glorious." [11]

These beautiful gardens and holy places which were raised up by the pen of Bahá'u'lláh lie on the north side of Mount Carmel, looking across the Bay of Haifa toward the white sands of 'Akká. Here on the north side of the mountain is being built all the future institutions of the Bahá'í Faith at its world center. This is the day and the place which David promised in his Psalms when he spoke of the mountain of God:

". . . on the sides of the north, the city of the great King." [12]

Ezekiel echoes the same promise given by Isaiah, Hosea, Micah, Daniel, Jeremiah, Zephaniah, Zechariah and Malachai:

"And, behold, the glory of the God of Israel came from the way of the east: and his voice was like the noise of many waters: and the earth shined with his glory. . . . And the glory of the Lord came into the house by way of the gate whose prospect is toward the east." [13]

Bahá'u'lláh, Whose name means the *Glory of the Lord,* or the *Glory of God,* came to Israel from His homeland, Persia, which lies directly east of the Holy Land. His Herald, the Báb, foretold His coming and prepared the way for Him. Báb is a word which means *the Gate.*

When Ezekiel had this vision of the last days, he said:

"I saw it were the appearance of fire. . . . This was the appearance of the likeness of the glory of the Lord. And when I saw it, I fell upon my face. . . ." [14]

The people at the time of Christ denied Jesus because they said that Moses had talked with God. Christ was plainly inferior. No station could equal that of the Interlocutor: He Who talked with God. Now in the time of Bahá'u'lláh, the people deny Him, saying: Christ is the Son of God. Bahá'u'lláh is plainly inferior. Nothing could equal the station of the Son of God.

George Townshend, sometime Canon of St. Patrick's Cathedral, Dublin, late Archdeacon of Clonfert, wrote in this book, *Christ and Bahá'u'lláh:*

"It has long been generally believed that Jesus Christ was a unique incarnation of God such as had never before appeared in the religious history. . . . This tenet made the acceptance of any later Prophet impossible, to a Christian. Yet there is nothing in Christ's own statements, as recorded in the Gospel, to support this view, and it was not generally held during His lifetime. . . .

"In spite of Christ's promise of further revelation of Truth, through the Comforter, through His own return, through the Spirit of Truth, the Christian church regards His revelation as final, and itself as the sole trustee of this religion. There is no room for the Supreme Redeemer of the Bible to bring in great changes for the establishment of the Kingdom of God. . . .

"Well might Christ warn His followers that false prophets would arise and misinterpret His teachings so as to delude even the most earnest and intelligent of His believers: from early times the Christians have disputed about Christian truth in councils, in sects, in wars."

Will Durant in *The Age of Faith* states that more Christians were killed by their fellow Christians during the dispute over the meaning of the Trinity than were slain during all the martyrdoms of Pagan Rome.

Bahá'u'lláh pointed to the words of Christ:

"For the Son of Man shall come in the glory of His Father." [15]

The meaning of the station of the "Son" and that of the "Father" was explained by Christ Himself in beautiful and simple language in His parable of the Vineyard. In fact, the whole history of religion, Bahá'u'lláh's Teachings tell us, can be found in this one parable:

"A certain man planted a vineyard, and set a hedge about it, and digged a place for the winefat, and built a tower, and let it out to husbandmen, and went into a far country.

And at the season he sent to the husbandmen a servant, that he might receive from the husbandmen of the fruit of the vineyard.

And they caught him, and beat him, and sent him away empty.

And again he sent unto them another servant; and at him they cast stones, and wounded him in the head, and sent him away shamefully handled.

And again he sent another; and him they killed and many others; beating some, and killing some.

Having yet therefore one son, his wellbeloved, he sent him also last unto them, saying, They will reverence my son.

But those husbandmen said among themselves, This is the heir; let us kill him, and the inheritance shall be ours.

And they took him and killed him, and cast him out of the vineyard. What shall therefore the lord of the vineyard do? He will come and destroy the husbandmen, and will give the vineyard unto others." [16]

The meaning is this: The vineyard is the earth, the man who planted it is God, and the husbandmen to whom it was let out are the people of the earth, especially their leaders.

The servant who was sent by God to claim the fruit was a Messenger or Prophet of God. The fruit He came to gather was the hearts of the people given in love for God and for their fellowman.

They beat the Prophet (servant) and drove Him off. So God sent another Prophet (servant) unto the world (vineyard) to claim His right from His creation. But the people (husbandmen) stoned them, beat them, and killed them. Always dealing thus with God's Messengers.

Finally the owner (God) sent his son (Christ) into the vineyard (earth) thinking surely they will honor Him and at last know the truth. But they crucified Him.

Thereupon the owner (God) sent the Lord of the vineyard (Bahá'u'lláh), representing the Father Himself into the vineyard (earth).

His Mission was to destroy the wicked husbandmen who did not acknowledge and serve God, and to give the vineyard (earth) out to those who were worthy of the Truth of God.

This is the outward symbol of the inward truth explaining the meaning of a gradually unfolding religion, and of the station of the Son (Christ) and the Father (Bahá'u'lláh). One is not greater than the Other. Both are equal. The fullness of Their Message depends upon the age and the receptivity of the people to whom They appear. Their purpose and spirit is one, Their love for Each other great.

Bahá'u'lláh has written:

> "Bethlehem is astir with the Breeze of God. We hear her voice saying: 'O most generous Lord! . . . The sweet savors of Thy presence have quickened me, after I had melted in my separation from Thee. Praised be Thou in that Thou hast raised the veils, and come with power in evident glory.'" [17]

Bahá'u'lláh was twice imprisoned in the land of His birth, Persia. He was scourged by the priests in the prayer-house at Amul. He was poisoned in the Black-pit prison in Tihrán, into which He was hurled. He was stoned on two separate occasions. His shoulders were lacerated by two hundred-pound chains. He was driven into exile to Baghdád, across the icy mountains in the midst of winter, possessionless, without proper food or clothes. There, another attempt was made on His life. He was cruelly persecuted during His further banishment to Constantinople and Adrianople. In the latter city He was twice poisoned. Shipped in bondage to 'Akká, He was cast into a cell.

At last Bahá'u'lláh reached the Holy Land and walked where the feet of Christ had walked.

NOTE SEVEN

All the Faiths of the world speak of a great "last day" when God will rule the earth and all the sheep will be gathered together into one flock. Christ Himself said: "And other sheep I have, which are not of this fold: them also I must bring, and they shall hear my voice; and there shall be one fold and one shepherd." [1]

In the Book of Zechariah it is expressed in yet another way:

"And the Lord shall be king over all the earth: in that day there shall be one Lord, and his name one." [2]

Although the name of every prophet up until the present time has appeared in various forms in the different languages of the world, the name Bahá'u'lláh is never spoken other than in this one form which is used throughout the earth.

In speaking of the last day, the Book of Habbakuk states:

"For the earth shall be filled with the knowledge of the *glory of the Lord*, as the waters cover the sea." [3]

The great American Negro educator, George Washington Carver, said that he believed that it was Bahá'u'lláh of Whom Habbakuk spoke when he uttered these prophetic words.

In NOTE ONE of this APPENDIX, we mentioned Leonard H. Kelber of Stuttgart, Germany. He and his followers awaited Christ's return in those fateful years between 1843-1845. When Christ did not appear as they expected, Kelber and his followers sold their possessions, chartered a boat, and sailed to the Holy Land. This colony of Christians, German Templars, settled at the foot of Mount Carmel. They were convinced from their study of the Scriptures that the "Glory of God" would appear on the side of Mount Carmel in the last days. In the stones above their doorways they carved the words: "Der Herr ist Nahe: The Lord is near."

They arrived in 1863, the very year when in far off Baghdád, Bahá'u'lláh made His public declaration to the world that He was the Promised One of all Ages, the "Father" foretold for the time of the end. Bahá'u'lláh was driven into exile until He reached the prison of 'Akká, and in the last years of His life He walked on the side of Mount Carmel. He looked down upon that colony of Christians who were waiting for the appearance of the "Glory of God."

His name, Bahá'u'lláh, when translated into English, means "The Glory of God."

In the Revelation of St. John the Divine, that disciple associated the Glory of God with the new Jerusalem, saying:

"And I John saw the holy city, new Jerusalem. . . . And the city had no need of the sun . . . for the Glory of God did lighten it." 4

At the time of the coming of the Bahá'í Faith, there were seven of the old revealed religions extant, with followers supporting them. This does not count philosophies and sects separately, such as were established by great reformers like Confucius and Luther. These seven great historical religions are those with a Book, a Prophet, and an historical civilization. They were as follows:

1. Sabean: Prophet, unknown. Date—5,000 B.C.*
2. Hindu: Prophet, Krishna. Date—2,000 B.C.*
3. Jewish: Prophet, Moses. Date—1330 B.C.
4. Zoroastrian: Prophet, Zoroaster. Date—1,000 B.C.*
5. Buddhist: Prophet, Buddha. Date—560 B.C.
6. Christian: Prophet, Christ. Date—1 A.D.
7. Islámic: Prophet, Muhammad. Date—622 A.D.

From the first of these great religions, Sabeanism, to the last, Islám, there was a cycle of 5,000 years. During this period, each of these religions looked forward to the "last days," or "day," when their own Faith would have its final fulfillment. Each of these pure and holy religions was a step in the progressive unfolding of the one great religion of God, divine and indivisible.

---

* Date is approximate, as authorities differ.

These seven religions were spoken of by Isaiah in one of his prophecies, which was to be fulfilled in the day of the "one fold and one shepherd." Isaiah wrote:

"And in that day seven women shall take hold of one man, saying, We will eat our own bread, and wear our own apparel: only let us be called by thy name, to take away our reproach." [5]

With the coming of Bahá'u'lláh, each of these seven women (religions) *do* eat of their own bread and wear their own apparel. It is one of the basic principles of the Bahá'í Faith that the spiritual, or underlying truths, ("food" and "apparel") are the same in every religion. These inner truths are not altered. It is only the outer teachings which are changed according to the needs of the people in the day in which each new prophet appears.

A basic teaching of Bahá'u'lláh is that the foundation of all religions is one. These "seven women" (religions) can take hold of "one man" (Bahá'u'lláh) and accept Him, confident that they are losing none of the pure, beautiful truths upon which they were founded.

This same remarkable prophecy of Isaiah, which foretells the unity of all the great religions in the "last days," also gives the promise of a *new* name by which God's Faith will be known. The prophecy says: "Let us be called by *thy name*," meaning the name of the new Prophet. Bahá'u'lláh is the name of the Prophet. His followers are called Bahá'ís, meaning followers of Bahá'u'lláh, the "Glory of God."

Bahá'u'lláh is the Promised One of all religions. He fulfilled by His coming the promise given to each of these Faiths in their own sacred Scripture: [6]

"To Israel He was neither more nor less than the incarnation of the 'Everlasting Father,' the 'Lord of Hosts' come down 'with ten thousand saints'; to Christendom, Christ returned 'in the glory of the Father'; to Shí'ah Islam, the return of the Imám Ḥusayn; to Sunní Islám, the descent of the 'Spirit of God' (Jesus Christ); to the Zoroastrians, the promised Sháh-Bahrám; to the Hindus, the reincarnation of Krishna; to the Buddhists, the fifth Buddha."

Isaiah referred to Bahá'u'lláh as: The "Glory of the Lord," the "Everlasting Father," the "Prince of Peace," the "Rod come forth out of the stem of Jesse," Who "shall judge among the nations," Who "shall assemble the outcasts of Israel."

David sang of Bahá'u'lláh as the "Lord of Hosts" and the "King of Glory."

Daniel proclaimed His appearance as the "Day of the Lord." Malachi described it as "the great and dreadful day of the Lord" when "the Sun of Righteousness" will "arise, with healing in His wings."

To Bahá'u'lláh's coming, Zoroaster must have referred when He foretold a period of three thousand years of conflict which must precede the advent of the World-Saviour, Sháh-Bahrám, Who would "usher in an era of blessedness and peace."

Bahá'u'lláh alone is meant by the prophecy "attributed to Gautama Buddha, Himself, that 'a Buddha named Maitreye, the Buddha of universal fellowship' should, in the fullness of time, arise and reveal 'His boundless glory.'"

To Bahá'u'lláh the Bhagavad-Gita of the Hindus referred, calling Him the "Most Great Spirit," the "Tenth Avatar," the "Immaculate Manifestation of Krishna."

To Bahá'u'lláh, Jesus, the Christ, referred as the "Prince of this world," the "Comforter" Who will "reprove the world of sin, and of righteousness, and of judgement," the "Son of Man" Who "shall come in the glory of His Father," the "Lord of the Vineyard," the "Spirit of Truth," Who "will guide you to all truth."

To Bahá'u'lláh, Muhammad alluded in His Book as the "Great Announcement." He declared the Day of Bahá'u'lláh to be the Day whereon "God" will "come down" "overshadowed with clouds," the "Great Day," the "Last Day," the day "when the earth shall shine with the light of her Lord."

The Book of Revelation referred to Bahá'u'lláh as the "Glory of God," as "Alpha and Omega," "the Beginning and the End," "the First and the Last."

To the hour of Bahá'u'lláh's appearance, St. Paul alluded as the hour of the "last trump," the "trump of God."

St. Peter spoke of Bahá'u'lláh's day as "the times of refreshing," the "times of restitution of all things, which God hath spoken by the mouth of all His holy Prophets since the world began."

The Báb extolled Bahá'u'lláh as the "Lord of the visible and invisible," "the Omnipotent Master," the "Essence of Being," the "sole Object of all previous Revelations, including the Revelation of the Qá'im [the Báb] Himself."

Bahá'u'lláh is the source of joy and thanksgiving to all the religions and Prophets who preceded Him. He is the seal of their labor, the fulfiller of their promises, the blessed object of all their hopes. He was indeed destined by the finger of God, to be the Author of the day of the "one fold and one shepherd."

All the Books of the past which had been sealed were opened by Him, and their truth made clear to men. In that historical record of the Bahá'í Faith, *God Passes By*, written by Shoghi Effendi, the first Guardian of the Bahá'í Faith, and great-grandson of Bahá'u'lláh, it is stated:

"Foremost among the priceless treasures cast forth from the billowing ocean of Bahá'u'lláh's Revelation ranks the Kitáb-i-Íqán (Book of Certitude), revealed within the space of two days and two nights. . . . [it] broke the 'seals' of the 'Book' referred to by Daniel, and disclosed the meaning of the 'words' destined to remain 'closed up' till the 'time of the end.' " [7]

"The Word of God hath set the heart of the world afire," Bahá'u'lláh proclaims; "how regrettable if ye fail to be enkindled with its flame!" [8]

Linking His own Faith forever with that of Christ, Bahá'u'lláh wrote movingly: "O Bethlehem! . . . Tell Me then: Do the sons recognize the Father, and acknowledge Him, or do they deny Him, even as the people aforetime denied Him (Jesus)?" [9]

The Pen of Bahá'u'lláh has called out to all mankind to have "eyes that will see" and "ears that will hear" in this day. To the question: "Have the verses been sent down?" He answers, "Say: 'Yea, by Him Who is the Lord of the heavens!' 'Hath the Hour come?' 'Nay, more; it hath passed. . . . He, the True One, hath appeared with proof and testimony. . . .' " [10]

"We, in truth, have opened unto you the gates of the Kingdom," Bahá'u'lláh calls out. "Will ye bar the doors of your houses in My face?" [11]

Bahá'u'lláh calls to the "pure in heart" who are seeking for the healing Word of God:

"I bear witness, O friends! that the favor is complete, the argument fulfilled, the proof manifest and the evidence established. Let it now be seen what your endeavors in the path of detachment will reveal." [12]

"He that hath an ear to hear, let him hear."

EPILOGUE

"Let no one, while this system is still in its infancy, misconceive its character, belittle its significance or misrepresent its purpose. . . . The source from which it derives its inspiration is no one less than Bahá'u'lláh Himself [God's Messenger for this day]. . . . Its seed is the blood of no less than twenty thousand martyrs who have offered up their lives that it may be born and flourish."

Unlike the religion of Christ, unlike all the religions of the past, the followers of Bahá'u'lláh in every land, "wherever they labor and toil, have before them in clear, in unequivocal and emphatic language, all the laws, the regulations, the principles, the institutions, the guidance, they require for the prosecution and consummation of their task. . . . Therein lies the strength of the unity of the [Bahá'í] Faith . . . that claims not to destroy or belittle previous Revelations, but to connect, unify and fulfill them."

"The Call of God when raised, breathed a new life into the body of mankind," said 'Abdu'l-Bahá, "and infused a new spirit into the whole creation. It is for this reason that the world hath been moved to its depths, and the hearts and consciences of men been quickened. Erelong the evidences of this regeneration will be revealed, and the fast asleep will be awakened." [1]

Since the day that 'Abdu'l-Bahá, the son of Bahá'u'lláh, spoke these words, Shoghi Effendi, the Guardian of the Faith, executed and carried out a world-wide teaching plan during which, up to 1959, Bahá'í literature was translated into two hundred and forty-four languages. Bahá'í schools, National Headquarters, and properties are to be found in every continent.

The National Assemblies of the Bahá'í Faith have been given legal recognition by the leading countries of the world. The Bahá'í Faith has been recognized as one of the non-governmental agencies attached to the United Nations.

The world center of the Bahá'í Faith is in Haifa, Israel, on the side of Mount Carmel, the "mountain of God." Professor Norman Bentwich in his article on Palestine, said of the Bahá'í Faith, "Palestine [now, Israel] may indeed be now regarded as the land of not three but four faiths, because the Bahá'í creed, which has its center of faith in 'Akká and Haifa, is attaining to the character of a world religion. . . . it is a factor making for international and inter-religious understanding."

The magnificent Bahá'í gardens, Shrines and holy places are a center of beauty and pilgrimage which attract Bahá'ís and visitors from all parts of the earth.

Bahá'í Temples are being erected in Africa, Australia and Europe. They already have been raised up in Asia and America. The beautiful Bahá'í House of Worship in the United States of America has been called "the first new idea in architecture since the thirteenth century."

There is hardly a country, territory or island of the sea where the Word of Bahá'u'lláh has not been taught. Like a mighty wind of God, this Faith has swept across the face of the planet. It began on May 23, 1844. In a little over a hundred years, it has spread to over five thousand centers in every corner of the earth, fulfilling the prophecy of Habbakuk for the last days.

"For the earth shall be filled with the knowledge of the glory of the Lord [Bahá'u'lláh], as the waters cover the sea." (2:14)

Great figures from all walks of life have paid tribute to this young, encouraging, uplifting religion.

1. "If there has been any prophet in recent times, it is to Bahá'u'lláh that we must go."

(the Rev. T. K. Cheyne, British Clergyman)

2. "The Bahá'í Cause is one of the great moral and social forces in all the world today."

(Eduard Beneš, former President of Czechoslovakia)

3. "Not alone China, but the whole world needs these Teachings."

(Y. S. Tsao, former President of the University of Shanghai)

4. "I regard it as one of the noblest of the world's religions."

(Dr. R. F. Piper, Philosophy Dept., Syracuse University)

5. "The Bahá'í Faith. . . . accepts all great Prophets gone before, it destroys no other creeds and leaves all doors open."

(Dowager Marie of Rumania)

6. "They [the Bahá'ís] have done more to bring interreligious understanding to the world than any other religious group."

(Dr. Paul Anderson, President of the Pennsylvania College for Women)

7. Dr. Pitrim A. Sorokin of Harvard University has called the Bahá'í Faith: ". . . this highly spiritual and moral religion."

8. Dr. Herbert Adams Gibbons, American historian, writes of the Bahá'í teachings: ". . . they form an unanswerable argument and plea for the only way that the world can be made over. If we could put into effect this program, we should indeed have a new world order."

9. D. V. Lesney, famous scholar: "Bahá'u'lláh is a Savior of the Twentieth Century."

"The time fore-ordained unto the peoples and kindreds of the earth is now come. The promises of God, as recorded in the holy Scriptures, have all been fulfilled." "The Lord is come in His great glory!" "He, verily, is the One Whom ye were promised in the Books of God. . . . How long will ye wander in the wilderness of heedlessness and superstition. Turn your hearts in the direction of your Lord, the Forgiving, the Generous."

"Every Prophet hath announced the coming of this day . . . "This Day is God's Day! . . . Happy is he who hath renounced this world, and clung to Him. . . ."

"Bestir yourselves, O people, . . . for the promised hour is now come. Beware lest ye fail to apprehend its import. . . ."

"Night hath succeeded day, and day hath succeeded night, and the hours and moments of your lives have come and gone, yet none of you hath, for one instant, consented to detach yourself from that which perisheth. Bestir yourselves, that the brief moments that are still yours may not be dissipated and lost. Even as the swiftness of lightning your days shall pass, and your bodies shall be laid to rest beneath a canopy of dust. What can ye then achieve? How can ye atone for your past failure?"

"He Who is the Everlasting Father calleth aloud between earth and heaven. Blessed the ear that hath heard, and the eye that hath seen, and the heart that hath turned unto Him . . . "This is that which the Son (Jesus) hath decreed."—*Bahá'u'lláh*

REFERENCES

FOREWORD

E. G. Browne, Preface to *The Chosen Highway* by Lady Bloomfield, pp. v-vi.

PROLOGUE

1. Comte de Gobineau, *Les Religions et les Philosophies dans l'Asie Centrale*, p. 220.

CHAPTER ONE

1. James Henry Foreman, *Story of Prophecy*, pp. 310-311.
2. Nabíl *The Dawn-Breakers*, pp. 9-10, footnote 3; pp. 17-18, footnote 2.
3. Ibid., pp. 4, 9-10, 16.
4. Ibid., p. 59: and footnote.
5. Ibid., pp. 25-30; 40-46.
6. Revelation 11:4.
7. Qu'rán 39:68.
8. Ibid., p. 50.

CHAPTER TWO

1. Nabíl, *The Dawn-Breakers*, pp. 22-23.
2. Ibid., pp. 47-61.
3. Comte de Gobineau, *Les Religions et les Philosophies dans l'Asie Centrale*, p. 120.
4. Nabíl, *The Dawn-Breakers*, p. 61.

CHAPTER THREE

1. Nabíl, *The Dawn-Breakers*, pp. 65-66.
2. Ibid., pp. 67-69.
3. Ibid., p. 70.
4. Ibid., p. 85.
5. Ibid., pp. 87-91; p. 82, footnote 1.
6. Ibid., pp. 92-94.

CHAPTER FOUR

1. Nabíl, *The Dawn-Breakers*, p. 96.
2. Ibid., pp. 129-130.
3. Ibid., pp. 136-137.
4. Ibid., p. 138.
5. Luke 11:52.
6. A. L. M. Nicolas, Introduction to Vol. I, *Le Bayán Persan*, pp. 3-5.
7. Nabíl, *The Dawn-Breakers*, pp. 140-141.

- CHAPTER FIVE

1. Nabíl, *The Dawn-Breakers*, pp. 142-143.
2. Ibid., pp. 144-148.

CHAPTER SIX

1. Nabíl, *The Dawn-Breakers*, pp. 149-150.
2. (1) A. L. M. Nicolas, *Siyyid 'Alí-Muhammad dit le Báb*, pp. 203-207; 229-231.
   (2) *Les Livre des Sept Preuves*, translated by A. L. M. Nicolas, pp. 64-65.
3. Nabíl, *The Dawn-Breakers*, pp. 162-168.

CHAPTER SEVEN

1. Comte de Gobineau, *Les Religions et les Philosophies dans l'Asie Centrale*, p. 122.
2. Ibid., p. 120.
3. Ibid., p. 118.
4. Sir Francis Younghusband, *The Gleam*, p. 194.
5. *Journal Asiatique*, 1866, tome 7, p. 341.
6. Comte de Gobineau, *Les Religions et les Philosophies dans l'Asie Centrale*, pp. 120-122.
7. *Journal Asiatique*, 1866, tome 8, p. 251.
8. Siyyid Yahyáy-i-Dárábi, surnamed Vahíd.
9. (1) A. L. M. Nicolas, *Siyyid 'Alí-Muhammad dit le Báb*, p. 273.
   (2) Nabíl, *The Dawn-Breakers*, p. 171.

10. *Le Bayán Persan,* translated by Nicolas, vol. 1, p. 43.
11. A. L. M. Nicolas, *Siyyid 'Alí-Muhammad dit le Báb,* p. 234.
12. *A Traveller's Narrative,* translated by E. G. Browne, p. 8.
13. Nabíl, *The Dawn-Breakers,* pp. 172-177.
14. Ibid., pp. 188-189.

CHAPTER EIGHT

1. Nabíl, *The Dawn-Breakers,* pp. 75-76.
2. *Star of the West,* The Bahá'í Magazine, vol. XIV, p. 271 (Article by Jináb-i-Avárih).
3. Nabíl, *The Dawn-Breakers,* pp. 79-80.
4. Ibid., p. 77.
5. Ibid., p. 192.
6. Ibid., p. 235.
7. A. L. M. Nicolas, *Siyyid 'Alí-Muhammad dit le Báb,* p. 255.
8. Nabíl, *The Dawn-Breakers,* pp. 194-197.
9. *A Traveller's Narrative,* p. 11.
10. A. L. M. Nicolas, *Siyyid 'Alí-Muhammad dit le Báb,* pp. 367-373.
11. Nabíl, *The Dawn-Breakers,* p. 198.

CHAPTER NINE

1. Nabíl, *The Dawn-Breakers,* p. 99; footnote, *Le Bayán Persan.*
2. *The Táríkh-i-Jadíd,* translated by E. G. Browne, pp. 220-221.
3. Nabíl, *The Dawn-Breakers,* p. 203-215.

CHAPTER TEN

1. A. L. M. Nicolas, *Siyyid 'Alí-Muhammad dit le Báb,* p. 242.
2. Comte de Gobineau, *Les Religions et les Philosophies dans l'Asie Centrale,* pp. 131-132.
3. *Journal Asiatique,* 1866, tome 7, pp. 367-368.
4. Nabíl, *The Dawn-Breakers,* p. 232, footnote (Hájí Mu'inu's-Saltanih's narrative, p. 129).
5. Ibid., pp. 230-231.
6. Comte de Gobineau, *Les Religions et les Philosophies dans l'Asie Centrale,* p. 124.
7. *A Traveller's Narrative,* p. 16.

CHAPTER ELEVEN

1. Nabíl, *The Dawn-Breakers,* pp. 237-241, 243.
2. (1) Ibid., p. 239.
   (2) A. L. M. Nicolas; *Siyyid 'Alí-Muhammad dit le Báb,* p. 375.

CHAPTER TWELVE

1. *Journal Asiatique*, 1866, tome 7, p. 356.
2. Nabíl, *The Dawn-Breakers*, p. 249.
3. A. L. M. Nicolas, *Siyyid 'Alí-Muhammad dit le Báb*, pp. 365-366.
4. (1) *Táríkh-i-Jadíd*, p. 238.
   (2) Nabíl, *The Dawn-Breakers*, p. 248, footnote 1.
5. *A Traveller's Narrative*, Note V, p. 349.
6. Shoghi Effendi, *The World Order of Bahá'u'lláh*, p. 100.
7. Matthew 24:42.
8. *Les Livre des Sept Preuves*, translated by Nicolas, pp. 64-65.
9. (1) *Ibid.*, pp. 64-65.
   (2) Nabíl, *The Dawn-Breakers*, p. 249, footnote 1.
10. A. L. M. Nicolas, *Siyyid 'Alí-Muhammad dit le Báb*, pp. 365-367.
11. Shoghi Effendi, *The World Order of Bahá'u'lláh*, p. 100.
12. Bahá'u'lláh, *Epistle to the Son of the Wolf*, p. 171.
13. Preface to *Les Livre des Sept Preuves*, translated by Nicolas, pp. 12-13.
14. Nabíl, *The Dawn-Breakers*, pp. 254-260.

CHAPTER THIRTEEN

1. Nabíl, *The Dawn-Breakers*, Introduction by Shoghi Effendi, p. xxxiii.
2. *Journal Asiatique*, tome 7, p. 371.
3. Nabíl, *The Dawn-Breakers*, p. 303.
4. (1) *Ibid.*, p. 70.
5. *Ibid.*, pp. 309-311.
6. Luke 17:7.
7. Nabíl, *The Dawn-Breakers*, p. 313-322.
8. Mark 14:62.
9. Dr. T. K. Cheyne, *The Reconciliation of Races and Religions*, p. 62.
10. *A Traveller's Narrative*, Note M, p. 290.
11. A. L. M. Nicolas, *Siyyid 'Alí-Muhammad dit le Báb*, pp. 239-240.
12. Nabíl, *The Dawn-Breakers*, pp. 321-322, footnote 1.
13. *Ibid.*, p. 323.
14. Shoghi Effendi, *God Passes By*, pp. 81-82.
15. Nabíl, *The Dawn-Breakers*, p. 321.
16. C. R. Markham, *A General Sketch of the History of Persia*, pp. 486-487.
17. *Journal Asiatique*, 1866, tome 7, pp. 367-368.
18. Nabíl, *The Dawn-Breakers*, p. 525.

CHAPTER FOURTEEN

1. Nabíl, *The Dawn-Breakers*, pp. 324-329, 351.
2. A. L. M. Nicolas, *Siyyid 'Alí-Muhammad dit le Báb*, pp. 296-297.
3. *A Traveller's Narrative*, pp. 34-35.

4. Nabíl, *The Dawn-Breakers, Introduction* p. xxxiv.
5. E. G. Browne, *A Year Among the Persians,* p. 74.
6. *A Traveller's Narrative,* pp. 34-35.
7. *Journal of the Royal Asiatic Society,* October 1889, Art. 12, pp. 927-928.
8. A. L. M. Nicolas, *Siyyid 'Alí-Muhammad dit le Báb,* pp. 295-296.
9. *The Táríkh-i-Jadíd,* pp. 49, 107-108.
10. E. G. Browne, *A History of Persian Literature in Modern Times,* (A.D. 1500-1922), p. 399.
11. Nabíl, *The Dawn-Breakers,* pp. 358-359.
12. *The Táríkh-i-Jadíd,* pp. 106-109.
13. Nabíl, *The Dawn-Breakers,* pp. 379-383.
14. *A Traveller's Narrative,* Note F, p. 245.
15. Comte de Gobineau, *Les Religions et les Philosophies dans l'Asié Centrale,* p. 176.
16. T. K. Cheyne, *Reconciliation of Races and Religions,* p. 83.
17. Nabíl, *The Dawn-Breakers,* p. 416.
18. Comte de Gobineau, *Les Religions et les Philosophies dans l'Asie Centrale,* p. 181.
19. *The Táríkh-i-Jadíd,* pp. 81-83.
20. Comte de Gobineau, *Les Religions et les Philosophies dans l'Asie Centrale,* pp. 181-182.
21. *The Táríkh-i-Jadíd,* pp. 79-80.
22. Ibid., pp. 106-109.
23. Bahá'u'lláh, *The Kitáb-i-Íqán,* pp. 224-225.
24. Nabíl, *The Dawn-Breakers,* p. 429.
25. A. L. M. Nicolas, *Siyyid 'Alí-Muhammad dit le Báb,* p. 330.
26. Nabíl, *The Dawn-Breakers,* pp. 430-432.

CHAPTER FIFTEEN

1. *Memorials of the Faithful,* pp. 291-298.
2. A. L. M. Nicolas, *Siyyid 'Alí-Muhammad dit le Báb,* pp. 273-274.
3. Martha L. Root, *Táhirih the Pure,* p. 22.
4. (1) Nabíl, *The Dawn-Breakers,* pp. 81-82.
   (2) *Memorials of the Faithful,* pp. 291-298.
5. Nabíl, *The Dawn-Breakers,* pp. 269-271.
6. *Samandar manuscript,* p. 9.
7. Martha L. Root, *Táhirih the Pure,* p. 22.
8. Shoghi Effendi, *God Passes By,* p. 73.
9. Martha L. Root, *Táhirih the Pure,* pp. 24-25.
10. (1) Nabíl, *The Dawn-Breakers,* p. 272.
    (2) Ibid., footnote 1.
11. *A Traveller's Narrative,* Note Q, pp. 214-215 (or 310).
12. Nabíl, *The Dawn-Breakers,* p. 272, footnote 1.
13. Martha L. Root, *Táhirih the Pure,* pp. 25-26.
14. Nabíl, *The Dawn-Breakers,* p. 272, footnote 2.

15. Ibid., footnote 3.
16. Martha L. Root, *Táhirih the Pure*, pp. 30-31.
17. (1) Ibid., pp. 32-34.
    (2) Nabíl, *The Dawn-Breakers*, pp. 273-275.
18. Martha L. Root, Táhirih the Pure, p. 7.
19. Ibid., pp. 37-38.
20. (1) Shoghi Effendi, *God Passes By*, p. 74.
    (2) Nabíl, *The Dawn-Breakers*, p. 282.
21. *Journal Asiatique*, 1866, tome 7, p. 474.
22. Nabíl, *The Dawn-Breakers*, pp. 284-285.
23. Shoghi Effendi, *God Passes By*, pp. 32-33.
24. Nabíl, *The Dawn-Breakers*, pp. 288-298.
25. Martha L. Root, *Táhirih the Pure*, pp. 62-63.
26. Sir Francis Younghusband, *The Gleam*, pp. 202-203.
27. Comte de Gobineau, *Les Religions et les Philosophies dans l'Asie Centrale*, p. 150.
28. A. L. M. Nicolas, *Siyyid 'Alí-Muhammad dit le Báb*, pp. 446-447.
29. Nabíl, *The Dawn-Breakers*, pp. 621-629.
30. Martha L. Root, *Táhirih the Pure*, pp. 68-69.
31. Shoghi Effendi, *God Passes By*, p. 75.
32. Lord Curzon, *Persia and the Persian Question*, vol. I, p. 501.
33. Shoghi Effendi, *God Passes By*, p. 76.
34. Dr. T. K. Cheyne, *The Reconciliation of Races and Religions*, pp. 114-115.
35. Nabíl, *The Dawn-Breakers*, p. 285, footnote 2, (*Memorials of the Faithful*, p. 306).
36. Martha L. Root, *Táhirih the Pure*, p. 77, footnote 1.

CHAPTER SIXTEEN

1. *The Táríkh-i-Jadíd*, p. 115.
2. A. L. M. Nicolas, *Siyyid 'Alí-Muhammad dit le Báb*, p. 390.
3. Nabíl, *The Dawn-Breakers*, pp. 465-475.
4. A. L. M. Nicolas, *Siyyid 'Alí-Muhammad dit le Báb*, p. 391.
5. *The Táríkh-i-Jadíd*, p. 117.
6. Nabíl, *The Dawn-Breakers*, p. 476.
7. A. L. M. Nicolas, *Siyyid 'Alí-Muhammad dit le Báb*, p. 393.
8. Ibid., p. 406.
9. Ibid., p. 407.
10. Nabíl, *The Dawn-Breakers*, p. 647, footnote; pp. 481-496.
11. A. L. M. Nicolas, *Siyyid 'Alí-Muhammad dit le Báb*, p. 408.
12. *A Traveller's Narrative*, Note H, pp. 259-260.
13. Bahá'u'lláh, *The Kitáb-i-Íqán*, p. 188.

CHAPTER SEVENTEEN

1. Nabíl, *The Dawn-Breakers*, pp. 445-450.

2. *The Táríkh-i-Jadíd*, p. 254.
3. Nabíl, *The Dawn-Breakers*, pp. 449-453.
4. (1) Nabíl, *The Dawn-Breakers*, pp. 453-455.
   (2) *A Traveller's Narrative*, Note B, pp. 212-213; 215-216.
5. Nabíl, *The Dawn-Breakers*, pp. 455-464.
6. *A Traveller's Narrative*, Note B, p. 216-217.

CHAPTER EIGHTEEN

1. Nabíl, *The Dawn-Breakers*, pp. 504-505.
2. *A Traveller's Narrative*, p. 3.
3. Bahá'u'lláh, *Epistle to the Son of the Wolf*, pp. 151-159.
4. Shoghi Effendi, *The World Order of Bahá'u'lláh*, p. 100.
5. Dr. T. K. Cheyne, *The Reconciliation of Races and Religions*, pp. 65-66.
6. Bahá'u'lláh, *Epistle to the Son of the Wolf*, p. 160.
7. Nabíl, *The Dawn-Breakers*, pp. 12-13.
8. Isaiah 54-5.
9. Nabíl, *The Dawn-Breakers*, pp. 8-9.
10. Ibid., p. 72.
11. Ibid., pp. 41-42; footnote 2.
12. Ibid., pp. 227-228.
13. Ibid., pp. 228-229.
14. Ibid., 433.
15. Shoghi Effendi, *God Passes By*, p. 28.
16. Ibid., pp. 189-190.
17. Nabíl, *The Dawn-Breakers*, pp. 29-33; 593-594.
18. Ibid., p. 285.
19. Ibid., p. 86; 96.
20. Ibid., pp. 105-106.
21. Ibid., pp. 126-127.
22. Ibid., p. 292.
23. Ibid., pp. 341-349.
24. Ibid., pp. 293-295.
25. Dr. T. K. Cheyne, *The Reconciliation of Races and Religions*, p. 75.
26. Nabíl, *The Dawn-Breakers*, p. 298.
27. Ibid., pp. 284-286; 299; 460.
28. Ibid., p. 122.
29. Ibid., p. 465.
30. *The Táríkh-i-Jadíd*, p. 115.
31. Nabíl, *The Dawn-Breakers*, p. 432.
32. Ibid., p. 536.
33. Matthew 10:21.
34. Qur'án 80:34.
35. Nabíl, *The Dawn-Breakers*, pp. 552-554.
36. Ibid., p. 537.
37. A. L. M. Nicolas, *Siyyid 'Alí-Muhammad dit le Báb*, p. 335.

38. Nabíl, *The Dawn-Breakers*, p. 572-573.
39. Comte de Gobineau, *Les Religions et les Philosophies dans l'Asie Centrale*, pp. 200-201.
40. A. L. M. Nicolas, *Siyyid 'Alí-Muhammad dit le Báb*, p. 350.
41. Nabíl, *The Dawn-Breakers*, p. 561, footnote.
42. Ibid., p. 323, footnote; p. 539.
43. Ibid., p. 70.
44. Ibid., pp. 93-94.
45. Ibid., p. 123.
46. Ibid., Introduction by Shoghi Effendi, pp. xxx-xxxi.
47. Bahá'u'lláh, *Epistle to the Son of the Wolf*, p. 162.
48. Ibid., pp. 141, 152.
49. Nabíl, *The Dawn-Breakers*, p. 50.
50. Shoghi Effendi, *God Passes By*, p. 25.
51. Bahá'u'lláh, *Epistle to the Son of the Wolf*, p. 154.
52. Nabíl, *The Dawn-Breakers*, pp. 371-373.
53. Bahá'u'lláh, *Epistle to the Son of the Wolf*, pp. 156-157.
54. Shoghi Effendi, *The World Order of Bahá'u'lláh*, p. 101.

CHAPTER NINETEEN

1. *Les Livre des Sept Preuves*, translated by Nicolas, pp. 54-60.
2. A. L. M. Nicolas, *Siyyid 'Alí-Muhammad dit le Báb*, p. 387.
3. Nabíl, *The Dawn-Breakers*, p. 463.
4. Comte de Gobineau, *Les Religions et les Philosophies dans l'Asie Centrale*, pp. 210-213.
5. Ibid.
6. Nabíl, *The Dawn-Breakers*, pp. 500-504.
7. Ibid., pp. 321-322; and Note 4.
8. Ibid., pp. 506-507.
9. Dr. T. K. Cheyne, *The Reconciliation of Races and Religions*, p. 185.
10. Nabíl, *The Dawn-Breakers*, pp. 306-308.
11. Dr. T. K. Cheyne, *The Reconciliation of Races and Religions*, pp. 8-9.
12. Nabíl, *The Dawn-Breakers*, pp. 507-512.
13. Comte de Gobineau, *Les Religions et les Philosophies dans l'Asie Centrale*, p. 220.
14. *Journal Asiatique*, 1866, tome 7, p. 378.
15. Nabíl, *The Dawn-Breakers*, pp. 512-514.
16. M. C. Huart, *La Religion de Báb*, pp. 3-4.
17. A. L. M. Nicolas, *Siyyid 'Alí-Muhammad dit le Báb*, p. 375.
18. A. L. M. Nicolas, *Siyyid 'Alí-Muhammad dit le Báb*, pp. 203-204, 376.
19. Luke 22:42.
20. M. C. Huart, *La Religion de Báb*, pp. 3-4.
21. Nabíl, *The Dawn-Breakers*, p. 518.
22. A. L. M. Nicolas, *Siyyid 'Alí-Muhammad dit le Báb*, p. 377.
23. Nabíl, *The Dawn-Breakers*, pp. 520-521.

24. Comte de Gobineau, *Les Religions et les Philosophies dans l'Asie Centrale*, pp. 207-209.
25. Shoghi Effendi, *God Passes By*, p. 83.
26. Ibid., p. 83-85.
27. Amos 8:9.
28. (1) 'Abdu'l-Bahá, *Some Answered Questions*, p. 65.
    (2) Shoghi Effendi, *God Passes By*, pp. 53-54.
29. Nabíl, *The Dawn-Breakers*, Introduction, pp. xxxi-xxxii.
30. Shoghi Effendi, *God Passes By*, pp. 55-57.
31. 'Abdu'l-Bahá, *Some Answered Questions*, pp. 30-31.
32. Shoghi Effendi, *God Passes By*, p. 56.
33. Ibid.
34. M. J. Balteau, *Le Babísme*, p. 28.
35. E. G. Browne, article: "The Babís of Persia," *Journal of the Royal Asiatic Society*, 1899, p. 933.
36. (1) Shoghi Effendi, *God Passes By*, p. 55.
    (2) Nabíl, *The Dawn-Breakers*, p. 516, footnote.
37. Ibid., pp. 516-517, footnote.
38. A. L. M. Nicolas, *Siyyid 'Alí-Muhammad dit le Báb*, pp. 203-204, 376.
39. Nabíl, *The Dawn-Breakers*, p. 522.
40. Comte de Gobineau, *Les Religions et les Philosophies dans l'Asie Centrale*, pp. 224-225.
41. Nabíl, *The Dawn-Breakers*, pp. 651-654.
42. Mírzá Abu'l-Fadl, *Fara'id*, pp. 50-51.

APPENDIX, NOTE ONE

1. The Bahá'í World, vol. V, 1932-1934, p. 604.
2. James Henry Foreman, *Story of Prophecy*, pp. 310-311.
3. James Russell Lowell, "*The Crisis*," (1843).
4. Job 38:35.
5. Numbers 23:23.
6. Matthew 24:3, 13-14.
7. *Year Book and Guide to East Africa*, p. 44, (Ed. Robert Hale Ltd., London, 1953).
8. Luke 21:7.
9. Ibid., 21:24, 27.
10. Encyclopedia Americana, vol. 16, p. 31 (1944 Edition).
11. Shoghi Effendi, *God Passes By*, Introduction by George Townshend, p. IV.
12. Revelation 11:2.
13. James Henry Foreman, *Story of Prophecy*, p. 88.
14. Matthew 24:15.
15. (1) Daniel, 9:24, 25.
    (2) 'Abdu'l-Bahá, *Some Answered Questions*, p. 43.
16. Daniel 8:13, 14.

17. *Bible Reading*, edited by Review and Herald Publishing Co., Battle Creek, Michigan, U.S.A. p. 94.
18. Daniel 8:2, 7:13, 14.
19. Jeremiah 49:38.
20. Nabíl, *The Dawn-Breakers*, p. 49.
21. Jeremiah 5:21.
22. Matthew 13:11-16.
23. Ibid., 17:10; Mark 9:11.
24. Matthew 11:14, 15.
25. John 1:21.
26. Luke 1:15-17.
27. Matthew 17:10-13.
28. Ibid., 11:18.
29. Daniel 12:4; 8-9.
30. Isaiah 29:11-12.
31. I Corinthians 4:5.
32. II Peter 1:19-21.
33. *Tablets of 'Abdu'l-Bahá*, vol. III, p. 692.
34. Revelation 5:6, 9.
35. Daniel 7:10; 13-14.
36. Isaiah 62:2 and 65:15.
37. Revelation 2:17; 3:3, 12; 16:15.

APPENDIX, NOTE TWO

1. John 7:12.
2. Ibid., 6:66.
3. Matthew 24:23-24.
4. II Thessalonians 2:3.
5. II Peter 2:1-2.
6. Amos 8:11-12.
7. II Peter 3:3-4.
8. Mark 13:35-36.
9. Ibid., 13:37.
10. Matthew 24:48-51.
11. Ibid., 7:15-20.
12. *Bahá'í World Faith*, p. 440.
13. Shoghi Effendi, *The World Order of Bahá'u'lláh*, p. 65.
14. J. E. Esslemont, *Bahá'u'lláh and the New Era*, p. 147.
15. *Gleanings from the Writings of Bahá'u'lláh*, p. 101.
16. Ibid., p. 95.
17. J. E. Esslemont, *Bahá'u'lláh and the New Era*, p. 164.
18. Shoghi Effendi, *The Advent of Divine Justice*, p. 22.
19. (1) Ibid., pp. 21-22.
    (2) Bahá'u'lláh, *Tablet of Tarázát*, Taráz 3-4.
20. 'Abdu'l-Bahá, *Paris Talks*, p. 16.
21. 'Abdu'l-Bahá, *The Promulgation of Universal Peace*, p. 199.

22. *Gleanings from the Writings of Bahá'u'lláh*, p. 285.
23. *Bahá'í World Faith*, p. 189.
24. Zephaniah 3:8-9.
25. Shoghi Effendi, *The World Order of Bahá'u'lláh*, p. 204.
26. C. C. Hurst, *Heredity, the Ascent of Man*, pp. 32, 35, 131.
27. Arthur H. Compton, *The Freedom of Man*, pp. 121, 126.
28. *Washington Star*, Article 12, 1936.
29. *Bahá'í World Faith*, p. 195.
30. *A Traveller's Narrative*, Introduction by E. G. Browne, p. XXXIX.

APPENDIX, NOTE THREE

1. Sir James Jeans, *Through Space and Time*, pp. 102, 154.
2. *Encyclopedia Americana*, vol. III, 1944 Ed., p. 691.
3. Shoghi Effendi, *The Promised Day is Come*, pp. 40-41.

APPENDIX, NOTE FOUR

1. Nabíl, *The Dawn-Breakers*, p. 322.
2. Genesis 17:18, 20.
3. Shoghi Effendi, *God Passes By*, p. 94.
4. Isaiah 11:1, 10, 12.
5. Ibid., 11:11.

APPENDIX, NOTE FIVE

1. Shoghi Effendi, *God Passes By*, pp. 273-274.
2. Ibid., p. 276.
3. *The Bahá'í World*, vol. XII, 1950-1954, p. 225.

APPENDIX, NOTE SIX

1. Micah 7:2-4.
2. Ibid., 7:7, 9, 10.
3. Ibid., 4:10.
4. Ibid., 7:14.
5. Ibid., 7:12.
6. Ibid., 7:15.
7. Hosea 2:15.
8. Isaiah 65:10.
9. Ibid., 35:2.
10. Ibid., 35:1.
11. Ibid., 60:11-13.
12. Psalms 48:2.
13. Ezekiel 43:2, 4.
14. Ibid., 1:27-28.
15. Matthew 16:27.

16. Mark 12:1-9.
17. Shoghi Effendi, *The Promised Day is Come*, p. 106.

APPENDIX, NOTE SEVEN

1. John 10:16.
2. Zechariah, 14:9.
3. Habbakuk 2:14.
4. Revelation 21:1, 23.
5. Isaiah 4:1.
6. Shoghi Effendi, *God Passes By*, pp. 94-97.
7. Ibid., pp. 138-139.
8. *Gleanings from the Writings of Bahá'u'lláh*, p. 316.
9. Shoghi Effendi, *The Promised Day is Come*, p. 106.
10. Bahá'u'lláh, *Epistle to the Son of the Wolf*, pp. 131-132.
11. Shoghi Effend: *The Promised Day is Come*, p. 110.
12. *The Hidden Words of Bahá'u'lláh*, pp. 51-52.

EPILOGUE

1. Shoghi Effendi, *The World Order of Bahá'u'lláh*, p. 156; pp. 21-22; p. 169.